Gender and Schooling in the Early Years

Edited by

Janice Koch
Hofstra University

and

Beverly J. Irby
Sam Houston State University

INFORMATION AGE
PUBLISHING

Greenwich, Connecticut 06830 • www.infoagepub.com

Library of Congress Cataloging-in-Publication Data

Gender and schooling in the early years / edited by Janice Koch and Beverly
Irby.
    p. cm. – (Research on women and education)
  Includes bibliographical references.
  ISBN 1-59311-255-6 (pbk.) – ISBN 1-59311-440-0 (hardcover)
  1. Sex differences in education. 2. Early childhood education. 3. Gender
identity. 4. Educational equalization. I. Koch, Janice, 1947- II. Irby,
Beverly J. III. Series.
  LC213.G43 2005
  372.1822–dc22

                                                              2005013180

CONTENTS

FOREWORD

I'm just a girl
Take a good look at me
Just your typical prototype
Oh… I've had it up to here!
Oh… am I making myself clear?

(No Doubt, 2005)

China's 1.3 billionth citizen was born on January 6, 2005. It was a boy. The method of calculating the birth that was to represent this momentous occasion came under scrutiny and was contentious. China's *one child policy*, set in a society with high kudos being given to producing a son and with commensurate increases in power and wealth for the family associated with producing a male heir, has caused severe problems for Chinese society. Many people had called for this occasion to be marked with the birth of a girl. Already it has been estimated that the difference between boy:girl births has topped at 130:100 in some regions, whereas the world average is 105:100. It seems as though finding a partner for the boys is going to be problematic in future years, and this may or may not have a corresponding effect on the birth rate, the reduction of which is a high governmental priority.

The desire for male offspring is not limited to Asian families. Grieshaber (1998) has noted the strong desire of Australian women to produce a male heir to please their husbands, while noting that they would want a girl, or preferably one of each to maintain the status quo.

The social ramifications of the biological categories of sex (male and female) have been shown to have a significant impact on preferences that parents have for the offspring they produce, and thus the process can be regarded as starting even before the child is born. Once the child is born, the construction and maintenance of these categories becomes social, and

Gender and Schooling in the Early Years, pages vii–ix
Copyright © 2005 by Information Age Publishing
All rights of reproduction in any form reserved.

doing gender becomes socially constructed, impacting all aspects of the everyday lives of young children and their families. This is why a consideration of the issues surrounding gender in the early years is so necessary, and why this current volume is timely and vital to our understandings of the ways in which we interact and work with young children.

Much of the work on gender has been coupled with the concept of equity since it was apparent that girls were, in fact, being disadvantaged or discouraged from participating in activities and employment that were traditionally the domain of boys. It is nearly three decades since the first gender equity programs were implemented (e.g., Cohen & Martin, 1976; Davis, 1979). Significant inroads have been made during this time, so much so in fact that the Australian government has now called for strategies and policies to be developed so that boys are not disadvantaged in schooling, specifically related to their poor performance in literacy and English.

A consideration of equity and creating contexts in education that are both equitable and socially just should be a goal of all educators since it benefits all participants. This is one of the reasons why this particular book is relevant and can make a vital contribution to helping those interested in educating young children. The contents and issues addressed are both specifically related to gender and equity, but they also encompass and describe educational settings (e.g., Reggio Emilia) that enable all participants to feel empowered to learn and who feel valued for their contributions. These ideas need to be voiced from the early years so that children grow up realizing that equity and social justice are a natural and integral part of our lives, and our behavior should be based on the ideals of equality of opportunity and maximizing individual potential.

Traditionally, *doing gender* involves judgments about a person. From a very early age we complement children based on the ways in which they might exemplify the qualities of either the masculine or the feminine. In this way a dualism has been created, and it has become important for children to get their gender *right* so that they can be regarded as normal. However, in some societies (Lorber, 1994) there are more categories with variations, including *male women* and *female men*. Thus, it is apparent that the context of gendered behavior is important, and the work of Davies (e.g., 1989) has illustrated the ways in which some young children are able to use different gender positions according to the context in which they find themselves and that these will vary if they are in the presence of adults or peers. Furthermore, what is regarded as being socially acceptable in terms of behavior changes. Over the last two decades, for example, we have observed that fathers have been taking a more active role in the parenting process, and women have extended their professional work into new arenas previously reserved for men.

While recognizing that gender is a major feature that constitutes the identity of a person, it is also evident that it is only one of the attributes, along with others such as race, ethnicity, and class, that contribute to the multiple identities that individuals create for themselves in the course of their lives. This volume will stimulate discussion around the issues of gender and equity in the field and assist us to critically interrogate hitherto unjust gendered practices that are detrimental for realizing one's full potential. It is vital and timely and will act as a catalyst for discussion so that teachers and parents may examine their practices and create contexts for learning and growing that are socially just and equitable for all children.

—Nicola Yelland
School of Education, Victoria University
Melbourne, Australia

REFERENCES

Cohen, M., & Martin, L. (1976). *Growing free: Ways to help children overcome sex-role stereotypes.* Washington, DC: Association for Childhood Education International.

Davies, B. (1989). *Frogs and snails and feminist tales: Preschool children and gender.* Sydney, Australia: Allen & Unwin.

Davis, W. (1979). *Towards a non-sexist classroom.* Adelaide, Australia: Department of Education, Women's Advisory Unit.

Grieshaber, S. (1998). Constructing the gendered infant. In N. Yelland (Ed.), *Gender in early childhood* (pp. 16–35). London: Routledge.

Lorber, J. (1994). *Paradoxes of gender.* New Haven, CT: Yale University Press.

No Doubt. (n.d.). *I'm just a girl* [Song lyrics]. Available at: http://www.sing365 .com/music/lyric.nsf/Just-A-Girl-lyrics-No-Doubt/F8B6AA23140B5E2A48256 8B9000D0BAB

INTRODUCTION

The Early Childhood Environment: An Exploration of Gender Issues

Janice Koch
Beverly J. Irby

In a recent newspaper cartoon that shows Cinderella talking to her fairy godmother, the caption reads, "Forget the royal ball; can you send me to Harvard?" The Cinderella social stereotype for young girls does not ring as true today as it may have many years ago as girls grow into young women with intellectual aspirations that render marital economic dependency unnecessary. Both girls and boys seek achievement in the public sphere as a means to prepare themselves for the broader adult world of earning a living and caring for oneself. As the editors of this second volume of the series on *Research on Women and Education,* we chose to focus on the early years and present young girls and young boys as they try to make sense of their gendered identities while negotiating the complex world of school.

As Volume I of this book series stated, gender equity is defined as parity between males and females in the quality-of-life, academic, and work outcomes valued by our society. The purpose of the field of gender equity is to develop, implement, and evaluate the success of strategies, programs, and policies designed to promote those outcomes. Klein, Ortman, and Friedman (2002) explained that

> Although there is no one legislatively mandated or commonly accepted definition, most would agree with the following: To be *equitable* is to be fair and just, free from bias or favoritism. The term *gender equity* means just that: to be

Gender and Schooling in the Early Years, pages xi–xiii

fair and just toward both men and women, to show preference to neither, and concern for both. (p. 4)

Attaining gender equity, in and through education, means achieving equitable outcomes for females and males in all that is of value to individuals and society. Additionally, this should encompass attempts to rethink what we value to include frequently neglected strengths and roles traditionally associated with women.

In this volume, gender and schooling in the early years addresses a broad range of issues including, but not limited, to gender equity in education. We explore, for example, the complex world of play in Fromberg's chapter and are reminded that for young children, play involves issues of power and hierarchy in ways that parallel the role of gender in society. Miletta's study of preschool children in northern Italy, at Reggio Emilia, reveals a story of classroom interactions where gender differences are not part of the equation for the youngsters. Her chapter begs the question, "How does this environment empower all children, regardless of gender?" Two chapters provide a lens to the Montessori setting for young children. Wilgus studies the gendered patterns of young women teaching at a Montessori school, while Irby, Rodriguez, and Lara-Alecio explore the intersections of culture and gender at a bilingual Montessori public preschool. Further examining the preschool years, Plaster and Schiller address the current brain research and examine the ways in which the adults that staff early child care programs, and the environments that they offer, play an important role in the development of our children.

Extending the study of gender and schooling for young children, Polnick and Funk examine the early education of girls and boys in the block corner as they develop mathematical skills. Plevyak provides a lens on the development of scientific interest for young children as she explores issues of gender and science. Irby, Brown, and Yang explore the role of gender in creating developmentally appropriate early childhood assessment practices. While Robles-Pina and Butler examine gender issues in school violence from the earliest grades, Warner and Barrera provide a chapter devoted to the role of educators in communicating gender equity to parents. Finally, Turner-Muecke explores the role of mentoring in creating leaders in early childhood education.

Issues addressing gender identity, gender development, and gender stereotyping are complex and multifaceted. This volume seeks to highlight these complexities by shedding light on the diverse contexts that influence the development of girls' and boys' gendered identities in school. Teachers need to encourage both boys and girls to express themselves with words and appropriate actions. Many boys, as well as some girls, will use their bodies to intimidate or bully, and teachers must intervene and ask them to express their feelings and share their thoughts. The notion that "boys will be boys" often condones inappropriate physical behavior in the early grades that often leads to problems in later grades. Girls, compared to boys, tend to be shy and quiet in group discussions. Boys' hands fly up and often are out of control as body movements frequently dominate boy communication. Teachers must encourage girls to participate and speak so they can be heard. The expression of feelings and thoughts in a public sphere begins in school. Both "bad boys" and "silent girls" (Gallas, 1998) are lost to the learning community in the early grades, and that isolation discourages appropriate development of communication skills.

Examining the gender issues in an early childhood classroom requires that teachers explore their students' socialization by observing how they are communicating with each other; evaluate their students' achievement in all subject areas through the lens of gender; and ask themselves, "Are the females and males in my classroom limited by the gendered expectations of the school, the society, or the particular culture to which they belong?" Asking this question and seeking authentic answers is part of the journey of creating a gender-equitable classroom environment.

This volume represents the first attempt, in our experience, to represent multiple voices around the issues of gender and schooling in the early years. We anticipate that this volume on gender and schooling in the early years will serve all who seek to provide equitable learning environments in their classrooms, in the hopes that all children can realize the full expression of their capabilities.

REFERENCE

Gallas, K. (1998). *Sometimes I can be anything: Power, gender, and identity in a primary classroom.* New York: Teachers College Press.

CHAPTER 1

THE POWER OF PLAY

Gender Issues in Early Childhood Education

Doris Pronin Fromberg

Play is an arena in which young children can feel powerful. When children self-select an activity, they view it as play. When a teacher requests them to participate in the same activity, they view it as work (King, 1992). The context of gender in society parallels the context of play in school as an issue that involves power, a sense of identity, communication, and opportunity. This chapter considers the dynamics of play and power in relation to gender issues in early childhood and concludes with some implications for teachers. Within the larger field of types of play, this chapter gives particular attention to sociodramatic play because of its dynamic character. The framework of sociodramatic play offers an opportunity for adults to understand and assess how young children use power and reflects the players' understanding of gender issues.

A DYNAMIC DEFINITION OF PLAY

Play is a dynamic process that lends itself to a fluid definition (see Fromberg, 2002). Play exists *in relation to* particular physical, cognitive (meaningful), and social contexts. It is both a noun and a verb form that includes the following contextual characteristics:

Gender and Schooling in the Early Years, pages 1–27

Play is a voluntary activity that occurs for its own sake and exists *in relation to* a particular context.

Play is meaningful to the player, and young children's imaginative play grows out of their personal experiences. *The variety of surface forms in which children represent meanings conform to specific underlying processes.*

Play is symbolic in that it represents experiences. *The underlying play structures* facilitate the variety of surface forms in which children represent their experiences.

Play is rule-governed. The rules of play emerge as children collaboratively build their play. Children organize themselves within the play framework. *There* is an ongoing, dynamic relationship between underlying rules and their multiple meaningful, observable representations.

Play is pleasurable even when dealing with serious themes. As they play, children experience a sense of satisfaction that transcends the moment. The *relationship* between the play frame and the satisfaction of the play content contributes to the sense of pleasure.

Play is episodic. Young children respond smoothly to one another's actions while they appear to be sharing similar unwritten episodic "scripts"[1] that they have developed together. Young children emphasize the activity rather than the "outcomes" (Dewey, 1933). *The emphasis on activity is an ever-changing process.*

Play is one condition for learning in early childhood that serves as a kind of lymphatic function because it integrates emotional, social, and cognitive learning. Children bring their prior experiences to their play and, through interactions with others, can modify, extend, and expand their learning.

TYPES OF PLAY

Young children engage in solitary or social play with objects or play with others using their imaginations. The extensive literature on children's play outlines the following forms of play.

Functional play, with body movements or objects, focuses on explorative, often repetitive activity, as in the case of sensory exploration. Functional play predominates during infancy.

Constructive play, alone or with others, involves the imaginative use of objects to create a variety of three-dimensional forms, as in building with blocks or constructing mobiles. Sometimes, children who build collaboratively with blocks engage in sociodramatic play during the building, and sometimes the building is preliminary to sociodramatic play. Constructive play begins in later infancy and in the toddler years.

Sociodramatic play occurs when two or more individuals enter a pretend-play frame together and move in and out of the play frame to negotiate their "scripts." Although the "scripts" have implicit play rules, the rules are flexible and subject to ongoing negotiation; sociodramatic play is a particularly powerful form in which children use both imagery and communication about their imagery in seamless ways. *The oscillation between imagery and communication about the imagery is the arena in which the potential for learning takes place.*

Sociodramatic play begins during toddlerhood and becomes more complex as young children's language skills develop. At the same time, children's language skills expand and flourish during sociodramatic play.

Games with rules may be as simple as tossing an object or a ball back and forth during toddlerhood or following the rules of board games during the preschool years (3–4 years) and beyond. Young children feel comfortable about applying the rules flexibly until the primary grades when they become increasingly meticulous about compliance with rules.

The classic sequence of social play development includes first solitary play; then parallel play; then onlooker play; and, finally, social play (Parten, 1932). On the surface, this continuum has served many researchers as a basis for categorizing children's play. However, rather than a deficit, solitary play may be essential to concentration for children of primary age (Cole & LaVoie, 1985; Eddowes, 1991; Rubin & Howe, 1986; Voss, 1987). Therefore, it is useful to focus on dynamic processes rather than on linear structures when examining issues of play, power, and gender.

RESEARCH ON GENDER AND PLAY

A consideration of the relationship of gender and play suggests that most authors assume only two genders. Scholars, however, also have found within-gender variation (Maccoby, 1998; Thorne, 1993).[2] Thus, there are questions to consider concerning a model of gender as a continuum rather than a polarity.

These considerations serve as a context when considering the polarity expressed in many research findings. At the same time, young children may be having a fluid experience of gender-based characteristics rather than merely culturally sanctioned gender stereotypes in early childhood. With the caution to consider play behavior as a continuum of possible experiences, the report of representative research literature summarized in Table 1.1 provides prototypes of young male and female styles of play.

Table 1.1.   Prototypes of Young Male and Female Styles of Play

Male	Female
Engage in shorter play episodes that focus on acceptance of their suggestions	Engage in longer play episodes that value focus on interaction; balance their perspective with others
(Black, 1989; Gilligan, 1982; Sheldon, 1992)	
Distractable and competitive during problem-solving projects	Oblivious to distractions, even when engaged in collaborative problem-solving projects
Value autonomy and individual control	Expectation of group development
(Hattie, Marsh, Neill, & Richards, 1997; Rankin, 1998, in Edwards, Gandini, & Forman, 1998)	
Object/power orientation	Internal experience; relational
Third-person stance	Speak through a character
(Rabbie, Goldenbled, & Lodewijkx 1992; Wolf, Rygh, & Altshuler, 1984)	
More fluent play	More flexible, original, and collaborative
(Gonen, Uzmen, Akcin, & Ozdemir, 1993)	
Tendency toward immediate entry	Tendency toward planning beforehand
(Project Zero/Reggio Children, 2001)	
Use separate knowledge	Use connected knowledge
(Belenky, Clinchy, Goldberger, & Tarule, 1986)	
Receive less adult proximity and more corrections; punished more harshly; receive more adult attention for assertive behavior	Receive more adult physical proximity, comments, and questions; Tend to follow the teacher
Outdoor play away from school building	Play is closer to school building and adults
(Bradley & Gobbart, 1989; Caldera, Huston, & O'Brien, 1989; Carpenter, Huston, & Spera, 1989; Eron, 1992; Fagot, 1988; Golomb, Gowing, & Friedman, 1982; Hughes, 1999; Roggman & Peery, 1989; Serbin, 1978; Thorne, 1993)	
Block play, superhero, adventure, and transportation themes predominate	Housekeeping themes, art, and dress-up predominate
(Elgas, Klein, Kantor, & Fernie, 1988; Fagot & Leve, 1998; Garner, 1998; Maccoby & Jacklin, 1974; Paley, 1984; Trawick-Smith, 1994)	
More creative	Less proximity to creative play
(Clark, Griffing, & Johnson, 1989)	
Larger variety of toys; more toys educationally oriented; toys oriented away from home; more rough-and-tumble play and play fighting	Narrower range of toys; domestic themes and miniatures
(Hughes, 1999; Pellegrini & Kato, 2002; Tracy, 1987)	

Table 1.1.   Prototypes of Young Male and Female Styles of Play (Cont.)

Male	*Female*
Did not receive nonrequested stereotypically girls' toys	Received nonrequested toys that were stereotypically boys' toys

(Hughes, 1999)

Male	*Female*
Used toys to mark gender differences at 4 years of age	Willing to play with stereotypical toys and use a greater variety of materials

(Duveen & Lloyd, 1990; Garner, 1998)

Male	*Female*
Roles had more status, and boys were less willing to play stereotypical female roles after 4 years of age Older boys played less with younger sisters	Engaged in more sophisticated constructive play when playing with boys; girls were willing to play with stereotypical boys' toys Older girls played more than did boys with younger brothers

(Goldstein, 1995; Greif, 1976; Honig, 1998: Oden & Hall, 1998; Pellegrini & Perlmutter, 1989; Ramsey, 1998; Thorne, 1993)

Male	*Female*
Primary-age boys treated girls as "contaminated" and mocked boys who engaged in cross-gender friendship	Exempted boys from ridicule and viewed them as tough

(Thorne, 1993)

Male	*Female*
More rough-and-tumble play, games with rules, and games involving spatial relations (except boys from separated/divorced families)	More sedentary and sociodramatic pretend play, often with housekeeping themes

(Blurton Jones, 1976; Dodge & Frost, 1986; Henniger, 1985; Humphreys & Smith, 1984; Kier & Fouts, 1989; Paley, 1984; Parker, 1984; Pellegrini, 1987, 1998; Volma & van Eck, 2001)

Male	*Female*
Preference for stereotypically male toys, demonstrated superior performance on tasks requiring spatial skills, and attained higher scores on mathematics and science achievement tests	Preference for stereotypically female toys and evidenced superior verbal skills

(Hughes, 1999)

Male	*Female*
More chasing games	When chased, there was less bodily engagement or physically rough play

(Thorne, 1993)

Male	*Female*
More group sports and games in larger groups that require strategic planning and competition; longer lasting play requiring more skill	More "chumships" beginning at age 4; more variety of shifting alliances and some large groups, depending on context

(Hughes, 1999; Maccoby & Jacklin, 1974; Thorne, 1993; Whiting & Edwards, 1988)

Male	*Female*
Games more competitive, active, and adventuresome	Games more passive and consumerist

(Freitag, 1998; Pinker, 2002)

Table 1.1. Prototypes of Young Male and Female Styles of Play (Cont.)

Male	*Female*
Preferred transportation toys	Preferred storybooks and drawing
	(Pan, 1994)
Humor more expressive	Humor more receptive and verbally aggressive
More exuberant, teasing, clowning	
	(Bergen, 1998; Honig, 1998)

Rough-and-Tumble Play

Researchers in general have found that rough-and-tumble play—playing at fighting within the play framework—is more typical among boys than girls. When children play at fighting, they demonstrate an understanding of the unacceptable nature of uncontrolled aggression. Rough-and-tumble play entails aggressive themes without aggression, violence, or malicious intent. Children signal their intent by smiling, teasing, and relaxed body language and gestures. Although not dangerous in itself, it has the potential to become aggression on rare occasions (Pellegrini, 1998). Posture, gesture, facial expression, verbiage, and body tension signal the rare transformation of rough-and-tumble play into aggression. Researchers, however, have found that aggression on playgrounds during "recess" (when children are able to self-select their pastimes) occurs less than 2–3% of the time (Pellegrini & Smith, 1993).

Although rough-and-tumble play gives children the chance to safely explore aggression and hazards, female teachers tend to feel uncomfortable with the boisterous nature of rough-and-tumble play and its physical closeness, however lacking in danger of injury. Nevertheless, learning to engage in self-organization and self-motivation, build autonomy, and resolve aggression are important early learnings that can take place during play. During rough-and-tumble play, young children have the chance to build their own motives for ethical, fair, and peaceful resolution of differences and interpersonal problems. Researchers have concluded that primary school–age boys demonstrate appropriate ways to express care and intimacy during their rough-and-tumble play (Reed & Brown, 2000). The children have an opportunity to learn alternative ways to deal with disagreements and conflicts. When teachers forbid rough-and-tumble play or exploration of aggressive themes, children usually move their antisocial feelings underground, for example, a block or a finger becomes a toy gun. A survey suggested that overcontrolled, overscheduled, and pressured children are more prone to volatility and violence (Doyle, 1999).

Some educators and researchers who have observed war play (Carlsson-Paige & Levin, 1987), extensive superhero play (Newkirk, 2002; Paley, 1984), and a variety of conflicts among preschool children (Vaughn, Vollenweider, & Bost, 2003) saw the episodes as learning opportunities. Some teachers role played and discussed alternative, mutually satisfying ways to resolve disagreements (Carlsson-Paige & Levin, 1987; Paley, 1984). Some teachers view such occasions as opportunities to build on children's choices of topics as the basis for developing literacy themes and bring reluctant-to-read boys into the mainstream of literacy learning (Newkirk, 2002).

Rough-and-tumble play that exists on the aggression continuum, without emerging into aggression, differs from bullying, a form of aggression. Physical bullying, more typical among boys, is an attempt to establish dominance and can be an aggressive strategy that boys, more than girls, use in order to gain entry into a new group. Girls tend to use rumor and social ostracism as forms of bullying (Ma, 2001; Pellegrini & Bartini, 2000).

Games and Toys

Games. Games can also reflect a form of socially acceptable aggression in that "games differ in the level of competition and often contain elements of cooperation, [yet] nearly all modern games involve some form of contest, which by itself is a symbolic expression of aggression" (Reid, 1993, p. 327). Children can feel powerful while playing games and tend to reflect gender exploration and identification. In effect, boys tend to engage in more competitive games and imaginative play (Hasse, 2002). In turn, males appear to predominate in adult careers in physics, attributable by Hasse (2002) to their comparatively more playful and imaginative outlooks.

Toys. Researchers have found that toddlers as young as 18 months to 2 years of age reflect gender-typed toy preferences (Goldstein, 1994). It is consistent, therefore, that the parents of primary-age children who had strong gender-stereotyped attitudes selected traditionally gender-linked toys (Pan, 1994). Among middle-class mothers of kindergarten-age children in Taiwan, "More than half the sample reported that boys were not forbidden to engage in 'girl's play' or gender-specific activities and vice versa" (Pan, 1994, p. 44). This, of course, implies that half of the mothers did forbid boys to engage in "girl's play" or did not deal with the question.

The impact of toy selection appears to impact broader attitudes that children hold. For example, children correlated gender-linked toys with occupations (Singer, 1994). "Both girls and boys presented more varied ideas for improving [stereotypically] masculine toys. It appears that these toys had more potential for unique or creative use" (Singer, 1994, p. 22).

NATURE–NURTURE ISSUES

The issue of nature and nurture surfaces in understanding the development of gender-stereotypic play. The statement, "Sex is biological. Gender is cultural" (Eugenides, 2002, p. 489) can provide a helpful distinction when considering gender issues and the play of young children. Nevertheless, there is a likely interaction between biology and culture. For example, Jared Diamond's (1997) interdisciplinary work highlights the complexity involved in the evolution of human culture and behavior. It is important to keep in mind the context of complexity when considering both biological arguments and social learning/cultural context arguments that theoreticians and researchers consider when they try to understand and explain their observations concerning gender-stereotypic play.

The Biological Model

The biological model has been influenced by current genetic research and takes the position that nature plays a significant role in human behavior. Building upon genetic factors such as DNA and human cultural history, one reviewer summarizes genetic predispositions as follows:

> [Males are] better at mentally rotating objects and maps, women are better at remembering landmarks and the positions of objects. Men are better throwers; women are more dexterous. Men are better at solving mathematical word problems, women at mathematical calculation. Women are more sensitive to sound and smells, have better depth perception, match shapes faster, and are much better at reading facial expressions and body language. Women are better spellers, retrieve words more fluently, and have a better memory for verbal material.... Men have a higher tolerance for pain and a greater willingness to risk life and limb for status, attention, and other dubious rewards. (Pinker, 2002, p. 345)

Although another reviewer contends that it is apparent that males tend to have a genetic predisposition for upper body strength and females to have a distinct reproductive function, it is possible that historical patterns have built upon these genetic distinctions (Maccoby, 1998). A further review of genetic research suggests that the predispositions of nature are designed to be highly malleable by nurture (Maccoby, 1998; Ridley, 2003). In this view, "learning itself consists of nothing more than switching genes on and off" (Ridley, 2003, p. 55). For example, the human predisposition to learn to speak needs exposure to language during the critical early years of life. Within this model, gender identity and expectations undergo similar sociocultural, environmental influences.

The Cognitive-Developmental Model

The cognitive-developmental model primarily reflects the views of psychologists. This view takes the position that gender identity development is "interwoven with play and other forms of communication" (Fagot & Leve, 1998, p. 191). A summary of research indicates that children establish gender identity between 18 months and 2 years of age (Davies, 1989). Another summary of research suggests that the development of gender identity appears to be apparent in children between 2 and 4 years of age and "a preference for same-sex playmates has not yet developed in the second year of life" (Maccoby, 1998, p.17). "Thus, the characteristics that children of the two sexes develop in the course of interaction with their parents may well carry over, to some degree, to the way the children behave in interaction with same-sex playmates" (Maccoby, 1998, p. 147). In a parallel study, anthropologists have found that children select same-gender playmates beginning at 4 years of age (Whiting & Edwards, 1988). Psychologists who studied the free play of 4- and 5-year-olds "suggest that individual differences in degree of exposure to same-sex peers makes a difference in children's [academic competence]" (Fabes, Martin, Hanish, Anders, & Madden-Derdich, 2003, p. 857).

In summary, there may be a significant confluence between gender identity (a cognitive attainment), the selection of same-gender playmates (a social corollary), and the reinforcement of culturally sanctioned gender stereotypical play themes by playmates, as well as parents and the media. The development of gender identity and gender-segregated play groups is also likely to be influenced by the differential toys, activities, and clothing that adults provide for them.

The Sociocultural Model

The sociocultural model grows out of the work of social scientists. This perspective emphasizes the significance of specific cultural contexts on children's development of gender-oriented play behavior that emerges from the children's development of their gender identity.

In agricultural societal settings, the continuum of play, play-work, and work can be fluid for 2- to 6-year-olds. Bloch and Adler (1994) found that thematic play appeared to be "directed" with girls engaging in cooking, domestic cleaning, marketing, and child care while boys engaged in more thematic play related to cars/transportation and hunting activities. With girls doing more responsible work with less playing when closer to home and boys doing less work in general, with more opportunities to play and working farther from home, "The emergence of the gender division of labor...leads to...inequitable consequences..." (Bloch & Adler, 1994, p. 166; see also Greishaber, 1998). It is conceivable that a combination of imitation of other children and adults, as well as the provision of toys and encouragement by other children and adults, leads to the early and continuing selection of gender-typed toys by boys and girls. The appearance of boy or girl models in media advertisements for toys also support the gender identification of toys (Levin, 2003).

To summarize, cultural contributions to the development of gender identity and gender-oriented play include the following:

- expectations of parents;
- the degree of physical vigor with which adults and older children play with younger children;
- the provision of differential playthings;
- the differential modeling of behavior at home, in gender-segregated play groups, and in the community; and
- the differential modeling of gender-specific behavior in the media.

Print and television advertisements for toys that depict children of a particular gender tend to lead to those toys being selected by children of the same gender (Schwartz & Markham, 1985). In the majority of instances, advertisers and merchandisers appear to reinforce gender-stereotypic toys by their depiction of boys or girls playing with them or with the placement of toys in separate areas with pink predominating in the girls' toy section (Schwartz & Markham, 1985). When the illustrations on packages are gender-neutral, or after seeing their same-gender model using a toy, both boys and girls are likely to select the toy, with girls spending more time with it (Schwartz & Markham, 1985).

In an anthropological study of middle- and working-class black and white children in the United States, the children from working-class homes in North Carolina were more likely to have narrower choices of toys that had more static uses (Heath, 1983). Such static uses for toys might contribute to the lower aspirations of children from these working-class homes. A related finding in Australia is that the adult provision of toys was predictably categorical for boys as contrasted with girls, but that middle-class children had more options (Davies, 1989).

THE DYNAMICS OF SOCIODRAMATIC PLAY

The research on children's play, particularly sociodramatic play, offers relevant support to the perspective that play is a valuable process in children's development. The preponderance of findings suggest that sociodramatic play significantly influences social competence, linguistic development, and cognitive development; there are mixed findings concerning the influence of sociodramatic play on creativity and problem solving (Fromberg, 2002).

Script theory defines the process within which children plan and then engage in sociodramatic play together. The content of sociodramatic play grows out of children's "event knowledge," their life experiences. The process of sociodramatic play involves a kind of grammar in which, based upon prior event knowledge, young children play out their themes within a predictably unpredictable structure. The unpredictability of the play structure occurs within the negotiations in which children engage that oscillate between metacommunication (planning) and imagery (playing). For example, a child will communicate about the play outside of the play frame (e.g., "You be the baby, and I'll be the doctor") (metacommunication) and immediately "become" the doctor while the "baby-player" seamlessly performs the role of the baby (imagery enactment). The predictability of the script is that the children engage in imagery within the same theme. The unpredictability of the script is the particular prior experience (event knowledge) or personal imagination that each child may represent while playing the respective roles. For example, the doctor may be more or less benevolent or nurturing and the baby may be more or less cooperative, or may present play symptoms to which the doctor may need to adjust (e.g., provision of a play hypodermic, bandages, or crutches). Within the varied unpredictable surface forms of the play, the basic predictable patient–doctor medical script relationship becomes enacted. Either player, without predictability, may involve other play roles in their script, such as an attendant, friend, or parent figure.

Thus, the players clearly represent their motives and thought processes within their play interactions (scripts). A major feature to highlight includes the dynamic movement between metacommunication (planning the play) outside the play framework about their mutual script building and the immediate communication (becoming their scripted roles) between the players within the play framework. The complexity of this dynamic process reflects the *phase transitions* between metacommunication and communicative imagery during which ideas are exchanged, change of script content can occur, and mutual learning can emerge. Within this phase transition process (the script's movement between metacommunication and imagery), script development is a form of collaborative oral playwriting, a powerful support for ongoing literacy development. The oscillation process reflects the complexity of "phase transitions," the arena in which there is potential for learning. It is worth mentioning that the oscillating process can become disturbed if power relations become unbalanced.

IMPLICATIONS FOR TEACHERS OF YOUNG CHILDREN

Scaffolding

Teachers have the potential to intervene and discourage play or influence learning through the process of scaffolding. Scaffolding, as outlined by Lev Vygotsky (1987), lies in the zone of proximal development, the "next step" that adults can take to support and challenge children. It is worth considering that such scaffolding requires the professional competence of an informed professional teacher who has both a strong knowledge base about how children learn, as well as significant social, aesthetic, and physical knowledge of the world.

Scaffolding also requires the development of trust between a professional teacher and young children. If children are too busy coping with stress and defending against a sense of failure or threat (Bruner, 1966; Goleman, 1995), the challenge of new learning may feel more hopeless than hopeful.

Within sociodramatic play, an adult can serve to scaffold opportunities by becoming part of the pretend play in a sensitive manner. Although sociodramatic play is a venue for assessing children's understandings, feelings, and social competence, it is highly vulnerable to destruction if adults intrude with too much metacommunication.

A successful scaffold has occurred when teachers have wanted to help girls feel welcome in the blocks area, for example, and found that girls were more likely to enter this area when the female teacher was present (Serbin, 1978). The blocks area provides opportunities for building the visual-spatial skills that are so relevant to understanding mathematical problems and physical science problems.

Inasmuch as girls are underrepresented in the fields of science and mathematics, scaffolding and modeling of gender-neutral activity is relevant. In addition, multiple "peer models may be especially helpful with students who hold self-doubts about their capabilities..." (Schunk, 1987, p. 170). "Observing several peers engaging in the same behavior may lead children to conclude that activities are appropriate for them to perform" (Schunk, 1987, p. 165).

Teachers can plan with, encourage, and scaffold girls to participate in building with blocks and to engage in group games and sports. Scaffolding might mean that adults can employ seamless strategies such as entering the play frame, inviting girls to enter, observing them, and perhaps beginning to play with the girls if necessary. For example, "Where could we use this block? Please hand me a block that is large enough to reach across both of these blocks." The adult then withdraws to an observer's role as soon as possible in order to support children's experience of power within the play frame. The teacher's sense of playfulness and sense of humor can support such initiatives. The adult who can enter seamlessly into—and soon exit from—young children's oral playwriting validates and demonstrates respect for the children's power to engage in this collaborative narrative. *Thus, power relations and instructional strategies—part of the cultural context—within a classroom also can support gender expectancies and the aspirations of children.*

Scheduling

It is during the scaffolding process, when phase transitions take place, that opportunities exist for children to learn and transform their thinking, skills, and attitudes. At a time when minimalist and standardized tests nudge school administrators to push for increasingly narrow teaching toward the tests, time for sociodramatic play in school settings has been sharply reduced or eliminated from kindergarten and the primary grades.

Therefore, early childhood teachers, from the earliest years throughout the primary grades, need to advocate for and ensure a schedule that includes sufficient time for significant script building to take place. One researcher suggests that a minimum of 30 minutes is necessary (Christie, Johnsen, & Peckover, 1988). Another researcher found that boys needed a minimum of 30 minutes of block play before they were able to approach more sedentary art activities with a reasonable degree of concentration (Paley, 1984). In order to provide sufficient time for young children to engage in significant sociodramatic play as well as other creative and intellectual experiences, the early childhood schedule profits from long blocks of time (from 45 to 75 minutes) in order for young children to develop the collaborative sociodramatic play scripts as well as other important experiences, such as creating artwork, doing creative writing, building with small and floor-based construction materials, pursuing science experiments, engaging in social studies projects, and self-selecting fine-quality trade books to read. One preschool teacher, anxious to see that boys, as well as girls, engaged in art experiences and sedentary table-based construction, began each activity period by closing the sociodramatic play areas (including floor blocks) for 30 minutes; then, when she matched the class clock to the wall clock, children knew that they could enter the sociodramatic play areas which were open for the remaining 45 minutes of the general morning activity period.

Teachers can help all children by providing opportunities for unstructured development of their own ways to solve problems "...if they accord respect and allow time for the knowledge that emerges from firsthand experience" (Belenky et al., 1986, p. 229). In general, the provision of time for unstructured play can help children to resist cultural stereotypes of gender (Yuen & Shaw, 2003). However, there are different ways to interpret "structured" activities. For example, if boys tend to play at a greater distance from adults and if their activities include more play that is "structured" by superhero media themes, then the boys function within an alternative "structure" that serves to stereotype gender roles. If girls tend to play nearer to adults, then it might appear that they are engaged in approved activities that are subject to adult standards of "structure." Therefore, teachers need to be in touch with the variety of themes in which children engage in order to access the significance of children's play.

SPACE PLANNING AND UTILIZATION

The utilization of space also can serve to support sociodramatic play and other opportunities for problem solving. It is helpful to place the sociodramatic props/housekeeping play area and the blocks area adjacent to one another and to maintain open traffic patterns between them. Consider moving props from either area into the other from time to time, or creating some themes and props that cut across these areas. Props that support such themes as toy store, post office, restaurant, airport, spaceship adventures, or hospital play tend to expand opportunities for both boys and girls to integrate their play with one another as well as to expand their use of event knowledge and language skills. Another example is that of "a social scientist (Donna Barnes) [who] has designed playful activities around the Thanksgiving theme that reflect the important role of colonial women" (Fromberg, 2002, pp. 153–154).

There is a body of research that finds children increase their literacy skills when they engage in a variety of sociodramatic play themes that integrate opportunities for literacy (e.g., labels, signs, appointment books, menus, receipts, and so forth) (Christie, 1991; Dodge & Frost, 1986; Levy, Schaefer, & Phelps, 1986; Morrow, 1990; Neuman & Roskos, 1991; Schrader, 1989, 1990; Vukelich, 1991). At the same time that a variety of props helps to extend children's opportunities for conceptual and language use, it is possible to observe the limits of children's event knowledge when—regardless of themes suggested by props—they include familiar family-based elements such as food preparation and child care (Fromberg, 2002). In effect, the out-of-school experiences and community attitudes toward gender roles is a strong source of event knowledge that children bring into their play. It is significant, therefore, that teachers take a proactive role in providing for egalitarian opportunities for children in school.

The City and Country School in New York City uses blocks as the representational centerpiece in the curriculum study of community resources; both girls and boys throughout the early childhood and elementary school years observe community activities, discuss their observations, and see the teacher write down their findings and plans for representation through block building. They then integrate visual arts and writing, solve technical problems, measure and compare structures, and study science as part of the community study. Boys and girls participate together in these activities. Another factor in the successful integration of girls with blocks is the plentiful provision of blocks. It is worthwhile to consider the quantity of resources when attempting to influence equitable access. For example, when teachers provide equivalent access or double the amount of available blocks, boys and girls use the blocks, although often in same-gendered dyads (Rogers, 1985). On the one hand, providing sufficient space for imaginative play and constructive play improves the opportunities for access. On the other hand, insufficient space or materials can contribute to competition and strife.

GENDER-NEUTRAL MATERIALS AND LANGUAGE

Unexamined and cultural patterns of behavior and use of language can reinforce gender-stereotypic play activities. Therefore, it is helpful when teachers select toys, equipment, and materials that serve multiple functions and might encourage both boys and girls to use them. When ordering toy figures, it is useful to have apparel that is androgynous as well as egalitarian. In this way, children can structure their own use of gender-neutral materials, such as blocks, clay, art materials, gender-neutral jigsaw puzzles, board games, and so forth. It is also useful to maintain gender-neutral toys by noticing and removing stereotypical labels or advertisements. At the same time, teachers who reflect thoughtfully on their use of gender-neutral language with young children can be proactive in undoing hierarchical stereotypes (see Mac Naughton, 1998).

One of the hallmarks of pretend play that helps children to extend learning and that helps teachers to assess development is the extent to which children can decontextualize props and use their imaginations. For example, a block can become a gun, a stethoscope, or a feeding spoon. When adults provide more realistic materials, such as toys that are detailed replicas of real things, the children appear to be less open to symbolic substitutions. Researchers have found that children who were less able to substitute props for real items did not achieve as much academic success as children who were able to engage in symbolic substitutions (Smilansky, 1968). Moreover, when adults presented unstructured toys before structured toys, children engaged in more extended symbolic play (McGhee, Etheridge, & Berg, 1984). In turn, academic achievement improved after teacher intervention to model and encourage pretense (Freyberg, 1973; Smilansky, 1968).

Some researchers have found that there was no gender difference in the amount of pretend play, although the themes vary, while others have found that "girls' pretend play is more symbolic and abstract.... Girls are more likely to use nonrealistic props.... This may be due to maturation; boys may simply be less ready cognitively to symbolize in this abstract way" (Trawick-Smith, 1994, p. 336).

Using gender-identified toys, one investigator asked children to suggest new or innovative ways to use them (Rosenfeld, 1975). The investigator found that both girls and boys presented more varied ideas for improving the masculine-stereotyped toys because they had more potential for unique and creative use. This finding supports the idea that adults can support imaginative play by carefully selecting toys that have the potential for multiple and interpretive uses.

GROUPING

Grouping is another way to provide egalitarian access to resources. One teacher-researcher describes communal play writing in which all children in the class must participate or the activity would not take place and in which some children role play another gender (Gallas, 1998). Others suggest that teachers group children on the basis of the children's subject matter interests as well as plan opportunities for children to work with a variety of different children in small groups or pairs (Edwards et al., 1998).

"The term borderwork helps conceptualize interaction across stereotyped gender boundaries" (Thorne, 1993, p. 64). Some teachers who planned for boys and girls to work together with computers, even with software that was gender-neutral, found that, "boys appear to focus more often on the computer work whereas girls concentrate more on the group process...[and the] girls working in mixed pairs get less chance to work on the computer" (Volma & van Eck, 2001, pp. 621–622) than boys, who take over the mouse. Therefore, when teachers plan for cross-gender groups, it is helpful to provide time for group process and to place computers where children can talk more together.

Teacher planning, modeling, and encouragement can contribute to reducing barriers. From a planning standpoint, for example, teachers would not set up girls' and boys' lines, teams, or label activities as girls' or boys' activities. From a modeling standpoint, teachers would engage with children in a variety of areas, for example, inviting girls as an underrepresented group to participate alongside the teacher in the construction activities. From an encouragement standpoint, the usual eye contact, teacher proximity, encouraging nods, and explicit discussion of participation would be relevant; one kindergarten teacher-researcher actually developed a kind of mantra that children adopted, "You can't say you can't play" (Paley, 1992).

MODELING

Thoughtful teachers attempt to model gender-neutral language. For example, they ask children to retrieve outdoor clothing or line up by the color of clothing, type of shoe, initial letter of names, and so forth, rather than as "girls and boys." When children see models of players or workers that cut across genders and across age groups, there is the potential to counteract stereotypes. However, it makes sense to provide multiple models that include a focus on the role of power relations. For example, just as some teachers pay more overt attention to boys' contributions and accomplishments, a subtle influence of teacher modeling resides in a finding that "white teachers directed more verbal praise and criticism and nonverbal praise toward males..." (Simpson & Erickson, 1983, p. 183).

Books also can provide models of egalitarian perspectives. Consider selecting books that provide egalitarian premises. When a book depicts stereotypic behavior, discuss the issues of fairness and accuracy, for example, "What might you do if someone told you that you could not do that because only girls/boys were permitted?"

Classroom resource visitors can provide additional models that counter stereotypes and support egalitarian outlooks, for example, a mother who is a physicist, sculptor, police detective, pilot, or construction worker; and a father who is a data processor, jewelry artist, or ballet dancer.

> Roles are learned when one identifies with models...unsuccessful as well as successful ones.... Roles are learned, then, when an individual imitates cognitive scripts displayed by models with whom he or she identifies. Many of these scripts are expressions of social norms, varying from time to time and culture to culture. Others are individual scripts, specific only to the model in question. (Bjorkqvist & Niemala, 1992, pp. 4, 15)

Social competence that can lead toward improving the expectations that children have for their immediate and distant futures can grow with role playing. "Playing with roles entails treating roles as things to be explored, complicated, transformed, and experimented with. This kind of creative enactment and playfulness with roles can help children to develop a "meta-level" awareness of social roles..." (Duncan & Tarulli, 2003, p. 287). In this way, teachers' modeling, along with their encouragement and appreciation of children's role playing, has the potential to expand the present and future possibilities that children might consider for themselves.

Teachers' modeling and providing time and space for role playing also can serve to offer children specific strategies for entering and maintaining play episodes. Researchers have found that the use of systematic scaffolding to support socially competent strategies and modeling with puppets can influence the cognitive development of 4- and 5-year-olds (Choi & Kim, 2003). Also, for those teachers who want to foster cross-gender play, modeling and role playing can serve as additional strategies for influencing such integration. Sensitive teachers enter the play frame by taking a role within an ongoing play script, modeling an extension of ongoing interaction, or suggesting that another child might assist the players by bringing in a new prop or "wondering if" something might happen next.

ASSESSMENT

The thematic content of young children's play reveals their developing category systems and understanding of events. If assessment focuses on children's development of meanings, it would make sense to value different forms and products. For example, by observing sociodramatic play, it is possible to observe children's career and life expectations as a category for assessment. If girls or boys consistently enact the limitations of stereotyped roles, then the sensitive teacher might consider ways to use curricular variables and the strategies, discussed above, to try to influence more egalitarian concepts and aspirations.

Thoughtful teachers recognize that the distinctive and different profile of strengths for some children will be apparent in their representational competences. The thematic content of children's play reveals their developing category systems, gender roles and expectancies, and understandings of events.

When children play outdoors, teachers can learn more about children's personal cultures and event knowledge. For example, children's language on the playground may "complement school literacies" (Grugeon, 2001, p. 114). In this respect, an observant teacher may build on children's preoccupations as an entry into school literacy.

PARENT INVOLVEMENT

The strong influence of broader cultural influences on gender and play makes it reasonable for school personnel to enlist parents in support of egalitarian opportunities for young children to play. In order to strengthen the egalitarian purposes in schools, school personnel have involved parents through individual conferences and group meetings that include purposeful analysis of advertisements for toys and the potential value of playthings that have varied and imaginative uses.

It is helpful for teachers to support parents in legitimizing parents' pretend play with their children. For example, researchers Jerome Singer and Dorothy Singer (1979) "found that high-imagination children reported greater contact with parents who modeled or provided specific opportunities for fantasy play. High-imagination children manifested a capacity to wait quietly for a longer period of time, reporting fantasy play as they did so. They also scored higher in imaginative storytelling, made more analogic kinds of statements, and were more persevering than low-fantasy children" (cited in Fromberg, 1999, p. 40). A related study by other researchers found that "in the areas of self-control and fantasy play levels, both boys and girls who received systematic child-centered group play sessions are likely to significantly outperform children who receive no play treatment" (Trostle, 1988, p. 104). Parents can find such information to be suggestive about helpful ways to interact with their children.

Newsletters are another useful "way to educate parents about gender issues and the value of cooperation between the sexes ... by [including] brief accounts of cooperative play and conflict resolution that have taken place in [the] classroom" (Schlank & Metzger, 1997. p. 214). At the same time, school personnel would keep in mind and be sensitive to the cultural pressures that parents, as well as children, experience that cause them to invest considerable energy in maintaining gender boundaries.

CONCLUDING STATEMENT

The finding that children appear to be less open to symbolic substitutions when they begin to use more realistic materials (see McGhee et al., 1984) has particular implications in the context of the contemporary pressure for a test-driven, narrowly conceived, skills-based curriculum. In effect,

> beginning children's school activities with paper-and-pencil tasks and work books may limit their ability to extend symbolic representation and its implicit potential for connection making. This finding implies that mathematical and scientific learning that depends on understanding physical and material relationships, as well as writing potential that depend upon imagination, may prosper when play with [unstructured] objects takes place and suffer when limited provisions exist. (Fromberg, 1992, p. 149)

A curriculum that includes opportunities for young children to play with a variety of materials, props, and themes empowers the players, whereas a workbook-oriented curriculum renders children relatively powerless. Within a workbook curriculum, boys often are preferentially disempowered even more than girls within the current cultural stereotype of the more acquiescent female and the more assertive male. For example, some boys' expectations for themselves as readers may be influenced by fear of peer group rejection (Best, 1983).

Gender-sensitive teachers are culturally sensitive teachers who plan for intentional teaching that provides for egalitarian access to education and expectations. Therefore, it is valuable for teachers and parents who prefer that all children have great expectations in their lives to be vigilant and sensitive in supporting a broad range of possibilities for all children to learn.

When teachers embrace the power that resides in the complexity and unpredictability of young children's play, they are in a position to both see and support play as a form in which children represent what they know and can do. The systemic complexity and predictably unpredictable, situation-specific nature of children's play and gendered behavior offers many phase transitions that can become opportunities for teacher intervention and children's learning.

In this era of assessment, public policy mandates that educators present data to account for what students know and can do. Narrowly designed paper-and-pencil tests are being used to measure minimalist standards. In a different conception of assessment, there are multiple forms of representation that can help educators to understand what young children know and what they can do with their knowledge.

Children's play, particularly sociodramatic play, is a dynamic form of representation that illuminates ways in which young children learn and what they understand. It is worthwhile for educators to provide intentional opportunities—through planning, scheduling, scaffolding, provisioning, modeling, and enjoying—for children to use their imaginations and their power to play and learn. The provision for play in early childhood education is both intellectual and ethical teaching.

NOTES

1. See psychologists (e.g., Nelson et al., 1986) who have collaborated with linguists and specialists in artificial intelligence (e.g., Schank & Abelson, 1977).

2. Steven Pinker (2002), who strongly favors a biological orientation to gender differences, suggests that there are male and female characteristics that overlap within a Bell curve model, with gender-specific characteristics manifested in the tails of the curve (pp. 344–345).

REFERENCES

Belenky, M. F., Clinchy, B. M., Goldberger, N. R., & Tarule, J. M. (1986). *Women's ways of knowing: The development of self, voice, and mind.* New York: Basic Books.

Bergen, D. (1998). Play as a context for humor development. In D. P. Fromberg & D. Bergen (Eds.), *Play from birth to twelve and beyond: Contexts, perspectives, and meanings* (pp.324–337). New York: Garland.

Best, R. (1983). *We've all got scars: What boys and girls learn in elementary school.* Bloomington: Indiana University Press.

Bjorkqvist, K., & Niemala, P. (1992). New trends in the study of female aggression. In K. Bjorkqvist & P. Niemala (Eds.), *Of mice and women: Aspects of female agression* (pp. 3–16). New York: Academic Press.

Black, H. (1989). Interactive pretense: Social and symbolic skills in preschool play groups. *Merrill-Palmer Quarterly, 35*(4), 379–397.

Bloch, M. N., & Adler, S. M. (1994). African children's play and the emergence of the sexual division of labor. In J. L. Roopnarine, J. E. Johnson, & F. H. Hooper (Eds.), *Children's play in diverse cultures* (pp.148–178). Albany: State of New York University Press.

Blurton-Jones, N. (1976). Rough-and-tumble play among nursery school children. In J. S. Bruner, A. Jolly, & K. Sylva (Eds.), *Play—Its role in development and evolution* (pp. 352–362). New York: Basic Books.

Bradley, B. S., & Gobbart, S. K. (1989). Determinants of gender-typed play in toddlers. *Journal of Genetic Psychology, 150*(4), 453–455.

Bruner, J. S. (1966). *Toward a theory of instruction.* Cambridge, MA: Harvard University Press.

Caldera, Y. M., Huston, A. C., & O'Brien, M. (1989). Social interactions and play patterns of parents and toddlers with feminine, masculine, and neutral toys. *Child Development, 60,* 70–76.

Carlsson-Paige, N., & Levin, D. E. (1987). *The war play dilemma: Balancing needs and values in the early childhood classroom.* New York: Teachers College Press.

Carpenter, C. J., Huston, A. C., & Spera, L. (1989). Children's use of time in their everyday activities during middle childhood. In M. N. Bloch & A. D. Pellegrini (Eds.), *The ecological context of children's play* (pp.165–190). Norwood, NJ: Ablex.

Choi, D. H., & Kim, J. (2003). Practicing social skills training for young children with low peer acceptance: A cognitive-social learning model. *Childhood Education, 31*(1), 41–46.

Christie, J. F. (1991). *Play and early literacy development.* Albany: State University of New York Press.

Christie, J. F., Johnsen, E. P., & Peckover, R. B. (1988). The effects of play period duration on children's play patterns. *Journal of Research in Childhood Education, 3*(2), 123–131.

Clark, P. M., Griffing, P. S., & Johnson, L. G. (1989). Symbolic play and ideational fluency as aspects of the evolving divergent cognitive style in young children. *Early Child Development and Care, 51,* 77–78.

Cole, D., & LaVoie, J. C. (1985). Fantasy play and related cognitive development in 2- to 16-year-olds. *Developmental Psychology, 21*(1), 233–240.

Davies, B. (1989). *Frogs and snails and feminist tales: Preschool children and gender.* Sydney, Australia: Allen & Unwin.

Dewey, J. (1933). *How we think: A restatement of the relation of reflective thinking to the educative process.* Boston: D.C. Heath.

Diamond, J. (1997).*Guns, germs and steel: The fates of human societies.* New York: Random House.

Dodge, M. K., & Frost, J. L. (1986). Children's dramatic play: Influence of thematic and nonthematic settings. *Childhood Education, 62*(1), 166–170.

Doyle, L. (1999, August 22). Killers among us. *New York Times Magazine,* pp. 13–14.

Duncan, R. M., & Tarulli, D. (2003). Play as the leading activity of the preschool period: Insights from Vygotsky, Leont'ev, and Bakhtin. *Early Education and Development, 14*(3), 271–292.

Duveen, G., & Lloyd, B. (1990). A semiotic analysis of the development of social representations and the development of knowledge. In G. Duveen & B. Lloyd (Eds.), *Social representations and the development of knowledge* (pp. 27–46). New York: Cambridge University Press.

Eddowes, A. E. (1991, Fall). The benefits of solitary play. *Dimensions,* pp. 31–34.

Edwards, C. P., Gandini, L., & Forman, G. (1998). The hundred languages of children: The Reggio Emilia approach—Advanced reflection. In C. P. Edwards, L. Gandini, & G. Forman (Eds.), *The hundred language of children* (2nd ed., pp. 457–466). Norwood, NJ: Ablex.

Elgas, P. M., Klein, I., Kantor, R., & Fernie, D. E. (1988). Play and the peer culture: Play styles and object use. *Journal of Research in Childhood Education, 3*(2), 142–153.

Eron, L. D. (1992). Gender differences in violence: Biology and/or socialization. In K. Bjorkqvist & P. Niemala (Eds.), *Of mice and women: Aspects of female aggression* (pp. 89–97). New York: Academic Press.

Eugenides, J. (2002). *Middlesex.* New York: Farrar, Straus & Giroux.

Fabes, R. A., Martin, C. L., Hanish, L. D., Anders, M. C., & Madden-Derdich, D. A. (2003). Early school competence: The roles of sex-segregated play and effortful control. *Developmental Psychology, 39*(5), 848–858.

Fagot, B. I. (1988). Toddlers; play and sex stereotyping. In D. Bergen (Ed.), *Play: A medium for learning and development* (pp.133–135). Portsmouth, NH: Heinemann.

Fagot, B., & Leve, L. (1998). Gender identity and play. In D. P. Fromberg & D. Bergen (Eds.), *Play from birth to twelve and beyond: Contexts, perspectives, and meanings* (pp. 197–192). New York: Garland.

Freitag, P. J. (1998). Games, achievement, and the mastery of social skills. In D. P. Fromberg & D. Bergen (Eds.), *Play from birth to twelve and beyond: Contexts, perspectives, and meanings* (pp. 303–312). New York: Garland.

Freyberg, J. T. (1973). Increasing the imaginative play of urban disadvantaged children through system training. In J. L. Singer (Ed.), *The child's world of make-believe: Experimental studies of imaginative play* (pp. 129–154). New York: Academic Press.

Fromberg, D. P. (1992). How can I be sure children are learning if all they do is play all day? In D. M. Murphy & S. G. Goffin (Eds.), *Project Construct: A framework for curriculum and assessment* (pp. 147–157). Columbia: University of Missouri & the Missouri State Department of Elementary and Secondary Education.

Fromberg, D. P. (1999). A review of research on play. In C. Seefeldt (Ed.), *The early childhood curriculum: Current findings in theory and practice* (3rd ed., pp. 27–53). New York: Teachers College Press.

Fromberg, D. P. (2002). *Play and meaning in early childhood education.* Boston: Allyn & Bacon.

Gallas, K. (1998). *"Sometimes I can be anything": Power gender and identity in a primary classroom.* New York: Teachers College Press.

Garner, B. P. (1998). Play development from birth to age four. In D. P. Fromberg & D. Bergen (Eds.), *Play from birth to twelve and beyond: Contexts, perspectives, and meanings* (pp.137–145). New York: Garland.

Gilligan, C. (1982). *In a different voice: Psychological theory and women's development.* Cambridge, MA: Harvard University Press.

Goldstein, J.H. (1994). Sex differences in toy play and use of video games. In J. H. Goldstein (Ed.), *Toys, play, and child development* (pp. 110–129). New York: Cambridge University Press.

Goldstein, J. (1995). Aggressive toy play. In A. D. Pellegrini (Ed.), *The future of play theory* (pp.127–147). Albany: State University of New York Press.

Goleman, D. (1995). *Emotional intelligence.* New York: Bantam.

Golomb, C., Gowing, E. D. G., & Friedman, L. (1982). Play and cognition: Studies of pretense play and conservation of quantity. *Journal of Experimental Child Psychology, 33,* 257–279.

Gonen, M., Uzmen, S., Akcin, N., & Ozdemir, N. (1993). *Creative thinking as 5–6 year old kindergarten children. Building bridges: International collaboration in the 1990s.* Warwick, UK: Warwick University International Early Year Conference Proc. (ERIC Document Reproduction Service No. PS023789 ED 392 516)

Greif, E. B. (1976). Sex role playing in pre-school children. In J. S. Bruner, A. Jolly, & K. Sylva (Eds.), *Play—Its role in development and evolution* (pp. 385–391). New York: Basic Books.

Greishaber, S. (1998). Constructing the gendered infant. In N. Yelland (Ed.), *Gender in early childhood* (pp. 15–35). New York: Routledge.

Grugeon, E. (2001). 'We like singing the Spice Girl songs...and we like Tig and Stuck in the Mud': Girls' traditional games on two playgrounds. In J. C. Bishop & Curtis (Eds.), *Play today in the primary school playground: Life, learning and creativity* (pp. 98–114). Philadelphia: Open University Press.

Hasse, C. (2002). Gender diversity in play with physics: The problem of premises for participation in activities. *Mind, Culture, and Activity, 9*(4), 250–269.

Hattie, J., Marsh, H. W., Neill, J. T., & Richards, G. E. (1997). Adventure education and Outward Bound: Out-of-class experiences that make a difference. *Review of Educational Research, 87*(1), 43–87.

Heath, S. B. (1983). *Ways with words: Language, life, and work in communities and classrooms.* New York: Cambridge University Press.

Henniger, M. L. (1985). Preschool children's play behaviors in an indoor and outdoor environment. In J. L. Frost & S. Sunderlin (Eds.), *When children play* (pp. 145–149). Wheaton, MD: Association for Childhood Education International.

Honig, A. S. (1998). Sociocultural influences on gender-role behaviors in children's play. In D. P. Fromberg & D. Bergen (Eds.), *Play from birth to twelve and beyond way: Contexts, perspectives, and meanings* (pp. 338–347). New York: Garland.

Hughes, F. P. (1999). *Children, play, and development* (3rd ed.). Boston: Allyn & Bacon.

Humphreys, A. P., & Smith, P. K. (1984). Rough-and-tumble in preschool and playground. In P. K. Smith (Ed.), *Play in animals and humans* (pp. 241–266). New York: Basil Blackwell.

Kier, C. A., & Fouts, G. T. (1989). Sibling play in divorced and married-parent families. *Journal of Reproductive and Infant Psychology, 7,* 139–146.

King, N. (1992). The impact of context on the play of young children. In S. Kessler & B. Swadener (Eds.), *Reconceptualizing the early childhood curriculum* (pp. 42–61). New York: Teachers College Press.

Levin, D. E. (2003). *Teaching children in violent times: Building a peaceable classroom* (2nd ed.). Washington, DC: National Association for the Education of Young Children.

Levy, A. K., Schaefer, L., & Phelps, P. C. (1986). Increased preschool effectiveness: Enhancing the language abilities of 3- and 4-year-old children through planned sociodramatic play. *Early Childhood Research Quarterly, 1,* 133–140.

Ma, X. (2001). Bullying and being bullied: To what extent are bullies also victims? *American Educational Research Journal, 38*(2), 251–370.

Maccoby, E. E. (1998). *The two sexes: Growing up apart, coming together.* Cambridge, MA: Harvard University Press.

Maccoby, E. E., & Jacklin, C. T. (1974). *The psychology of sex differences.* Stanford, CA: Stanford University Press.

Mac Naughton, G. (1998). Improving our gender equity 'tools': A case for discourse analysis. In N. Yelland (Ed.), *Gender in early childhood* (pp.149–174). New York: Routledge.

McGhee, P. E., Etheridge, L., & Berg, N. A. (1984). Effect of toy structure on preschool children's pretend play. *Journal of Catholic Education, 144,* 209–217.

Morrow, L. M. (1990). Preparing the classroom environment to promote literacy during play. *Early Childhood Research Quarterly, 5*(4), 537–554.

Nelson, K., et al. (1986). *Event knowledge: Structure and function in development.* Mahway, NJ: Erlbaum.

Neuman, S. B., & Roskos, K. (1991). The influence of literacy-enriched play centers on preschoolers' conceptions of the functions of print. In J. F. Christie (Ed.), *Play and early literacy development* (pp. 167–187). Albany: State University of New York Press.

Newkirk, T. (2002). *Misreading masculinity: Boys, literacy, and popular culture.* Portsmouth, NH: Heinemann.

Oden, S., & Hall, J. A. (1998). Peer and sibling influences on play. In D. P. Fromberg & D. Bergen (Eds.), *Play from birth to twelve and beyond: Contexts, perspectives, and meanings* (pp. 266–276). New York: Garland.

Paley, V. G. (1984). *Boys and girls: Superheroes in the doll corner.* Chicago: University of Chicago Press.

Paley, V. G. (1992). *You can't say you can't play.* Cambridge, MA: Harvard University Press.

Pan, H. L. W. (1994). Children's play in Taiwan. In J. L. Roopnarine, J. E. Johnson, & F. H. Hooper (Eds.), *Children's play in diverse cultures* (pp. 31–50). Albany: State of New York University Press.

Parker, S. T. (1984). Playing for keeps: An evolutionary perspective on human games. In P. K. Smith (Ed.), *Play in animals and humans* (pp. 271–293). New York: Basil Blackwell.

Parten, M. (1932). Social participation among preschool children. *Journal of Abnormal and Social Psychology, 27*(2), 243–269.

Pellegrini, A. D. (1987). Rough-and-tumble play and social problem solving flexibility. *Creativity Research Journal, 5*(1), 12–26.

Pellegrini, A. D. (1998). Rough-and-tumble play from childhood to adolescence. In D. P. Fromberg & D. Bergen (Eds.), *Play from birth to twelve and beyond: Contexts, perspectives, and meanings* (pp. 401–408). New York; Garland.

Pellegrini, A. D., & Bartini, M. (2000). A longitudinal study of bullying, victimization, and peer group affiliation during the transition from primary school to middle school. *American Educational Research Journal, 37*(3), 699–725.

Pellegrini, A. D., & Kato, K. (2002). A short-term longitudinal study of children's playground games across the first year of school. Implications for social competence and adjustment to school. *American Educational Research Journal, 39*(4), 991–1015.

Pellegrini, A. D., & Perlmutter, J. C. (1989). Classroom effects on children's play. *Developmental Psychology, 25*(2), 289–296.

Pellegrini, A. D., & Smith, P. K. (1993). School recess: Implications for education and development. *Journal of Research in Childhood Education, 63*(1), 51–67.

Pinker, S. (2002). *The blank slate: The modern denial of human nature.* New York: Viking.

Project Zero/Reggio Children. (2001). *Making learning visible: Children as individual and group learners.* Cambridge, MA: Harvard Graduate School of Education/ Reggio Children.

Rabbie, J. M., Goldenbled, C., & Lodewijkx, H. F. M. (1992). Sex differences in conflict and aggression in individual and group settings. In K. Bjorkqvist, & P. Niemala (Eds.), *Of mice and women: Aspects of female aggression* (pp. 217–228). New York: Academic Press.

Ramsey, P. G. (1998). Diversity and play: Influences of race, culture, class, and gender. In D. P. Fromberg & D. Bergen (Eds.), *Play from birth to twelve and beyond: Contexts, perspectives, and meanings* (pp. 23–33). New York: Garland.

Rankin, B. (1998). Curriculum development in Reggio Emilia: A long-term curriculum project about dinosaurs. In C. P. Edwards, L. Gandini, & G. Forman (Eds.), *The hundred language of children* (2nd ed., pp. 213–237). Norwood, NJ: Ablex.

Reed, T., & Brown, M. (2000, Fall–Winter). The expression of care in rough and tumble play of boys. *Journal of Research in Childhood Education, 15*(1), 104–116.

Reid, S. (1993). Game play. In C. E. Schaefer (Ed.), *The therapeutic powers of play* (pp. 323–328). Northvale, NJ: Jason Aronson.

Ridley, M. (2003). What makes you who you are. *Time, 161*(22), 54–60, 63.

Rogers, D. L. (1985). Relationships between block play and the social development of children. *Early Child Development and Care, 20*, 245–261.

Roggman, L. A., & Peery, J. C. (1989). Parent-infant social play in brief encounters: Early gender differences. *Child Study Journal, 19*(1), 65–79.

Rosenfeld, E. F. (1975). *The relationship of sex-typed toys to the development of competency and sex-role identification.* Paper presented at the annual meeting of the Society for Research in Child Development, Denver, CO.

Rubin, K. H., & Howe, N. (1986). Social play and perspective taking. In G. G. Fein & M. Rivkin (Eds.), *The young child at play* (pp. 113–125). Washington, DC: National Association for the Education of Young Children.

Schank, R., & Abelson, F. (1977). *Scripts, plans, goals and understanding: An inquiry into human knowledge structures.* Hillsdale, NJ: Erlbaum.

Schlank, C. H., & Metzger, B. (1997). *Together and equal: Fostering cooperative play and promoting gender equity in early childhood programs.* Boston: Allyn & Bacon.

Schrader, C. T. (1989). Written language use within the context of young children's symbolic play. *Early Childhood Research Quarterly, 4*(2), 25–244.

Schrader, C. T. (1990). Symbolic play as a curricular tool for early literacy development. *Early Childhood Research Quarterly, 5*(1), 79–103.

Schunk, D. H. (1987). Peer models and children's behavioral change. *Review of Educational Research, 37*(3), 149–174.

Schwartz, L. A., & Markham, W. T. (1985). Sex stereotyping in children's toy advertisements. *Sex Roles, 12*(1/2), 157–170).

Serbin, L. (1978). Teachers, peers, and play preferences: An environmental approach to sex typing in the preschool. In B. Spring (Ed.), *Perspectives on nonsexist early childhood education* (pp.79–93). New York: Teachers College Press.

Sheldon, A. (1992). Conflict talk: Sociolinguistic challenges to self-assertion and how young girls meet them. *Merrill-Palmer Quarterly, 38*(1), 95–117.

Simpson, A. W., & Erickson, M. T. (1983). Teachers' verbal and nonverbal communication patterns as a function of teacher race, student gender and student race. *American Educational Research Journal, 20*(2), 183–198.

Singer, J. L. (1994). Imaginative play and adaptive development. In J. H. Goldstein (Ed.), *Toys, play and child development* (pp.6–26). New York: Cambridge University Press.

Singer, J. L., & Singer, D. (1979). *The value of imagination.* In B. Sutton-Smith (Ed.), *Play and learning* (pp. 195–218). New York: Gardner.

Smilansky, S. (1968). *The effects of sociodramatic play on disadvantaged preschool children.* New York: Wiley.

Thorne, B. (1993). *Gender play: Girls and boys in school.* New Brunswick, NJ: Rutgers University Press.

Tracy, D. M. (1987). Toys, spatial ability, and science and mathematics achievement: Are they related? *Sex Roles, 17*(3/4), 115–138.

Trawick-Smith, J. (1994). *Interactions in the classroom: Facilitating play in the early years.* New York: Merrill Macmillan.

Trostle, S. L. (1988). The effects of child-centered group lay sessions on social-emotional growth of three- to six-year-old bilingual Puerto Rican children. *Journal of Research in Childhood Education, 3*(2), 93–106.

Vaughn, B. E., Vollenweider, M., & Bost, K. K. (2003). Negative interactions and social competence of preschool children in two samples: Reconsidering the interpretation of aggressive behavior in young children. *Merrill-Palmer Research Quarterly, 49*(3), 247–278.

Volma, M., & van Eck, E. (2001). Gender equity and information technology in education: The second decade. *Review of Educational Research, 71*(4), 613–634.

Voss, H. G. (1987). An empirical study of exploration-play sequences in early childhood. In D. Gorlitz & J. F. Wohlwill (Eds.), *Curiosity, imagination, and play* (pp. 152–179). Hillsdale, NJ: Erlbaum.

Vukelich, C. (1991). Materials and modeling: Promoting literacy during play. In J. F. Christie (Ed.), *Play and early literacy development* (pp. 215–231). Albany: State University of New York Press.

Vygotsky, L. (1987). Imagination and its development in childhood. In R. S. Rieber & A. S. Carton (Eds.), *The collected works of L. S. Vygotsky* (Vol.1, pp. 339–349) (N. Minick, Trans.). New York: Plenum Press.

Whiting, B. B., & Edwards, C. P. (1988). *Children from different worlds: the formation of social behavior.* Cambridge, MA: Harvard University Press.

Wolf, D. H., Rygh, J., & Altshuler, J. (1984). Agency and experience: Actions and states in play narratives. In I. Bretherton (Ed.), *Symbolic play: The development of social understanding* (pp. 195–217). New York: Academic Press.

Yuen, F. C., & Shaw, S. M. (2003). Play: The reproduction and resistance of dominant gender ideologies. *World Leisure Journal, 45*(2), 12–21).

CHAPTER 2

GENDER ISSUES

Focusing on the Importance of Early Care and Education Programs in Center-Based Settings

Elizabeth Plaster
Pam Schiller

The preconditions for educational quality, equity and efficiency, are set in the early childhood years, making attention to early childhood care and development essential to the achievement of basic educational goals. (UNESCO, 2000, Paragraph 20)

Gender equity in early care and education of children is more than making sure girls have the same opportunities as boys; it is about eliminating the stereotypes and barriers that limit the choices and opportunities of both sexes that keep them from reaching their potential and being able to contribute fully to society. True respect for equity leaves no one behind and builds on the strengths of every member of the community.

There have been two significant events in recent years that have had a major impact on our awareness and understanding of the importance of the complexities of the developing child from birth to age 5 and the critical role of quality early care and education. These events are: (a) the

Gender and Schooling in the Early Years, pages 29–37
Copyright © 2005 by Information Age Publishing
All rights of reproduction in any form reserved.

advent of technology and its contribution to understanding how the
human brain works and (b) the significant change in the dynamics of our
workforce. As we begin to bridge the gap between neuroscience and education, we must first find ways to educate parents, teachers, politicians, and
society in general about the significance of early brain development and
the overall well-being of children in America.

During the first 3 years of life, responses to outside stimulation forge
connections that form the wiring in the brain. Critical factors that stimulate optimum brain development are healthy relationships in which children receive warm and responsive care and positive age-appropriate
stimulation. This sets the stage for how children will continue to learn and
interact with others throughout life. A child's formation of sense of self,
including sexual identity and attitudes, is part of this process that begins
at birth. With the advent of technology we now have the capacity to look
inside the human brain while an individual is alive. We are no longer
dependent on the limited knowledge we could access through autopsies.
One of the most intriguing findings of modern technology is the difference in not only the structure of the male and female brain, but also in
the way each sex approaches learning. Here are a few examples of the
findings for typical males and females. Females tend to have more sensitive hearing. Males have better depth perception and distance vision.
Females excel at visual memory. Males react more extremely to extreme
temperatures. Females react more quickly and acutely to pain. Males
approach problem solving from whole to part. Females approach problem
solving part to whole.

It is clear that instruction needs to be differentiated for males and
females. We may have gone too far with "gender-bias-free" thinking. If we
are going to make application of what we are learning from neurological
research, we may have to change our thinking. Equity should not be
defined as giving everyone the same opportunities to begin, but rather give
everyone the opportunity for equal outcomes. Our educational system
needs a drastic overhaul. A "systems approach" would go a long way in creating an environment of equal opportunity (Farai & Sheinfeild, 1988;
Kimura, 1992).

As recently as a generation ago, most young children were cared for by a
parent in the home. The change in the dynamics of the workforce, as
reflected by the number of children no longer cared for in the home, is
not only a result of more women choosing to be involved in careers but
also a result of the increased divorce rate and the significant number of
women and men choosing not to marry when they have children.

Large numbers of adult females are raising children on their own, often in
poverty or welfare-dependency. In 1991, there were 11.7 million female-

headed families in the United States, and 36 percent of them, 4.2 million, were poor. Female-headed families made up more than half of all poor families in the country in contrast to 1959, when fewer than two million female-headed families lived in poverty, and constituted only 23% of all poor families. (U.S. Bureau of the Census, 1992)

Today, approximately 53% of the families with children under age 6 are categorized as living in families with "all parents working"; that is, either a two-parent family where both parents work or a single-parent family where the sole parent works (Kids Count Census Data Online, 2004). About three-quarters of infants and toddlers of employed mothers are primarily cared for by someone other than a parent while their mother is working, with approximately 25% in center-based care. Findings from national studies demonstrate that almost half of the families with working parents chose center-based programs for their 3- and 4-year-old children (Urban Institute, 2001).

The current brain research regarding the dramatic growth and development that occurs in children between birth and age 5 and the differences in the way males and females approach learning, in concert with the change in workforce dynamics (fewer children cared for at home, increase in poverty) clearly demonstrates that early childhood care and education programs, including the adults that staff these programs and the environments that they offer children, play an important role in the development of our children (Bowman, Donovan, & Burns, 2001).

ROLE OF PARENT IN GENDER DEVELOPMENT

A child's earliest exposure to gender identity and what it means to be male or female comes from parents (Santrock, 1994). The parent–child relationship has effects on development that last well into adulthood. The internalization of parental messages regarding gender has been observed in 2-year-old children (Weinraub et al., 1984). Parents frequently provide subtle messages regarding gender that are internalized by the developing child. Several studies, including those by Hargreaves and Colley (1986) and Snow, Jacklin, and Maccoby (1983), indicate that parents treat sons and daughters differently from birth. Parental attitudes, warmth, and support are key factors in the development of a child's sense of self and self-worth. Parents who have more egalitarian, democratic, uncensored, open attitudes regarding gender are more likely to foster this attitude in their children. Democratic parents are found to be highly encouraging when it comes to supporting achievement and developing a sense of self-worth in both their sons and daughters (Sedney, 1987). Children whose mothers work outside the home often have a less traditional sex-role orientation and a stronger sense of their ability to make choices that are not hindered by gender (Davies & Banks, 1992). Individuals that have a more democratic viewpoint regarding gender have been found to have higher self-esteem. The most important influence on the educational attainment of children is the education level of the mother (Lewis, 1996). Economic hardships and low income can reduce the child's self-esteem if these conditions reduce the emotional or supportive qualities of the parent's home. "The pressure that limited economic resources can place on marital relationships can, in turn, translate into negative parent–child relations and lower levels of self-esteem" (Axinn, Duncan, & Thornton, 1997).

IMPORTANCE OF PARENT PARTNERSHIP

Research in gender equity and achievement strongly supports the notion that quality early care and education (ECED) programs with strong parent involvement components produce positive outcomes for children. Parents, when involved meaningfully as partners with staff of ECED programs, not only play a crucial role in their child's continuing development, but also contribute to enhancement of the quality of the programs themselves. Parental attitudes and expectations for quality ECED programs can increase demand for a more egalitarian approach in the classroom. Though quality ECED programs can serve not only to prepare children to succeed in school and in life, but also to prepare parents to acquire the information and advocacy skills necessary to make them engaged and effective advocates on behalf of their children in future years, the staff must be knowledgeable and well trained in this area (Lubeck, Jessup, deVries, & Post, 2001). Parents must be educated regarding the characteristics of quality ECED programming and this programming must be affordable for parents.

QUALITY EARLY CARE AND EDUCATION PROGRAMS

Though quality, nationally accredited, nonstate or federally funded ECED programs exist in the United States, only 12 states require college credits or a Child Development Associate's Credential (CDA) or Child Care Professional Credential (CCP) for employees (Barnett, 2003). Though there are alternative pathways to a 4-year degree, Bowman and colleagues (2002) argued in *Eager to Learn* that "there exists a serious 'mismatch' between the preparation (and compensation) of early childhood teachers and the expectations for their jobs: i.e., helping children to optimize their developmental potential and to set the stage for success in the school years and beyond." There is also a national debate on the standards and teacher training that should be required for professionals in early childhood. The inadequate compensation and the lack of governmental support of a comprehensive national early care and education system is a very visible reminder of the endemic inequity of our society, particularly in regard to women and children.

GENDER EQUITY IN THE EARLY CHILDHOOD CLASSROOM

There are two components to gender identity: sexual identity, which is biological, and role identity, which is cultural (Derman-Sparks, 1989). Children need adult help to understand that their gender identity is not dependent on what they like to do, what they wear, or how they communicate or express their feelings. Adults can encourage children to go beyond stereotypic gender roles, try new behaviors, and challenge existing biases and sexual stereotypes. It is important for teachers to involve and educate families regarding the importance of gender equity and engage their support as some children may experience some emotional conflict during the process of expanding their ideas of social norms.

Learning centers in early childhood classrooms offer staging areas for social interactions between peers, a major area in which gender role development takes place. Peer groups often perpetuate gender-type play and interactions, thus providing opportunities for children to examine the fairness and equity of their play. By expanding play options and storylines, teachers can find creative ways to assist children in discovering the contradictions between their ideas and their own experiences and engage in problem solving.

STRATEGIES THAT PROMOTE GENDER EQUITY

1. Reorganize learning centers to encourage different interactions. This can be achieved by:
   - Maintaining a balance of males and females in centers.
   - Pairing the block center (typically male dominant), sand center, or water table with the dramatic play center (typically female dominant). Incorporate materials that create connections between these centers (i.e., a restaurant with a dishwashing area or food preparation area, a furniture factory, or a chicken farm that produces and sells eggs to grocery stores). MacNaughton (1994) observed the following strategies were used to increase

the participation of girls in the block center: "girl's day in the block center," adding more "traditionally feminine" accessories, fusing the centers together (as previously discussed), and increasing adult monitoring. In his study, the strategies only provided short-term success, primarily because it focused on increasing the interest of the girls in blocks without addressing the greater issue of the blocks as a space of traditional male dominance. This means that children need support in understanding what it means to be a normal male or female, and teachers need to find ways to more equally distribute the power between the sexes in the different centers. Grouping children, strategically connecting centers, giving boys and girls ideas for nonsexist storylines, and increasing the focus on the inappropriateness of discriminatory behavior while supporting more democratic play can encourage both sexes to begin to better understand equalitarian play and to begin to examine ways to share power (Derman-Sparks, 1989). Children become social activists themselves as they work through and discuss these issues.

2. Removing or covering the traditional dramatic play center props (stove, refrigerator) with paper, and creating centers that are appealing to both sexes (i.e. circus tent, pizza parlor, grocery store, etc.). Introduce the roles and responsibilities of the different workers in these settings and encourage cross-gender choices.

3. Expanding the dress-up props to include clothing and accessories for both genders. Typically female apparel can be more appealing than male apparel. It is important to give careful attention to selecting more interesting male apparel items (i.e. add construction clothing, colorful ties, interesting hats, etc.).

4. Offering field trips to businesses that honor and respect employees of both sexes.

5. Utilizing math concepts to enhance the understanding of the activities and relate them to "real life."

6. Inviting parents to come in, participate in the role play, and share information regarding their own work.

7. Using nonbiased fiction and nonfiction literature to inspire and motivate children to create a more intricate and expanded environment. Include opportunities for writing (i.e., making lists and signs, creating books, taking dictation, etc.) that engage and involve both boys and girls.

8. Modifying learning for typical males and females in accord with differences in approaches to learning as stated by early brain development research. Teach males using a whole-to-part approach. Teach

females using a part-to-whole approach. General curriculum approaches favor females, therefore males are more likely to be in need of curriculum modifications.

THE ROLE OF LITERATURE IN GENDER BIAS

In imaginative or dramatic play, the use of power is heavily implicated in the storylines used by young children. Many of these storylines come from children's literature. Teachers must understand how to analyze children's books for sexism and racism so that they can select books that address diversity in families, gender roles, disabilities, ethnicities, and racial identifications and begin to introduce antibiased storylines. Bias-free books, both fiction and nonfiction, should be used to support the themes that instigate play and instructional strategies. As children act out storylines, the teacher's role is to facilitate the balance of power. She must be vigilant in observing and evaluating the impact of power on the play (i.e., who has it, how did they get it and maintain it, what is the impact?). Researchers Walkerdine (1988) and Davies (1990) suggested that the storylines used in play are central to how power relationships between boys and girls are established:

1. Different storylines are used by boys and girls. Girls use traditional feminine (passive, nurturing) storylines (Barbie dolls and My Little Pony figures) to determine how girls should act. Boys use traditional masculine storylines (powerful, aggressive, expansive, dominant) storylines (super heroes, G.I. Joe dolls) to define their concepts of how boys should act.

2. When boys and girls interact with their traditional storylines it leads to play situations that end in unequal power relations.

They also suggested that the role of the teacher is to observe how power relationships are being created and maintained and help children understand how to create storylines that give everyone opportunities for power. This encourages children to recognize and value each other, leading to a better understanding of democratic interactions.

IMPLICATIONS FOR FURTHER STUDY

This chapter focused on implications of two significant events that have an impact on gender equity: (a) the advent of technology and its contribution to understanding how the human brain works and (b) the significant change in the dynamics of our workforce. Although each of these events is important, there are other issues that impact gender bias in the early childhood setting: the lack of male role models in child care centers, curriculum strategies aimed specifically at the deeper issues of fairness versus unfairness, curriculum adjustments to a problem-solving model as opposed to the traditional model of convergent thinking, and better training for parents and all personnel that work with young children. Each of these topics needs expanded study to determine how they impact gender equity and what solutions or strategies can be employed to help us move beyond their influence.

REFERENCES

Axinn, W., Duncan, G. J., & Thornton, A. (1997). The effects of parents' income, wealth, and attitudes on children's completed schooling and self-esteem. In G. J. Duncan & J. Brooks-Gunn, (Eds.), *Consequences of growing up poor* (p. 521). New York: Russell Sage Foundation.

Barnett, W. S. (2003). *Better teachers, better preschools: Student achievement linked to teacher qualifications.* National Institute for Early Education Research Policy Facts.

Bowman, B., Donovan, M. S., & Burns, S. (Eds.). (2002). *Eager to learn: Educating our preschoolers.* Washington, DC: National Academy Press.

Davies, B., & Banks, C. (1992). The gender trap: A feminist postculturealist analysis of primary school children's talk about gender. *Journal of Curriculum Studies, 24,* 1–25.

Derman-Sparks, L. (1989). *Anti-bias curriculum: Tools for empowering young children.* Washington, DC: National Association for the Education of Young Children.

Farai, J., & Scheinfield, A. (1988). Sex differences in mental and behavioral traits. *Genetic Psychology Monographs, 77,* 169–229.

Hargreaves, D., & Colley, A. (1986). *The psychology of sex roles.* London: Harper & Row.

Head Start Performance Standards and Other Regulations, Revision 5, (2000). Washington, DC: U.S. Department of Health and Human Services, Administration on Children and Families, Head Start Bureau.

Kids Count Census Data Online. (2004). Retrieved January 29, 2005, from www.aecf.org/kidscount/census

Kimura, D. (1992). Sex Difference in the Brain. *Scientific American,* pp. 119–125. Retrieved from http://www.aecf.org/cgi-bin/aeccensus

Lewis, A. C. (1996). Breaking the cycle of poverty. *Phi Delta Kappan, 78,* 3.

Lubeck, S., Jessup, P., deVries, M., & Post, J. (2001). The role of culture in program improvement. *Early Childhood Research Quarterly, 16*(4), 499–523.

MacNaughton, G. (1994, September). *It's more than counting heads in block play: rethinking approaches to gender equity in early childhood curriculum.* Paper presented at the 20th Triennial Conference, Perth, Australia.

Santrock, J. (1994). *Child development* (6th ed.). Madison, WI: Brown & Benchmark.

Sedney, M. A. (1987). Development of androgyny: Parental influences. *Psychology of Women Quarterly, 11,* 311–326.

Snow, M. E., Jacklin, C. N., & Maccoby, E. E. (1983). Sex of child differences in father–child interaction at one year of age. *Child Development, 53,* 227–232.

United Nations Educational, Scientific, and Cultural Organization. (April, 2000). *Education for all: Meeting our collective commitments.* Dakar, Senegal: Author.

U.S. Bureau of the Census. (1992). *Poverty in the United States: 1991* (Current Population Reports, Series F-60, No. 181). Washington, DC: U.S. Government Printing Office.

Walkerdine, V. (1988). *The mastery of reason.* New York: Routledge.

Weinraub, M., Clemens, L. P., Sachlott, A., Ethridge, T., Gracely, E., & Myers, B. (1984). The development of sex role stereotypes in the third year: Relationships to gender labeling, gender identity, sex-typed toy preferences, and family characteristics. *Child Development, 55,* 1493–1503.

CHAPTER 3

GENDER, AUTHORITY, AND MONTESSORI

Early Childhood Teachers' Choices of Interactional and Disciplinary Styles

Gay Wilgus

A recent study on coworker conflict in the early childhood classroom uncovered an intriguing challenge to the research literature's assertions regarding the interactional and disciplinary styles certain cultural and socioeconomic groups choose to use with young children. Specifically, the research literature reviewed suggests that adults from middle-class "white," "Anglo," and "North American" backgrounds demonstrate nonauthoritarian, democratic, noncoercive tendencies in their choices of disciplinary strategies when compared to adults from working-class minority backgrounds (Ballenger, 1992; Valdes, 1996; Wrigley 1995). However, in my study, five teachers, who describe themselves as "white and middle class" and taught in a private preschool in New York City, were relatively authoritarian and coercive in teacher–child interactions. For example, responding to a child who has asked, "Why can't I play with that toy now?" with "Because I said so!" rather than giving the child a viable reason in language she can comprehend, is a behavior that has traditionally been associated with adults from working-class minority groups. In the current study it was

Gender and Schooling in the Early Years, pages 39–60
Copyright © 2005 by Information Age Publishing
All rights of reproduction in any form reserved.

the middle-class, white preschool teachers who did this more often. Early childhood teachers' choices of disciplinary and interactional style with young children cannot be understood exclusively in terms of their culture, ethnicity, and socioeconomic class.

This challenge to the research literature caught my attention. It seemed clear that the literature's insinuation that adults' choices of interactional styles with children can be understood somewhat exclusively as a function of their class, cultural, and ethnic background was not sufficient to explain the phenomena I was witnessing. Clearly, factors other than, or in addition to, class and cultural background were involved. Identification of these seemed primary to the project of understanding why the middle-class white teachers I was observing did not "fit" the model painted by the research literature.

Gilligan, Rogers, and Tolman's (1991) work on the socialization experiences of adolescent girls provided a key inroad for this project. These researchers found that young women are often socialized in ways that convince them that their feelings, opinions, and ideas are not worthwhile, and therefore, they "don't know" anything. An adolescent socialization experience of this nature, combined with early experiences with authoritarian ideologies, seem to have played a significant role in the lives of the teachers I observed, particularly with reference to the decisions they made about the interactional styles they chose to use with children in the early childhood classroom. Thus, as will be elaborated upon later, the discourse on adolescent girls' socialization experiences provided a fruitful starting point for understanding the interactional styles of these teachers.

WHAT THE RESEARCH LITERATURE SUGGESTS WITH REFERENCE TO THE DISCIPLINARY BELIEFS AND PRACTICES OF PARENTS AND TEACHERS FROM MIDDLE-CLASS, WHITE BACKGROUNDS

A number of the studies suggest that teachers' and parents' choices of disciplinary and limit-setting styles are primarily a function of their socioeconomic, cultural, and ethnic backgrounds. Valdes (1996) asserted that in middle-class American families, children are usually the center of attention, are allowed to interrupt adult conversations whenever they want, and are permitted to disrupt adults' interaction with their play. By contrast, Mexican American children in her study were expected to defer to adult conversation and needs, and their mothers were highly critical of "Anglo" mothers they observed begging children to comply with their demands.

The Latina and Caribbean private caregivers in Wrigley's (1995) study perceived the American children they cared for to be "spoiled and bad-mannered" (p. 105) and believed it was their parents' excessive indulgence of their children that accounted for this. Wrigley points out that middle-class white parents seemed to believe that "encouraging children to know what they want and to feel free to ask (would) make them self-motivated, confident, and articulate" (p. 105). For example, one Salvadoran caregiver recounted how her employer allowed his child to use four tea cups, as she saw fit, rather than restricting her to the use of one. Wrigley notes that the father's actions were intended to encourage his daughter to develop her own tastes and opinions, while for the caregiver, this represented "indulgence run amok" (Wrigley, 1995, p. 102).

Cynthia Ballenger (1992) has also discussed the comparatively democratic, noncoercive interactional and disciplinary styles of "North American" preschool teachers. A Haitian American student in Ballenger's child development class challenged the developmental literature's assertion that when young children display aggression, anger, or other undesirable behaviors and feelings, it is the adult's job to name and discuss the child's feeling for her. This teacher commented that North American teachers "...frequently refer to children's internal states and interpret their feelings for them; for example, 'you must be angry, it's hard for you when your friend does that,' and so on" (Ballenger, 1992, p. 203), while she "makes no reference to the children's emotions" when disciplining children. As Ballenger noted, "North American teachers speak as if something like the child's 'enlightened self interest' were the ultimate moral guidepost" (p. 207).

In stark contrast to what the above-cited literature suggests, I noted the five teachers from middle-class, white backgrounds in my study to be coercive, authoritarian, and uncompromising in their disciplinary and other interactions with children.

DESCRIPTION OF THE STUDY

The findings described here were encountered incidentally during the course of a larger study on coworker conflict in the early childhood classroom. The larger study involved $2\frac{1}{2}$ years of observing the classroom practices of several private preschool teachers who self-identify as middle class and white. I equate these teachers with the "Anglo" or "North American" parents and teachers in the research literature. Teachers of Latino, working-class backgrounds were observed at a second site. The larger study identifies and discusses 10 categories of coworker conflict that occurred most frequently in these settings (Wilgus, 2002). Findings for the overall study are not discussed here.

LOCATION OF THE STUDY

The preschool is located in an affluent community in Manhattan. Families at the preschool are almost exclusively middle- and upper-middle-class and white. There is a heavy international presence, mostly European. One teacher reported that 2 years ago, six of the 10 children in her class were either European, Scandinavian, Israeli, or Asian. Although the school has funding for some publicly funded child care slots, these are rarely utilized. There are usually one or two Asian children in each classroom and very few African American children. Although a class of 4-year-old children had four African American children during the second year of this research project, this was exceptional. Generally there may be one African American child per class. Most parents work in professional fields, including investment banking, law, fashion design, architecture, real estate, theater, film, and television.

There are seven classrooms in total. There are 20 children in the three classrooms for 4- and 5-year-olds, 18 children in the three classes for the 3-year-olds, and 10 children in the two's class. There are two teachers in each classroom and, on average, one or two student teachers each day. Five of the head teachers are Montessori trained, as is the assistant director. Montessori certification in Early Childhood Education can be broadly described as follows:

> The Montessori approach is not just a method, it is a response to life. Early Childhood Montessori provides an environment that is enriched with materials that meet the developmental needs of today's child. In this specifically designed classroom, the child will learn at his or her own rate; for children want to work, want to master their own bodies, and their own selves.... We believe that the task of the adult is not to amuse or entertain the child but rather to prepare the environment, guide the child to it, and assist in the unfolding of the child's being. Our students learn the skills to help children develop personal responsibility and strong self-esteem.

> ...we value the importance of the age 2–6, and the importance of nurturing, developing, and supporting excellence in the adults who work with children in schools and child care centers.

> The academic phase offers rigorous instruction in Montessori philosophy, theory, and teaching strategies. The student receives supervised practice with Montessori materials and is exposed to various teaching styles. Course curriculum includes: Montessori philosophy and pedagogy, child development (including analytical, cognitive, emotional, and language), observation techniques, and classroom management. Montessori didactic materials and exercises for everyday living, sensorial activities, as well as language development, mathematics, geography, history, art, music, and natural sciences are presented and explained in full sequence.

The practicum phase is started after the academic phase. It is a nine-month internship of student-teaching. In most schools this is a paid position. The student teacher works in a Montessori early childhood classroom approved by [the certifying Montessori organization], under the direct supervision of a supervising teacher who is a Montessori certified early childhood teacher. Practicum sites in an...approved Montessori school are available throughout the United States. The student observes and participates in the growth and development of the children and the class; s/he also learns classroom management strategies and techniques from the supervising teacher. During the practicum phase the student teacher will receive three on-site consultation visits by a representative of [the certifying Montessori organization]. (http://www.cmteny.com/)

The other teachers at the Children's Center attended various well-known and respected teacher education programs. Several of the teachers interviewed commented on their surprise at discovering when they were hired that there was no "mission statement" for the school. Teachers were free to design their classroom environments and base their curricula on whatever educational philosophy they chose, a situation that teachers perceived as "both good and bad." While this arrangement left them with a significant amount of freedom, when conflict over philosophy and practice arose between either teachers or between teachers and administrators, there were no clear guidelines in place for resolving these conflicts.

Older children (ages 4–5, and some age 3) come from 9:00 am to 3:00 pm and have lunch and nap at school. Younger children (ages 2–3) come for half-day sessions, either from 9:00 am to 12:00 pm or from 1:00 to 4:00 pm. One or both parents usually bring the child to school for the morning session. Most children in the afternoon session are dropped off and picked up by private caregivers. A few private caregivers bring children at the morning arrival time. When children arrive they generally have "free play" or "work" time (the Montessori teachers' term) for 40 minutes to an hour, depending on the ages of the children. Children can utilize the "work areas" as they want. Classrooms generally include a block area, dramatic play area, "sensory table" for sand and water play, art area, a cozy corner with books, and a manipulatives (trains, Legos, peg boards) area.

The Montessori-trained teachers' classrooms are arranged differently from the classrooms of the other teachers. Specifically designed Montessori materials, including graded wooden cylinders in a frame, pairs of same-sized pitchers for pouring, and a series of pink blocks for making a tower, are located on individual shelves. The Montessori teachers' classrooms do not include a dramatic play area. Several of the Montessori teachers stated that this was because Montessori believed that it was unhealthy for children to engage in fantasy play. In fact, Montessori believed that imaginative and fantasy play behaviors were manifestations that the child was not being provided with the proper opportunities for turning inner chaos into order (Goffin, 1994). Along similar lines, "play" was perceived as an activity lacking purpose and order, whereas "work" was the desired and valued opposite: "ordered activity toward a determined end." Order in one's psychic life was assumed to represent a blossoming "evolution in inner life." Montessori believed that children's interactions with objects and materials should occur in an ordered, systematic way, not through free exploration. The ultimate goal was the child's development of sufficient self-discipline to accomplish a decided-upon goal. Purposeful, self-directed activity meant that a child was exercising self-control, and this reflected a development of will (Goffin, 1994).

After "free play" or "work time," children either go to "gym time," or for older groups, to the nearby park. "Meeting time" or "circle time" generally takes place for each group mid to late morning. During meeting time children sit in a circle to sing songs, discuss the day"s events and concerns, and read a book together. Children then have a snack and another free play session. For younger children the day usually ends here with parents or private caregivers arriving at around 11:50 to pick them up. Older children continue with lunch, then nap, then another "free play" and/or "gym" session before they are picked up at 3:00 pm. Two days per week the music teacher comes to do a one-half hour session with each group.

RESEARCH METHODOLOGY

The research data were collected through classroom observation and open-ended interviews with teachers and administrators. Teachers were formally observed during classroom activities for sessions of at least an hour, once per week, over a $2\frac{1}{2}$-year period. Teachers were each interviewed, at length, at three points during the study: once at the beginning of the study, again in the middle, and a third time at the end of the study. Interviews lasted anywhere from 45 minutes to 2 hours, depending on the amount of material the interviewee volunteered. All interview and observational data were recorded by the researcher in narrative form.

OBSERVATIONS: WHITE, MIDDLE-CLASS TEACHERS' INTERACTIONAL AND DISCIPLINARY STYLES WITH CHILDREN

Dalia

Dalia was the head teacher in a classroom of children who were $2\frac{1}{2}$ to $3\frac{1}{2}$ years of age at the beginning of the school year. She had completed a joint program from which she received a master's degree in Early Childhood Education and at the same time became Montessori certified. Other teachers at the school report that Dalia was primarily hired because of her expertise in Montessori. The administration expected and hoped that Dalia would instruct some of the teachers who were not Montessori trained. Two teachers reported episodes in which Dalia demonstrated authoritarian, rigid tendencies in her interactions with children.

Loretta, an assistant teacher in the "three's" classroom, described an incident she witnessed between Dalia and a child over which she was quite concerned. Loretta found a $2\frac{1}{2}$-year-old child standing at the top of a long stairwell, crying and frozen with fear at the prospect of descending. As she reflexively began to help the child down the stairs, she spotted Dalia standing at the bottom of the stairwell, looking up. "If you help him down, he's never gonna learn how to be independent," she insisted, shaking her head. "Montessori says the most important thing for kids is to learn to be independent" (May 20, 2000), she recited. Loretta chose to ignore Dalia and continued helping the child to the bottom of the stairwell. She was so disturbed by the incident she immediately sought out her co-teacher. The two women reported what Loretta witnessed to the assistant director.

Richard, Dalia's co-teacher, described another episode in which Dalia appeared overly rigid and uncompromising in her dealings with children. Jim, a $2\frac{1}{2}$-year-old, came into school extremely upset and crying one morning. The mother informed Richard and his co-teacher, Dalia, that Jim had not had breakfast. Richard suggested that perhaps some juice and crackers might help Jim calm down, but Dalia insisted that snack time was at 10:00 am and that Jim must wait until that time to eat. Richard says Jim's mother "pitched a fit...she started swearing at Dalia." Richard very calmly gave Jim some juice and a cracker, at which point Dalia became extremely angry and yelled at Richard, "You didn't support me!" (July 28, 2000).

With reference to the event, Richard stateed, "I'm not rigid. As a teacher you have to find a place between two standards, you have to compromise, find a middle ground between following the rules directly and doing whatever a parent or child is asking. You have to figure out the best thing to do for the child" (July 28, 2000). In an effort to offset the possibility of a repeat scenario, Richard began putting snacks out on a side table at the beginning of the day so children can go and get what they want when they are hungry.

Kelly

Kelly was the head teacher for a "3–4's" group at the Children's Center. Kelly also had a master's degree in Early Childhood Education, but she made a point of stating that her primary focus of study had been the Montessori method.

I once observed afternoon snack during which time the 18 children in the class were expected to sit silently in a circle on the floor. One serving plate of each snack food was passed around the circle for children to serve themselves. The children were obliged to sit quietly and wait until all 18 children had served themselves before beginning to eat. Kelly told me that this was the way that Montessori states meals should be conducted. Although Montessori does stipulate that children should wait until all the children have been served before beginning to eat (Montessori, 1964), I could not find in Montessori's writings where she advocates eating on the floor. Additionally, Kelly required all children to simultaneously say "Bon appetit, it's time to eat!" before eating.

Kelly told the children they must finish all the food on their plates before going to "gym time," meaning the leisurely eaters got less time to play in the gym. The tacit message to the children was that eating quickly was a good thing, while taking one's time to enjoy the snack resulted in a form of punishment.

One day a particularly disturbing incident occurred. A child, Eliza, had begun quietly weeping during "wash-up" time, just before snack. Although Kelly clearly noticed Eliza's crying—she looked directly at the child, then mumbled something under her breath to me about the child's inability to separate—Kelly did not otherwise acknowledge Eliza's distress. One by one, her classmates finished the snack and ran off to the gym while Eliza sat over her full plate. Kelly insisted in a cheerful tone sufficiently loud for Eliza to hear, but without addressing her directly, "Eliza should finish her snack so she could go to the gym." Eliza continued to quietly cry but Kelly ignored her. Unfortunately, I was obliged to leave before the situation came to any sort of resolution, but in total, I calculate the child was left crying for 25 minutes.

I later learned that Eliza had just been moved from another classroom at another school into Kelly's class. Apparently no plan for helping Eliza make this transition had been devised. She had been plopped into the classroom with a "sink or swim" send-off.

Like Dalia, Kelly used Montessori as a rationale for her refusal to address Eliza's crying. She quipped, "If she doesn't learn how to deal with her feelings on her own, she will never become independent, and Montessori says children's independence is the most important thing for learning" (May 13, 2000).

Callie

Callie, the assistant teacher in a "4's" class, was a woman in her mid-forties. She held a master's degree in Early Childhood Education and had just returned to teaching 2 years before after raising two sons. The first time I entered the Children's Center, I was immediately struck by the sound of Callie shouting admonitions at two boys in her classroom. "What are you doing?!! What makes you think you can do that?!! You know better than to do that!!! What's wrong with you?!! You act like you don't have any sense at all!! Cut it out!!" Other teachers complained that they could hear her throughout the day, barking in a similar tone, several classrooms away. In fact, a parent of a child at the school reported that a friend of hers had come to tour the school, thinking she would send her child there next year. This parent told other parents in the neighborhood that Callie's tone with the children was "consistently acerbic" and decided not to send her child to the school for fear that she might have Callie as a teacher. The parent also worried, "If she yells at children like that when she knows parents are watching, I can only imagine what she does when no parents are around!" (June 7, 2000).

Sally

Sally was the head teacher in a class of $2\frac{1}{2}$- to $3\frac{1}{2}$-year-olds. Sally also held a master's degree in Early Childhood Education and had recently completed a few of the courses for a Montessori training program but had not done any of the supervised student teaching.

Throughout most observations, regardless of where one was positioned in the school, Sally could be overheard shouting orders across the classroom at children. Gabrielle, who had taught the same group of children the year before, noted

> those children, last year, even when they were a year younger, didn't need to be
> yelled at. All I had to do was ask them "could you do this" or "could you please
> stop hitting him" and they would cooperate. Sometimes the noise level from

that classroom is so high I can't think! It's like she raises the ante for them…they have to scream at each other to be heard over her! (June 14, 2000)

Additionally, when children questioned Sally's rules, regulations, and demands (e.g., "Why can't I play with the paints?"), Sally's frequent response was a resounding "Because I said so." No explanation or rationale for the demand was offered to the children.

Sally also occasionally added shaming, humiliating remarks to her commands (e.g., "You are one of the bigger kids in the classroom so you ought to KNOW better!" or "no kids want to play with you anymore because you keep saying YOU have to have the stethoscope!") in an effort to coerce the child into complying with her demands. Additionally, on several occasions, Sally was observed snatching objects away from children at whom she was angry, while simultaneously snapping, "You may not grab things away from other children!" Here again, an obvious lack of interest in the child's perspective in situations involving limit setting is painfully evident.

Martha

Perhaps more remarkable than the authoritarian, coercive limit-setting style of Sally were the "snatching and grabbing" behaviors of Martha, the assistant director at the preschool. Like Dalia and Kelly, Martha had completed a Montessori training program. Martha was observed several times summarily taking children's transition objects—items brought from home to facilitate the home-to-school transition—away from them. One day Martha decided that a child in the three's class, Chloe, needed to give up her "lamby," as Martha believed "lamby" was preventing Chloe from participating fully in class activities. Thus Martha decreed that "lamby" should be banished to Chloe's cubby for the remainder of the day. For hours Chloe sat quietly in the book corner with a troubled look on her face. Nonetheless, "lamby" remained imprisoned in the cubby. In fact, Chloe's participation in class decreased even further. On another occasion, Martha decided to take matters into her own hands when a child was learning to separate from her mother. It was the child's second day at school so the parent had stayed on at arrival time at her teacher Loretta's request. This was intended to help the child "warm up" to the classroom and teachers, and to provide an opportunity for the parent to "endorse" the classroom and the teacher for the child. The mother had, in accordance with Loretta's guidelines, told her child that she would be leaving soon, to give the child an interval to adapt to the idea of being in the classroom without her. A few minutes later, the mother started to exit the classroom and the child began weeping, asking to be held. The mother picked up her child who continued to cry and, in fact, the mother began to cry herself. Observing the situation from the door, Martha marched over to the mother, pulled the child out of the mother's arms, and barked at the mother, "You need to leave!" Martha's proclamation only heightened the distress of both mother and child.

Millicent

Millicent identifies herself as Caribbean American; thus even though she describes herself as coming from a distinctively middle-class family, the previous discussions regarding the childrearing styles of "white," "Anglo," or "North American" teachers and parents are not easily applied to her. However, she is included in the study because I believe what she has to say about growing up in an authoritarian culture makes an important contribution to the discussion at hand.

Millicent was the head teacher in the 3–4's group. She held a master's degree in Early Childhood Education. She had had some training in the Montessori method through staff development workshops at the Children's Center. These workshops were held once per month and were led by teachers from the various classrooms. At least twice per year, these were led by Montessori-trained teachers like Dalia and Kelly, who shared their pedagogical techniques with non-Montessori-trained teachers.

Millicent explained that she has "lots of rules" for her classroom. She asserts,

> I like a quiet classroom where the kids are working; there are lots of rules in the classroom for behavior but I let them do alot on their own in the gym. I set limits from day one. I start with the Montessori work rugs and tell the children exactly what the rules are about working with them. (March 3, 2000)

Montessori work rugs are rectangular, about 3 × 2 feet. Children spread them on the floor then put their "work" on top of the rug. The rug is meant to delineate that child's work space. If another child approaches and attempts to "invade" the area of the rug, the working child is encouraged to say, "That's my work!"

Millicent continued, "I go through this everyday, religiously, with them. By Halloween, they 'get it.' I also tell them 'Don't run in the classroom...we use our words (to express our needs and feelings, rather than grabbing, hitting, biting, etc.)...we have a calm class, etc.' " When they go to the gym, Millicent says she tells them, "Don't take your shoes off if you can't put them back on yourself!" This rule is slightly tempered with "We will tell you which one goes on which foot but you still have to put them on yourself" (March 3, 2000).

Loretta, who worked with Millicent's group while she was on vacation, states that there are SO many rules in Millicent's classroom that the children are afraid to initiate any sort of activity on their own. Loretta described how her during her first day substituting for Millicent, children whom she (Loretta) had had in her classroom the year before, and whom she knew to be feisty, confident children, appeared timid and inhibited. They gathered quietly near Loretta and asked in what she described as almost fearful voices, "Is it okay if we take out the paints?"

Like Dalia, Millicent stated she believes that the most important mission she has in teaching young children is "to make the kids as independent as possible." She explained, "I make them clean up the messes they make. If they spill things, THEY clean it up" (March 3, 2000). Thus for Millicent, a significant piece of encouraging autonomy in children involves getting them to clean up the messes they make.

Along the same lines of Dalia's insistence that children should learn to negotiate long stairwells independently, Millicent expressed a staunch belief that children should solve their own emotional problems. In fact, she often leaves individual children who are upset to figure out what to do to help themselves. When parents have observed such scenarios, they have sometimes described Millicent's behavior as "indifferent and cruel." Once, some parents who were dropping off their children were disturbed upon observing that a child was crying in one corner of the room. Millicent was far away from the child, poignantly making no effort to comfort the child. Millicent maintained, "I wanted the child to come and ask for comfort" (July 12, 2000). The observing parent, however, believed that Millicent was simply being cold and harsh.

On another occasion, Millicent asked a child with some sort of developmental delay to hand out the plates at snack time. The child, owing to his delay, was unable to negotiate some aspect of this task and was consequently standing still, apparently confused and uncomfortable. A parent who observed this scenario later asked Millicent "Why didn't you help him?" Millicent responded she wanted the child to "let him figure it out for himself" (July 12, 2000); however, the parent was of the opinion that the nature of the child's developmental delay would not allow him to figure out how to accomplish the task on his own. She believed Millicent was being cruel to let him stand there frustrated and confused.

DISCUSSION

The challenge presented by these teachers' behaviors to the research literature, which paints middle-class white adults as democratic, nonauthoritarian, noncoercive disciplinarians, is obvious. Additionally, I found the rigidity, harshness, and authoritarianism in the interactional styles that Dalia, Kelly, Callie, Millicent, Sally, and Martha used with children disturbing. Having been a two's teacher for 7 years, and having found it largely unnecessary to employ limit-setting techniques that derived their power and effectiveness from shaming, humiliating, and frightening children, I was interested in investigating and understanding why these teachers chose to utilize such techniques. In examining my interview material, in which I had elicited as much autobiographical data as teachers were willing to volunteer, one particularly promising inroad surfaced: This centered on Gilligan and colleagues' (1991) work on the socialization experiences of adolescent girls. I began to suspect that perhaps these teachers' experiences as adolescent girls might have had profound significance for how they chose to interact with young children, as well as for their choices of general pedagogical method.

Gilligan and colleagues' (1991) *Women, Girls and Psychotherapy* presented evidence that adolescent girls are socialized in a way that encourages them to believe that their thoughts, feelings, and opinions are not worthy of consideration, that they "don't know" anything. Drawing on ethnographic data from a 5-year study on girls' development, Gilligan and colleagues describeed a tendency for girls who have entered adolescence to "revise the story of their childhood" and in the process frequently "name the relational life they have lived...as "false, illogical or stupid" (p. 7). She explains:

> This act of revision washes away the grounds of girls' feelings and thoughts and undermines the transformatory potential which lies in women's development by leaving girls-turning-into-women with the sense that their feelings are groundless, their thoughts about nothing real, what they experienced never happened or that they cannot understand their own experiences. (Gilligan et al., 1991, p. 7)

Gilligan asserted that the ultimate outcome of this experience is that girls become convinced that they "don't know." Grief (1979) has described how girls have received the message that their thoughts are not important as early as toddlerhood. In videotaped sessions of parents reading to or playing with $3\frac{1}{2}$-year-old children, she noted that both mothers and fathers are more likely to interrupt the speech of girls versus boys and that both parents "engaged in more simultaneous speech with daughters" (quoted in Honig, 1983, p. 63). As Grief noteed, "The message to girls is that they are more interruptable, which suggests, in a subtle way, that they are also not too important, or at least less so than boys" (pp. 6–7).

I wondered if Callie, Martha, Sally, Millicent, Dalia, and Kelly might have experienced this as adolescents. Perhaps owing to the fact that most of these women report being raised in either "strict Catholic environ-

ments" (Callie and Sally), Catholic (Martha) or "staunchly military" environments (Kelly), or in a culture where "they tell you every move to make"
(Millicent), these women experienced this washing away of feelings and
thoughts, this sense that their thoughts are about nothing real, more pro-
foundly than other adolescent girls.

During interviews, Callie and Sally expended considerable time
describing their experiences being raised in "very Catholic" (their words)
families and while attending Catholic school as children. On several occasions—both in interviews and in informal conversations with other teachers (e.g., at lunch time)—both Callie and Sally recounted how the nuns at
their schools had utilized corporal punishment. Both had been obliged to
"hold our hands out while the nuns slammed them with a paddle board."
Sally said this "hurt like hell!" She also described how she had been
obliged to sit in the corner with her face to the wall for half-hour periods
with her arms extended to the side. In sum, these teachers assert they were
clearly given the message that children ultimately have no right to question the demands—behavioral or otherwise—made on them by adults in
positions of power. One must always unquestioningly defer to the "wisdom" and judgment and authority of a higher power, to never presume
that she is in a position and that it is acceptable for her to make judgments
about what is good, bad, right, or wrong, and the right course of action in
any given situation.

Block's (1973) summary remarks regarding a cross-cultural study of childrearing suggested that the seeds for this perspective are planted much
earlier in a girl's life since their socialization

> ...tends to reinforce the nurturant, docile, submissive and conservative
> aspects of the traditionally defined female role and discourages personal
> qualities conventionally defined as masculine: self-assertiveness, achievement
> orientation, and independence. (quoted in Honig, 1983, p. 64)

Martha reported having been raised in a Catholic household but did not
comment on her school experiences. Although Millicent did not explicitly
discuss religion in her upbringing, she maintained, "I come from a culture
[Jamaican] where you are told everything—you're told how to think, how
to behave...so I believe I mix together my home culture and my formal
training when it comes to deciding how to be with young children." Kelly
also did not comment on her religious background but reported during
the first interview that she had been raised as an only child in "a military
household." She described her father as a "staunch military man" but said
her mother was "very unlike him." She said, "My mother let me do anything...she would set up these little activities for me at home...painting,
whatever...and then she would just let me explore." At first this fact

seemed to suggest that Kelly had experienced more freedom as a child—that is, more opportunities to assert herself and engage in self-directed explorations—than Callie, Sally, and Martha. However, in considering this later on, I realized that Kelly said her mother *set up* activities for her, then let her do "whatever I wanted." That is to say, it was Kelly's mother who decided which activities Kelly would have access to and then—in "setting up" this activity for her—outlined the precise parameters within which Kelly would be allowed to explore. Thus, she was given considerably less freedom than a child who is given opportunities to decide what sort of materials they themselves would like to work with, how she will obtain these materials, and then how she will engage with them.

Perhaps as a result of their early experiences with the Catholic Church, a military parent, or "a culture that tells you every move to make," these teachers were easy prey for adolescent socialization experiences that gave them the message that their opinions, feelings, and interpretations of their experiences and other phenomena did not matter. From what they report it seems these teachers, as young children in military, rigidly religious, or authoritarian cultures, were made to believe that it was wholly inappropriate for them to critically evaluate the ideas, rules, or other assertions of the adults and religious figures in their lives; that such evaluations and decisions should always be left to some higher authority—a parent, teacher, priest, nun, or someone else in a position of power. Typically, children who experience such early environments learn to comply with social rules not because someone explained the reasons behind specific social rules ("We don't bite other people because it hurts them!" "We don't put our feet on the lunch table because there might be dirt from outside on our shoes, and it will get on the food") so that the rule "makes sense" to them, but from fear of being punished by some powerful, external force; that is to say, they obey social rules "because the parent/the teacher/the nun or God said so." Perhaps this explains, at least in part, these teachers' espousal of nondemocratic, authoritarian, coercive interactional styles with children.

It seems feasible to propose that owing to their early childhood experiences, these women might have been particularly susceptible to voices in their socialization as adolescents, which encouraged them to believe that their opinions, feelings, and ideas are unimportant. What I am specifically suggesting here is that Callie, Martha, Sally, Dalia, Millicent, and Kelly's use of coercive, uncompromising, authoritarian interactional styles with children reflect a conscious or subconscious fear of daring to challenge the ideologies that were promoted by their parents, teachers, or other adults with power over them.

For a teacher who has been convinced in childhood and adolescence of the inappropriateness of questioning authority, democratic, nonauthoritarian interactional/educational styles with children could pose a particular threat. In fact, to this way of thinking, teachers who espouse nonauthoritarian educational ideologies might rightly be accused of leading children to believe that they will experience only "democratic" environments once they leave preschool—that they will be entitled to question rules and authority and to challenge these through their behaviors. This amounts to giving children an unrealistic, "false" education. Although one might learn in an early childhood master's degree program that constantly exerting one's authority over children is usually not in the best interest of children's social and emotional development—particularly with reference to children's learning how to regulate their own behaviors—how can this knowledge compete with the lurking threat of punishment by a powerful external force? What chance does developmental and social-emotional curriculum theory have of being given fair consideration in the face of such threats?

Callie, Martha, Sally, Dalia, Millicent, and Kelly's experiences with the Catholic church, a military parent, or an authoritarian culture early in life, combined with the experience of being socialized as an adolescent to believe she "doesn't know" and that her opinions and ideas are worthless, might likewise explain these teachers' fierce attachment to the Montessori method. Indeed, Montessori's writings readily lend themselves to interpretation of her method as authoritarian and rigidly formulaic. Montessori repeatedly spelled out in highly precise language as to what the teacher's exact role and actions are to be in interactions with children. In her section on "Education of the Intellect," she instructed:

> So, for example, touching the smooth and rough cards in the first tactile exercise, [the directress] should say "This is smooth. This is rough," repeating the words with varying modulations of the voice, always letting the tones be clear and enunciation distinct. "Smooth, smooth, smooth. Rough, rough, rough."... The teacher must always test whether or not her lesson has attained the end she had in view, and her tests must be made to come within the restricted field of consciousness, provided by the lesson on nomenclature.... If the child has not committed any error, the teacher may provoke the motor activity corresponding to the idea of the object: that is, to the pronunciation of the name. She may ask him "What is this" and the child should respond "Smooth." The teacher may then interrupt, teaching him how to pronounce the word correctly and distinctly, first, drawing a deep breath, and then, saying in a rather loud voice, "Smooth." When he does this the teacher may note his particular speech defect, or the special form of baby talk to which he may be addicted. (Montessori, 1964, pp. 225–227)

Might Callie, Millicent, Martha, Dalia, Sally, and Kelly's having been socialized as adolescents to believe they "don't know," that their opinions and ideas are not worthwhile, possibly account for these teachers' seeking out and clinging to the Montessori method? Might they perceive it as an ironclad pedagogical approach, one that dictates, in almost script-like fashion, every move they should make in any given interaction with children? Perhaps a pedagogical approach with some leeway space, one that allows or requires the teacher to sometimes critically evaluate rules (real or imagined) of the method for handling different situations with children, might present a frightening prospect for teachers like those described above; that is to say, for someone who has been convinced during her adolescent experiences that she must always inevitably defer to the judgment of a higher authority—that at bottom, she "doesn't know" anything.

A pedagogical method that lends itself to a fundamentalist, formulaic, unwavering interpretation might have particular appeal for such a person. That person may seek someone or something—an educational philosophy and/or a method that *seems* "to know." Perhaps this explains these teachers' choice of the Montessori method, in that, at least in the way they read her, she *seems* to know. In fact, in some of her writings, Montessori takes on an omniscient, god-like, authoritative tone, suggesting at the same time that teachers should be god-like. For example:

> Among these almost savage people [the inhabitants of the tenements in Rome where Montessori's Casa di Bambini were located]...has come a gentlewoman of culture, an educator by profession, who dedicates her time and her life to helping those about her! A true missionary, a moral queen among the people...." (Montessori, 1964, p. 62)

> When the teacher shall have touched...soul for soul, each one of her pupils, awakening and inspiring life within them as if she were an invisible spirit, she will then possess each soul, and a sign, a single word from her shall suffice; for each one will feel her in an alive and vital way, will recognize her and will listen to her.... They will look toward her who made them live, and will help and desire to receive from her new life. (Montessori, 1964, p. 116)

This authoritative, omniscient tone might make Montessori's method particularly appealing for early childhood educators who are in search and in need of some sort of "bible" that will dictate to them exactly what do in any situation with young children. They seek a script, a formulaic, prescriptive, rule book that dictates the teachers' every move in interactions with children. This choice frees them from the potential burden of questioning or critically evaluating "the method" and provides particular relief to someone who has been convinced they are not capable or competent to question.

In the course of writing, I recalled that Priscilla, one of the other teachers at the preschool, also reported having been raised in a "very Catholic" family. However, I remembered Priscilla as having been exceedingly democratic and noncoercive in her interactions with the 2- and 3-year-old children for whom she cared. Wanting to understand why Priscilla seemed to have escaped, seemingly unscathed, from her early experiences with Catholicism while the other teachers had not, I decided to share my findings with her. I thought perhaps her experiences at Catholic school had been qualitatively different from those of Callie, Martha, and Sally and this might explain her choice of less authoritarian disciplinary strategies with children. So I asked her to describe her experiences in Catholic school. She expounded

> Oh my God those nuns were horrible! They were all about shaming and humiliation and emotional abuse! We couldn't budge an inch...they expected to sit like this all day (sits up straight with hands folded on the table) and if we didn't they screamed at us. They were insane. And the clothes! Those outfits they wore back then....the huge, black, long robe and the headdress and they wore these big, long rosaries with these gigantic crosses hanging from them. I was scared to death of them. One day I was chasing a little boy in the playground and this nun came swooping down the staircase into the playground in that big black robe and it was terrifying! She looked like this huge vulture coming to get me. (August 24, 2000)

Priscilla continued:

> It was all about control.... They would make us put our heads down on the desk for 30 minutes, supposedly to rest, but it was just because they didn't have anything to teach us at that moment and they couldn't bear not to have total control over us.

> I went there for the first and second grade but then I told my parents they had to take me out and put me in public school—I insisted—I told them I wouldn't go back to school if they didn't so they let me go to public school. Even at the age of 7 I could tell this was a totally insane situation, that those nuns were completely insane and that it wasn't healthy to be around them. I mean they would start preaching to us about "the Lord Almighty" and they would start to cry—the tears rolling down their cheeks—and I would think "Get a life!" or something like that. No, I could tell there was something seriously wrong with them. My sisters (she is the second of four girls) stayed in Catholic school but I got out, and I was so glad I did! (August 24, 2000)

Taking into account the above, the biggest question for me became the following: Why is it that Priscilla—even at the age of 7—was able to see being humiliated and shamed by nuns at school as completely unacceptable and to speak up about it, to insist that she be removed from that situation while her sisters, and apparently Callie, Martha, and Sally, were not? I asked Priscilla how she might explain the fact that she knew it was best to "get out" but her older sister, who had been raised in the same environment by the same parents, did not. She said her older sister tended to be "very passive and accepting of the way things are." Priscilla added, "We're just temperamentally different—we always have been" (August 24, 2000).

IMPLICATIONS AND SUGGESTIONS FOR FURTHER RESEARCH

Investigation into this issue could potentially prove interesting and useful not only for early childhood teachers like those described above and their administrators, but also for the children with whom they work. Determining teachers' level of awareness of the potential relationships between the religious ideologies with which they were raised, as well as their adolescent socialization experiences and their beliefs about early education and their choices of interactional styles with children and classroom practice—particularly with reference to limit-setting and disciplinary strategies—might constitute a first step in this investigation. The discussions that might result from such investigation could provide more nuanced, in-depth understandings of these connections, possibly proving to be useful for the early childhood teacher educators and for the administrators who support these teachers' growth and professional development.

These understandings could prove useful to children in the early childhood classroom. Specifically, through professional development, early childhood teachers could be encouraged to investigate the connections between their childhood and adolescent experiences and their choices of pedagogical approaches and interactional styles with children. This might, in turn, encourage early childhood teachers to reflect upon, discuss, and question their use of rigid, coercive, authoritarian interactional styles with children. As a result, these teachers might consider more democratic, non-coercive interactional styles and become more sensitive and attuned to the needs of the children for whom they care. Such a scenario would obviously benefit the growth and development of the children in question. However, if—as I have suggested—these teachers cling to rigid dogmatic pedagogical methodologies because they have been conditioned to believe that they have no business questioning authorities and that their opinions are not worthy of consideration, an obstacle to this project looms large. To convince such teachers of the importance of examining and questioning their choices in early childrearing beliefs and practices, these teachers must somehow first be convinced that their opinions are viable and DO matter. That is to say, the "undoing" of the negative, repressive effects of these women's earlier experiences appears to be the primary task. Such a project will obviously require significant reflection, planning, ingenuity, and effort.

REFERENCES

Ballenger, C. (1992). Because you like us: the language of control. *Harvard Educational Review,* 62(2), 191–208.

Block, J. H. (1973). Conceptions of sex role: some cross cultural and longitudinal perspectives. *American Psychologist,* 28, 512–529.

Gilligan, C., Rogers, A., & Tolman, D. (1991). *Women, girls and psychotherapy: Reframing resistance.* New York: Haworth Press.

Goffin, S. (1994). *Curriculum models and early childhood education: appraising the relationship.* New York: Macmillan.

Grief, E. B. (1979). Sex differences in parent–child conversations: Who interrupts whom? Paper presented at the Biennial Meeting of the Society for Research in Child Development, San Francisco.

Honig, A. S. (1983). Sex role socialization in early childhood. *Young Children,* 38(5), 57–69.

Montessori, M. (1964) *The Montessori method.* New York: Schocken Books.

Valdes, G. (1996). *Con respeto: bridging the distances between culturally diverse families and schools: an ethnographic portrait.* New York: Teachers College Press.

Wilgus, G. (2002). *"Why don't you try letting her do it herself?": Ideological and practical conflict in the early childhood classroom.* Unpublished doctoral dissertation, City University of New York Graduate Center.

Wrigley, J. (1995). *Other people's children.* New York: Basic Books.

ADDENDUM

Montessori believed that the purpose of education, and of her method in particular, was to "revolutionize society by creating an educational environment that responded to children's innate nature and nurtured the child's complete spiritual and psychic actualization" (Goffin, 1994, p. 49). Montessori focused on the individual child's development, but only to enhance that child's eventual contributions to the social collective. The ultimate goal of her educational program was the better functioning of the whole society—not the simple enhancement of individual children's development. Her method was intended to "assure the spiritual and intellectual well-being of children and...(thus) transform the future of civilization" (Goffin, 1994, p. 50).

One of Montessori's intentions was to move educational ideologies and methods away from abstract philosophical bases and toward pedagogies derived from empirical, naturalistic observations of children. She was not interested in getting to know children as the unique individuals they were, but more as "member(s) of the species" (Goffin, 1994, p. 51). Keeping one's distance in the way, Montessori believed, created grounds for her assertion that the data gained from her "naturalistic observations" were objective and scientific. Accordingly, she believed her findings could be applied to all children, not just certain individuals.

If Montessori's pedagogy was to be based on empirical observations of children, she believed it necessary to train teachers to conduct these "scientific" observations. Thus, for Montessori, the task of training teachers primarily involved teaching them to "divest (themselves) of personality in order to become instruments of investigation" (Goffin, 1994, p. 50). Bordering on the fanatical, Montessori stated, "Let us seek to implant in the soul the self-sacrificing spirit of the scientist with the reverent love of the disciple of Christ, and we shall have prepared the spirit of the teacher" (Goffin, 1994, p. 50).

Montessori viewed children as spiritual as well as biological creatures who were "endowed with a plan of development, which was expressed through their spontaneous activity" (Goffin, 1994, p. 51). In order for this development to take place, a specifically prepared, orderly environment that "freed children's natural evolution from external obstructions" (Goffin, 1994, p. 51) was needed. Montessori believed that between the ages of 3 and 6 having the possibility for such experience was particularly important since "during these sensitive years, children's spontaneous activity is intrinsically motivated toward bringing their chaotic inner world into an orderly coherence, a prerequisite to the development of rational, intellectual thought" (Goffin, 1994, p. 51). This belief derived from Montessori's contention that children are "born in a state of physical and psychological chaos" (Goffin, 1994, p. 53). She moreover believed that "the child, left at liberty...ought to find in his surroundings something organized in direct relation to his internal organization which is developing itself by natural laws" (Goffin, 1994, p. 51). Accordingly, the classroom must be designed "to focus the child's activity toward the essential task of self-formation in accordance with the inherited plan." Thus the classroom must provide the child with the materials for self-education, that is, materials that correspond to the child's emerging inner life as determined by observation of the child's activities.

As a result of this overall experience,

> the spirit, organized in this manner under the guidance of an order which corresponds to its natural order, becomes fortified, grows vigorously, and manifests itself in the equilibrium, serenity, the self-control which produces the wonderful discipline characteristic of the behavior of our children. (Goffin, 1994, p. 51)

Significantly, Montessori believed that once this "sensitive period" was passed, these natural inclinations toward "bringing the chaotic inner world into orderly coherence" disappears (Goffin, 1994).

Although the teacher was not to intrude into the child's spontaneous activity, he or she was not to leave the children completely to their own devices. In particular, they were to discourage "ill-bred acts" and other generally inappropriate behaviors. Teachers' activities were likewise never to "provoke unnatural effort" in the child as this was seen to upset the child's "natural developmental ascent." Disruptive behaviors from children, Montessori held, were indications that a teacher had not properly constructed the learning environment, and thus the child's "innate disposition for orderly development" was being obstructed. Montessori believed that imaginative and fantasy play behaviors were also manifestations that the child was not being provided with the proper opportunities for turning inner chaos into order (Goffin, 1994).

Along similar lines, "play" was perceived as an activity lacking purpose and order whereas "work" was the desired and valued opposite: "ordered activity toward a determined end." Order in one's psychic life was assumed to represent a blossoming "evolution in inner life." Montessori conceived of her method as she did science—as "a carefully sequenced technique, not an ongoing process of discovery" (Goffin, 1994, p. 54). She believed that children's interactions with objects and materials should occur in some ordered, systematic way, not through free exploration. The ultimate goal was the child's development of sufficient self-discipline to accomplish a decided-upon goal. Purposeful, self-directed activity meant that a child was exercising self-control and this reflected a development of will (Goffin, 1994).

The above-described "scientific" nature of Montessori's pedagogical approach dictated that any child or teacher-initiated modifications would "annul its scientific validity" (Goffin, 1994, p. 55). Thus materials were to be used in a very specific, unchanging way, and teachers' instruction to children about how to "work" with these were likewise to be precise and unchanging.

The learning environment, like Froebel's kindergarten, included an accessible garden where children could care for plants, a large "work" room, a sitting room where children could interact, and a dining room with drawers and cupboards children could reach so they could set the tables themselves. Tableware included real china so that children could see what happened when they were dropped. Sinks were of children's height so they could wash their own hands and dishes. Tables and chairs were likewise child-sized so the children could move them without help. Cupboards for the didactic materials were child-sized so that children could choose materials as they saw fit then put these away when they were finished. Each child had a drawer for her personal possessions, and the room was decorated with pictures and flowers since Montessori believed "beauty promoted concentration and refreshed the spirit" (Goffin, 1995, p. 56).

CHAPTER 4

PREKINDERGARTEN BILINGUAL MONTESSORI EDUCATION

A Gendered Perspective

Beverly J. Irby
Linda Rodriguez
Rafael Lara-Alecio

Although the Montessori pedagogical approach is over a century old, it is remarkably relevant for social justice issues in the 21st century, specifically those issues related to poverty and gender equity. According to Kramer (1988), Maria Montessori was deeply concerned with social injustices for women and children; therefore, she concentrated her efforts on those women and children with low socioeconomic status (SES) (Standing, 1984). In this chapter, we share the thoughts of Montessori on justice related to gender, and we apply those concepts to a public school prekindergarten Montessori program that is predominately bilingual (Spanish/English) and that houses more than 90% low socio-SES children.

Gender and Schooling in the Early Years, pages 61–77
Copyright © 2005 by Information Age Publishing
All rights of reproduction in any form reserved.

JUSTICE AND MONTESSORI

Montessori indicated that justice was deeply rooted in the moral notion of human society. She said that the feeling of justice is born in the soul of the child, together with the understanding of the link between actions and the needs of the children around him. Furthermore, she suggested that the sense of justice is not inborn but becomes rooted in the human spirit, and its evolution may be studied by following the development of the child. She cautioned if that is not done then a very different idea of justice will arise. Montessori (1939) spoke of justice in the school as "distributive justice" in which all things should be alike for everyone. In other words, all children should share in the good things happening in a classroom. Montessori felt that injustice is realized when one person receives different treatment from another.

Modern schools, as they evolved based in their origins with Horace Mann and as a reflection of their growth within 20th century hegemonic society, have segregated, compartmentalized, and gendered the education of millions; furthermore, they have not specifically followed the development of the child (other than an approximation of age by grade level), nor have our schools fostered a sense of justice.

Apple (1990) indicated that schools are one of the hegemonic institutions that helps maintain the status quo: "Schools create and recreate forms of consciousness that enable social control to be maintained without the necessity of dominant groups having to resort to overt mechanisms of domination" (p. 3). Even before coming to school, a child's gap in educational achievement has been influenced by poverty, race/ethnicity, and home language (Lee & Burkam, 2002). Children of poverty, of course, have less and receive less in terms of a preprimary education; even with federally funded preschool programs for the underprivileged, all of those children do not attend due to space or lack of access due to their parents' lack of information about the programs. Within the influencer of poverty, race and ethnicity is a social control issue with the mentality still being that some races or ethnicities "deserve" rights, while others have to "earn" them; the children of the later group grow up in an already oppressed social milieu. Holding great social control over the recent immigrants is the prejudice of language. Many of the immigrants come from an oppressed economic and social situation, only to live in an even more layered social and economic oppression due to their ethnicity, immigrant status, and, most of all, language. If a child's parents do not know the language of the school (literally and figuratively), then the access to preschool programs will be limited. Additionally, if a child does not know the language of the school or has no head start with preschool programs in language acquisition and vocabulary development in either the native or the target language, he or she will already be 1–2 years behind upon entrance to kindergarten.

The major witness to the aforementioned societal influencers is the limited access young children have to "good" schooling. Society had many lessons related to domination and access 50 years ago with the court-ordered desegregation of schools—major reasons for the court order were access to an equal education. A sense of equity did not exist for the children attending an all-black school. Sometimes, society does not pay a great deal of attention to lessons learned because there are continuing problems of access and equity in schools, lingering even in the 21st century. For example, although research has demonstrated that access to good early childhood programs with appropriate curriculum and content, and in particular, good early childhood teachers, may help bridge this achievement gap by providing children from lower SES or from at-risk environments with social and academic experiences that correlate with school success (Caughy, DiPietro, & Strobino, 1994; Lee & Burkam, 2002; Peisner-Feinberg, Clifford, Culkin, Howes, & Kagan, 1999), *only* 10% of America's 3- and 4-year-olds attend high-quality early childhood programs. Montessori focused her initial work with poor children, but once again, a hegemonically controlled societal agenda for schools has not supported early childhood education, but has promoted her philosophy and method primarily for exclusive private education. For example, according to Ruenzel (1997), only 200 of the approximately 5,000 Montessori schools in the United States (4%) were funded under public education. Thus, the social injustice for which Montessori worked is not evidenced in the majority of the schools with her namesake, because general access to her unique approach is limited primarily to those who have the resources to afford private school education.

ACCESS TO EARLY CHILDHOOD PROGRAMS

According to the National Center for Educational Statistics (1998), only 50% of children living in households with incomes of $10,000 or less receive care and education from persons other than their parents, in comparison to 77% of children in households with incomes in excess of $75,000. Kagan (1989) indicated, "there are vast inequities regarding children's eligibility and access to programs. Children are segregated by income, with limited choices and resources for low-income families" (p. 234) and this situation "...does not reflect the law or spirit of our nation" (p. 235), nor does it reflect the spirit of Montessori. When considering accessibility and ethnic groups, Hispanic children in the United States (46%) are less likely to receive supplemental care and education than white (62%) and black (66%) children (NCES, 1998).

Access to Montessori education for children who are low SES, English language learners (ELL), and Hispanic is further limited due to the fact that materials for teaching in Montessori programs are currently developed primarily in English, and they are not specific to the Hispanic culture (Rodriguez, Irby, Lara-Alecio, & Galindo, 2000). Indeed, even in the literature there is a paucity of references to Montessori and low socioeconomic status and/or to Montessori and ELL Hispanic students and corresponding bilingual educational materials and programs. In an exhaustive review of literature, only two studies were found that related to low SES and Montessori (Jackson, 1980; Wheeler, 1998), while only four studies were found related to ELL students and Montessori (Jackson, 1980; Rodriguez, 2002; Rodriguez, Lara-Alecio, & Irby, 2000; Wheeler, 1998), and none of these considered gender. According to Rosanova (2000), bilingual Montessori programming itself is virtually unexplored by the American Montessori educational community. The best-known encyclopedia, *Encyclopedia of Bilingualism and Bilingual Education* (Baker & Jones, 1998), includes no topic on gender issues in its 738 pages. Additionally, the National Center for Education Statistics' *Trends in the Education of Girls and Women* (2004) includes no reference to education of English language learners. With regard to Montessori, only profiles or program descriptions of language immersion or bilingual dual-language Montessori programs were uncovered in the literature, with no reference to gender (Chattin-McNichols, 1990; Rosanova, 1997, 2000).

GENDER EQUITY ISSUES

Several academic issues revolve around gender in mainstream education. As early as second grade, both boys and girls express gender stereotyping by describing math as a male domain. By third grade, females, in comparison with males, rate their competence in mathematics lower—even when they receive the same or better grades. By sixth grade, girls see mathematics as less important and useful to career goals than boys do (Hanson, 1992). Several researchers have noted that girls tend to perform better than boys on measures such as readiness tests (Ellwein et al., 1991). Bianchi and McArthur (1993) found a higher incidence of delayed school entry, kindergarten retention, and repetition of first grade among boys. This indicates that sex differences in school entry and early school experience are important variables in an analysis of the accomplishments and difficulties of young children.

There are differences between boys and girls in emerging literacy and numeracy; higher percentages of girls have demonstrated each of the accomplishments. About 5–7% more girls than boys identify colors, count to 20 or more, and read or pretend to read. Girls are also more likely to recognize letters and write their own names by a slightly larger margin (about 9–11%). On average, girls demonstrated 3.7 of the five accomplishments, whereas boys demonstrated fewer, 3.3 on average. These findings are consistent with research demonstrating that boys score slightly but significantly lower on four commonly used tests of school readiness (Ellwein et al., 1991).

Boys have been determined to be more advanced than girls in mathematical reasoning, spatial ability, and mechanical ability; however, girls generally score higher on memory, perceptual accuracy, verbal fluency, and language tasks (Aiken, 1987). All preoperational children (before about age 7) need a lot of hands-on learning (Wardle, 2003); however, because of boys' abilities in math and mechanical skills and their limitations in memory and language, they specifically need multiple opportunities for hands-on learning rather than verbal instruction, literacy activities, and rote learning.

MONTESSORI PEDAGOGICAL APPROACH

The Montessori pedagogical approach was developed in Italy by Dr. Maria Montessori in 1906 to serve disadvantaged children (Kahn, 1995). Her first school, Casa dei Bambini (Casa del Niño, The Children's House), served 50 poor children from a Roman slum (Ruenzel, 1997). Montessori stated:

> The poor have not yet had proper consideration, and always there remains one class that is yet more completely ignored, even among the rich. Such is childhood! All social problems are considered from the point of view of the adult and his needs.... Far more important are the needs of the child. (Montessori, 1961, p. 120)

She later stated in the same essay,

> Suppose we set up in schools the same social improvement that we are so proud of achieving! Let us feed the children, give them playground, clothing, freedom of speech. (p. 121)

Montessori's words reflect the tradition of those for whom she had great admiration—Jean Jacques Rousseau, Johann Heinrich Pestalozzi, and Friedrich Froebel—all of whom emphasized the innate potential of children and their abilities to develop in environmental conditions of freedom and love (Lillard, 1972). Educational philosophies prior to Montessori's philosophy had not so centralized the child (Montessori, 1996). Demonstrating this centralization of the child, the faculty at a private Montessori school, Escuela Montessori de Montopolis (2000) in Austin, Texas, affirmed:

> The Montessori classroom is structured to enhance social and learning skills and emotional development. By experiencing the class as a functioning social community, the child is trained in the fundamental social qualities that form the basis of dependable citizenship. Children attending Montessori schools learn to work cooperatively within a group and develop self-discipline required to perform a task. The stimulating environment and contagious enthusiasm encourage the development of individual talents and interests. Children attain confidence through achievement. (p. 1)

According to Montessori (Britton, 1992), during the first 3 years children gain much information from their surroundings. From age 3 to 6, they begin to develop intellectual constructs for organizing what they learn through their sensory explorations. Montessori materials are purposefully colorful and attractive to enhance a child's motor coordination and sensory and intellectual development. Montessori's idea was, through these materials, a child would discover the pattern and harmony of life in all its facets, whether it were in practical life skills or in content subject areas.

Montessori (1976) organized the curriculum into the following components: mathematics, music, language, sensorial, practical living, physical exercise, geography, art, and science.

A MODEL FOR A MONTESSORI BILINGUAL EARLY CHILDHOOD/PREKINDERGARTEN PROGRAM

Like most public school preschool educational programs, which are funded with federal funds that support low-income children, the Keeble Early Childhood/Prekindergarten Center, Aldine Independent School District, Houston, Texas, has 93.5% of the children identified at or below poverty level. Of the over 700 children on the campus, 85% are Hispanic, 10% African American, and 5% Other. Sixty-two percent of the children are categorized as ELLs and are served in bilingual classrooms. Ten percent are served in special education. A characteristic of Keeble that sets it apart from most public school prekindergarten programs is that the entire program for *all* children on this campus is centered in the Montessori pedagogical approach and philosophy.

Focusing specifically on the use of Montessori in bilingual prekindergarten classrooms, we outline in the remainder of this chapter the program design and how it supports an environment of gender equality.

Program Design

Transitional bilingual education programs, in general, traditionally have served more than 33% of all students by providing them instruction in their native language, along with education in English as a second language (WATESOL, 1997). Although the transitional bilingual Montessori model has been implemented, a type of dual-language Montessori program is being considered. The teachers and principal at the campus have held the belief that if the native language is first instilled in the child with an additive value of English enhancement (and now additive Spanish enhancement) and a knowledge of when the child is ready to discover this aspect of language as Montessorians are so aware, then language development is much more in line with appropriate language acquisition theory and research. Additionally, they believe that such a program is needed that emphasizes child development, cultural values, and literacy through native language and additive English (Aiming High and Targeting Excellence, 1999) and Spanish.

According to Lara-Alecio and Parker (1994), the pedagogical guidance from bilingual theory to classroom practice "typically takes the form of general pedagogical principles, including the following:

- provide an emotionally supportive environment;
- emphasize quality of social interaction between teacher and student;
- ensure 'bilingual' status is not considered a disability;
- provide quality social interactions between teacher and student;
- provide multi-modality interactions with students;
- incorporate minority students' culture in teaching;
- guide and facilitate rather than control student learning;
- encourage student talk and independent learning;
- structure activities which facilitate quality interactions;
- encourage community participation in schooling;
- promote student intrinsic motivation;
- teach 'meaningful' content;
- develop prior competency in the home language; and
- continue to develop competencies in both languages." (p. 119)

Cummins (1980) indicated that content areas of instruction provide a rich source of comprehensible input for ELL children, who often experience anxiety and hostility toward learning in general and toward English in particular. Such attitudes reduce the amount of input that can be acquired and slow down the development of English as a second language (Cummins, 1980; Krashen, 1998). To overcome these obstacles, teachers and administrators at Keeble have appealed to the child's affect, demonstrating that they value their language and culture (Aiming High and Targeting Excellence, 1999).

Curriculum

Bilingual Montessori Language Model. The maturational/linguistic worldview of the young child with special foci on bilingualism is advocated by Saville-Troike (1973), McLaughlin (1978, 1987), and Chaudron (1988). The child begins to develop sounds and place those sounds in such an order until they may elicit a response from a parent or other significant adult. The child's first language is used as the primary mode of instruction, with 10% of the instructional time daily spent in the target language (additive English/Spanish model). This model is currently being revised to be aligned with dual language; in the restructuring, an English-speaking class will be paired with a Spanish-speaking class, and for 20% of the day the classes will mix for instruction in Spanish or English (calendar time, storytime, arts, physical education, science/social studies/health, and social time). Dual-language programs are designed to help all participating students become fluent in both English and in a second language (Lara-Alecio & Irby, 2001).

Since a Spanish language program was not developed for Montessori bilingual classrooms, a committee of bilingual teachers from the district was convened to develop such a program. The language program developed consists of four color-coded levels and the following components: presentation of the three-period lesson using sandpaper letters, matching sounds, object to initial sounds, initial sounds with pictures, puzzle with picture, lotto game, matching capital and lowercase letters, movable alphabet, spelling with objects, object to word, picture with syllable, and mystery words. The development of this program was a 3-year project. In the present transitional bilingual model, additive English occurs when the child has mastered concepts in his or her primary language. Additionally, additive English is used in content area centers, during storytime, and during music. An explanation of each curriculum component with bilingual education included is detailed in Table 4.1.

The bilingual teachers worked for 1 year prior to opening the school on the development of the language program for Montessori. They continued to work on curriculum development during the additional 10 days they were employed as bilingual teachers. Several of the teachers and the principal

Table 4.1.   Explanation of Curriculum Areas
of the Montessori Method for Bilingual Education

Curriculum Area	Explanation of Curriculum Area
Practical Life	This area deals with life skills such as hygiene, dressing, ordering surroundings, table manners, fine motor skills of turning or using a screwdriver, and the like. The practical life activities and materials help to develop motor control, sequencing, and concentration. All materials are explained to the children in their native languages. Sometimes enhancements of diversity and the celebration of the child's culture (traditions, food, music, customs) are added to the area. Examples are beans, rice, tortillas, or rolling pins.
Sensorial	Sensorial activities focus on awareness and understanding of one's environment as perceived through shapes, colors, dimensions, and textures. The activities are introduced in the child's native language with modeling of the activities step-by-step. Fabrics from various origins are included in the area. Smelling bottles are included and typical spices are included from the child's home (e.g., for Spanish speakers: garlic, onion, cilantro, or vanilla).
Math	Preschool children begin with verbal activities (e.g., songs, poems, and rhymes that relate to numbers) that progress to experiencing symbols, quantities, sets, and math functions. The activities and responses are in the child's native language. The Mayan numeric system is introduced to the children as a culturally inclusive activity. Names of the geometric figures, place value, calendar, numbers, and money are labeled in English and Spanish.
Culture	Beginning with verbal presentations, this area progresses to sensorial and memory experiences. Representations of geographic locations of where the children's original countries are displayed and studied. A cultural fair is included in the curriculum. Maracas and other cultural artifacts are included in this area. Parents are encouraged to bring cultural artifacts to share. The children's native language is used in teaching within this center.
Language	Preschool children work on vocabulary enrichment and sentence development. They also develop reading readiness skills by learning letters, shapes, sounds, and word construction, with a strong emphasis on phonics. The children then progress to reading and writing skills. Typical animals, people, and objects that relate to the culture are included in the area. For example, a cactus, a parrot, a sombrero, and other such cultural articles are used in the language development program, which includes color-coded containers with letters, sandpaper letters, puzzles, pictures, and the objects that relate to the children's culture. The letter sounds are taught in the child's native language.
Expression	These include arts, crafts, and music. The children are encouraged to create freely with paper and other materials, which they may cut, color, tear, tape, staple, fold, or manipulate by any creative means. In music, the focus is on the awareness of their voices. Music is introduced in the child's native language; traditional songs and rhymes are included. Multicultural art projects are included in the curriculum.

visited a Montessori all-Spanish program in Monterrey, Mexico, during the summer prior to opening the school. Materials for curriculum development were purchased that would be culturally appropriate for the children. Teachers were sensitive to the alterations in the language program so that the concepts remained Montessorian, but also that the concepts were linguistically and culturally appropriate. Teachers continued to work on curriculum development during the first year of the program for the 10 additional contracted days and for 6 paid Saturdays.

Montessori, Traditional Preschool Education, and Montessori Bilingual Preschool Education. Montessori varies from traditional early childhood education in several ways, and Montessori bilingual education varies slightly from both, Montessori mainstream preschool and traditional preschool. These variations can be viewed in Table 4.2.

Table 4.2.   Comparison of Montessori Preschool, Traditional Preschool, and Montessori Bilingual Preschool Education

Montessori Education	*Traditional Preschool Education*	*Montessori Bilingual Preschool Education*
Three-year span	All one age	Multiage 3–5
Motivated by self development	Teacher-motivated	Teacher-Child motivated
Nongraded	Graded	Graded, but multiage in that there are 3- to 5-year-olds, mixed
Self-correcting materials	Teacher-corrected errors	Self-correcting materials and teacher reteaching
Children learn by handling objects and teaching themselves	Teacher lectures	Group and individual lessons
Materials used for specific purposes with sequences of steps	Materials used in many ways without previous instruction	Materials used for specific purposes with sequences of steps
Child-centered learning environment	Teacher-centered	Child-centered learning environment
Recognition of sensitive periods	All children instructed the same	Instruction meets the needs of the individual child
		Development of additive English through the content areas
		Pre- and post-standardized tests
		Assessment in both languages
		Instruction in the primary language

HOW THE BILINGUAL MONTESSORI
PREKINDERGARTEN IS GENDER INCLUSIVE

Fifteen interviews with the bilingual prekindergarten female teachers were conducted in the program described. The interviews requested information regarding how they developed gender-inclusive classrooms within the bilingual education framework and the Montessori curriculum areas. Responses were analyzed by curriculum area category.

Practical life. Teachers noted that the materials were used interchangeably by the boys and girls. It was noted that within the Hispanic community, stereotypical behaviors are expected (i.e., women take care of household chores and men do mechanical chores or go outside the home to work). With reference to the Practical Life area, one teacher commented, "It is nice to see the boys setting the table and preparing the bouquet of flowers and the girls polishing shoes or managing a screw driver.

Because of the specific manner in which lessons are presented and the fair way in which children are treated, they do not notice any difference." Another teacher commented, "As a human in today's society, we usually assume and label certain material as either a boy or girl identity. We assume that only a particular gender can manage or operate the material. However, in the Montessori bilingual classroom, the attraction is based on the materials themselves—the color, shape, and texture." Another commented, "When

Figure 4.1.   Interests of boys are considered (but girls have a turn at using and working with the screwdriver as well).

switching out materials to be seasonal, I try and make sure that I include some sport-related activities to incorporate the interests of the boys as well as activities that girls typically prefer. Boys and girls both enjoy working in this area. If I notice there is a gender difference in who is using a center, I try to reevaluate and change things around to accommodate all needs. In this center, boys work with activities such as table setting and hanging clothes with clothespins, which are typically seen as activities girls would choose over boys. The children seem to enjoy this center equally." Other typical responses were: (a) "Many activities in this area have the goal of teaching left-to-right progression and strengthening fine motor skills for writing. These are all activities in which the children need to improve, and they are not gender specific—all children are expected to work here and participate" and (b) "promotes success for both girls and boys by allowing the child to work at his or her own pace as they develop their individual fine motor skills. An example would be sorting objects using fingers, then sorting with a large spoon, then smaller spoon, tongs, tweezers, etc."

Sensorial. Teachers generally observed the materials to be gender neutral. One commented, "All the sensorial material is gender-fair, and the material is not gender specific. The children learn colors, shapes, size, and counting one to ten. Girls and boys can easily work with materials such as the Brown Stair, which requires more strength, or the Knob Cylinders and Color Boxes, which require the use of fine motor skills."

Figure 4.2.   Boy and girl folding towels.

Figure 4.3.   Girl with Brown Stair. (Note the order on the shelf behind her. The teacher does not keep that order; the boys and girls do.)

Another indicated, "Sensorial activities help children perfect their senses. Each activity focuses on one sense, such as color, sound, smell, or texture. This is gender free. Sensorial materials give the children opportunities to explore their own senses. The materials we use in the bilingual classrooms are ones we try to also make culturally appropriate and relevant as well." Several teachers responded similarly, "In Sensorial you build a symbol and enjoy, thus, rendering the materials and activities as very individualized and accommodates all learning styles. There is an abundant opportunity for rich language experiences. Regardless of gender, maturity level, motor skills, or language development, the materials have an appropriate (fair) application."

Math. "The materials in this area have the ability to develop the concrete and the abstract thinking abilities of both boys and girls," said one teacher. One teacher stated, "The material on the math shelf has activity cards with pictures of boys, girls, and animals. We also include objects for counting that are gender neutral: animals, beans, cars, planes, flowers, frogs, and others. The children, regardless of their gender, enjoy them all. Boys and girls work the same with butterflies, as well as with little trucks in the number games. All other materials don't have any specific gender relation; that is why Montessori material is so wonderful for encouraging gender-fair activities."

Culture. A teacher stated, "The books we read in the native language in our classrooms depict stories about men and women performing anything they want to do." Another teacher said, "We present ideas, activities, famous people (including men and women), dress, and customs in a way that encourages respect and discourages stereotypes. Students are aware that people from both genders are excelling and working for the common good. They learn to appreciate the importance of people regardless of gender or color. Several teachers responded related to the international tour conducted by the entire school. A typical response follows, "The international tour allows the students to see what is important in other cultures and how other people live. The students learn that there are things that make people different, yet there are things that make people alike." "All students are exposed to science activities where boys and girls actively participate in the experiments. We try very hard to make certain the girls are not just cleaning up or recording the information," said one teacher. A teacher indicated, "All children are able to spread out, using their Montessori mats. They can use as much space as needed. Usually boys like to take up a lot of space, but with this arrangement, boys and girls have the space they need. Both boys and girls are taught to respect the materials, and they quickly learn that everything has its place. Anytime you can walk into our classrooms everything is in order."

Language. Teachers were very verbal about language. A typical response was, "Language includes materials that can be used by either girls or boys, showing no difference. Activities such as the fruit and vegetable baskets, opposites, sound recognition, and writing show no gender difference." One teacher stated, "Some lessons that teach positional words have girls, boys, men, and women on the cards." Another indicated, "At some point during the day, since we are trying to develop oral language, each student has an opportunity to talk. Talk is equal, and we try to ensure that all students have an equal opportunity to develop his or her language. Activities in the language center provide children the opportunity to develop language skills simultaneously. The language area focuses specifically on helping students develop verbal skills, visual perception, and small muscle coordination. Students gradually begin to gain an understanding that separate sounds can be blended to make meaningful words. The language area focuses on developing children's growth in phonics, and it is not gender specific."

Expression. The teachers noted, again, for this area, no gender bias. The teachers indicated that they used music to develop a child's listening skills. One said, "We use familiar music, poems, fingerplays, and rhymes that do not portray one gender over the other. All children join in the activities in multiple ways." Another stated, "Crafts are used in the classroom to develop motor skills. All children participate in the creation of artwork." A teacher indicated, "We have beach days and other special activities, and both boys and girls have equal access and are encouraged to participate in physical activities and dances. Additionally, we have physical education for all children on our campus in which equal-access sports are emphasized." Play is also a good way to increase brain development (synapse and dendrite growth) and increase speed of messages between all parts of the brain and nervous system, which is particularly important for boys (Berger, 2003).

SUMMARY, CONCLUSIONS, AND IMPLICATIONS

The Montessori bilingual curriculum is an integrated and sequential program and is considered gender-inclusive by the teachers. In summary, one of the teachers said, "All Montessori materials are created to develop the children fully. They help build stronger intellectual, spiritual, social, and emotional children in a safe environment. When children are working in a Montessori classroom, they have the free opportunity to choose any material of their own interest; boys and girls can work with the same material independently or in small groups." Another said, "I think overall the Montessori classrooms at Keeble do an excellent job in promoting both boys and girls in a nonstereotypical way; however, it is up to the teacher to make sure that he or she spends the appropriate time with all children, and gives extra help to those who need it, regardless of gender. In addition, the teacher needs to be aware of her own personal biases so this doesn't affect the child's developmental learning, regardless of gender. I believe I am aware that there are gender biases; I am aware of my classroom setting, my personal way of communicating with the students, and the activities provided to them. Furthermore, there are many other people, like our skills specialists, who are always trying to readjust and make materials appropriate for each child's success at Keeble." Boys often struggle to be successful in early childhood programs, as usually this is a female culture with mostly female teachers. They may tend to develop environments that cater to girls' enjoyment. But, in the Keeble Early Childhood Bilingual Montessori Program, both boys and girls are treated with equal respect, and boys, like girls, are considered daily in the curriculum and instruction in a gender-fair environment. Teachers are paying attention to the needs of both genders, not just "thinking" that the curriculum and their instruction is fair.

REFERENCES

Aiken, L. (1987). Sex differences in mathematical ability: A review of the literature. *Educational Research Quarterly, 10,* 25–35.

Berger, K. S. (2003). *The developing person. Through childhood* (3rd ed.). New York: Worth.

Britton, L. (1992). *Montessori play and learn.* New York: Crown.

Caughy, M. O., DiPietro, J. A., & Strobino, D. M. (1994). Day-care participation as a protective factor in the cognitive development of low-income children. *Child Development, 65*(2), 457–471.

Chattin-McNichols, J. (1990). *What does research say about Montessori?.* Unpublished doctoral dissertation, Seattle University.

Chaudron, C. (1988). *Second language acquisition.* Cambridge, UK: Press Syndicate of the University of Cambridge.

Cummins, J. (1980). The cross-lingual of language proficiency: Implications for bilingual education and the optimal age issue. *TESOL Quarterly, 14,* 175–187.

Escuela Montessori de Montopolis. (2000). [Online]. Available: http://www.main.org/escuela/montes.htm

Hanson, K. (1992). *Teaching mathematics effectively and equitably to females.* New York: ERIC Clearinghouse on Urban Education.

Jackson, S. (1980). *Formative evaluation of a bilingual Montessori preschool program.* Unpublished doctoral dissertation, University of Texas.

Kagan, S. L. (1989, February). Early care and education: Tackling the tough issues. *PhiDelta Kappan, 70*(5), 433–439.

Kahn, D. (1995). *What is Montessori preschool?* Cleveland, OH: North American Montessori Teachers' Association.

Kramer, R. (1988). *Maria Montessori a biography.* Chicago: Chicago Press.

Krashen, S. (1998). *A note on Green's a meta-analysis of the effectiveness of bilingual education.* Available at http://ourworld.compuserve.com

Lara-Alecio, R., & Parker, R. (1994). A pedagogical model for transitional English-bilingual classrooms, *Bilingual Research Journal, 18*(3&4).

Lara-Alecio, R., & Irby, B. J. (2001). Bilingual and English as a second language programs. In G. Schroth & M. Littleton (Eds.), *The administration & supervision of special programs in education* (pp. 77–96). Iowa: Kendall/Hunt.

Lee, V. E., & Burkam, D. T. (2002). *Inequality at the starting gate: Social background differences in achievement as children begin school.* Washington, DC: Economic Policy Institute.

Lillard, P. (1972). *Montessori a modern approach.* New York: Schocken Books

McLaughlin, B. (1978). *Second-language acquisition in childhood.* Hillside, NJ: Erlbaum.

McLaughlin, B. (1987). *Theories of second-language learning.* London: Edward Arnold.

Montessori, M. (1939). *The second plane of education.* Retrieved February 27, 2004, from http://www.montessori-ami.org/4people/4bmariala1939a.htm

Montessori, M. (1961). *To educate the human potential.* India: Kalakshetra Publications.

Montessori, M. (1976). *From childhood to adolescence.* New York: Schocken Books.

Montessori, M. (1996). *Formacion del hombre.* 6a Impresion. Mexico: Editorial Diana.

National Center for Education Statistics. (1998). *Characteristics of children's early care and education programs: Data from the 1995 national household survey* (NCES 98-128). Washington, DC: U.S. Government Printing Office.

Peisner-Feinberg, E. S., Clifford, R. M., Culkin, M., Howes, C., & Kagan, S. L.(1999). *The children of the cost, quality, and outcomes study go to school.* Chapel Hill, NC: Frank Porter Graham Child Development Center, NCEDL.

Rosanova, M.J. (1997). *Early childhood bilingualism in the Montessori children's house: Guessable context and the planned environment.* (ERIC Document Reproduction Service No. ED 409704)

Rosanova, M. J. (2000, Winter). Demand grows for bilingual program. *Public School Montessori, 12,* 14–15.

Ruenzel, D. (1997, April). The Montessori method. *Education Week.*

Saville-Troike, M. (1973). *Bilingual children: A resource document (Vol. 2).* Washington, DC: Center for Applied Linguistics.

Standing, E. M. (1984). *Maria Montessori, Her life and work.* New York: Penguin.

Wheeler, K. (1998). *Bilingualism and bilinguality: An exploration of parental values and expectations in an American sponsored overseas school.* Unpublished doctoral dissertation, University of Minnesota.

Wardle, F. (2003). *Introduction to early childhood education: A multidimensional approach to child-centered care and learning.* Boston: Allyn & Bacon.

WATESOL (1997). *How long does it take to become fluent in English?* WATESOL News.

CHAPTER 5

MANAGING DILEMMAS

Uncovering Moral
and Intellectual Dimensions of Life
in a Reggio Emilia Classroom

Alexandra Miletta

Two children are engaged in a heated argument in one corner of the room, and even though they are out of earshot of the teacher, she[1] can see that the anger and frustration could quickly escalate from a verbal to a physical manifestation. Meanwhile, she notices that once again a child who is frequently alone and withdrawn is staring into space, apparently doing nothing. The formerly harmonious block construction corner has degenerated into a shouting match, and the art project in progress on the table before her is desperately in need of cleaning as it is now time for lunch. The teacher must make split-second decisions that will bring all of these situations to a peaceful resolution.

Situations such as these are endemic and pervasive in teaching. Even experienced teachers struggle when faced with competing choices, and they describe the frustration of knowing there are no easy answers. They know that the consequences of their decisions and actions may have an impact on the well-being and growth of their students, something they care deeply

Gender and Schooling in the Early Years, pages 79–97
Copyright © 2005 by Information Age Publishing
All rights of reproduction in any form reserved.

about. Certainly there are many kinds of issues involving competing choices in teaching. But for certain teachers, it is the daily tasks of fostering positive relationships with and among students, and of developing their intellectual and moral capacities, that present the greatest challenges. These are often the most intriguing puzzles of teaching.

The teaching episodes analyzed in this chapter are part of a larger study that investigated the moral and intellectual dimensions of teaching by examining how teachers managed insoluble dilemmas of practice. The careful and close analysis of classroom life, with a particular focus on seeking a better understanding of pedagogical beliefs and practices that are influential in the moral and intellectual development of students, was undertaken by combining an ethnographic and collaborative approach with discourse analysis. In addition, the theoretical concept of manner in teaching (Fenstermacher, 2001), which helps clarify why teaching is an inherently moral activity, was used as a conceptual lens. Manner has been defined as human conduct that expresses virtue and is consistent with a relatively stable disposition or character trait (Fenstermacher, 1992). An underlying assumption in this research is that each classroom constructs its own unique culture and climate through language and patterns of interaction that, over time, converge into meaning and understanding.

A municipal preschool classroom of 5-year-old children[2] in Reggio Emilia, Italy, co-taught by two exemplary teachers, is the site for the study of the ways in which these particular teachers make use of teaching and learning opportunities as they arise in practice, either serendipitously or because the teacher planned for them, in order to manage ongoing dilemmas of practice, as well as how their students understand and respond to the teachers' intentions, and how these actions and interactions contribute to the classroom's harmonious climate. What is notable from a gender perspective is the absence of gender stereotyping, prejudice, or discrimination. Reggio Emilia is a city in northern Italy that has, over the past 30 years, built a system of early childhood education in municipal infant/toddler centers and preschools recognized by international scholars for its inspiration to educators everywhere (Corsaro & Emiliani, 1992; New, 1993). By examining classroom life in Italy, I sought to reveal culturally-based beliefs that have an influence on the moral and intellectual dimensions central to this research. As Ben Mardell found in Harvard University's Project Zero research in Reggio Emilia, cross-cultural comparisons allow for a fruitful inquiry into what he calls "cultural knots." "Encounters with the pedagogical practice of other cultures make explicit our generally implicit educational worldviews, allowing an opportunity to reflect on the conceptual basis of our teaching" (Mardell, 2001, p. 281). The cultural comparisons of interest to my research had more to do with the philosophical and conceptual foundations that informed the teachers' practice than with societal contrasts.

I also chose the Reggio Emilia site for two other reasons. As Carla Rinaldi (2001) wrote, "a personal and collective culture is developed that influences the social, political, and values context and, in turn, is influenced by this context in a relationship of deep and authentic reciprocity" (p. 38). Two values in particular were of interest to me: the holistic value of subjectivity and the value of difference. Second, the teachers in the municipal preschools are renowned for their theoretical stance on teaching as inquiry. Describing the schools as sites of "pedagogical research," two other Project Zero researchers, Mara Krechevsky and Janet Stork, explained:

> Teachers in Reggio Emilia see themselves as building knowledge through rigorous documentation of children's learning experiences. They are collectively engaged in an ongoing process of posing hypotheses and gathering data through careful observation, documentation, and interpretation. In this way, they use practice to create theory. (2000, p. 64)

I was excited by the prospect of conducting my research in a Reggio Emilia municipal preschool particularly because descriptions of the schools in the extant literature make them sound like the most idyllic educational settings imaginable for young children. For example, Howard Gardner has described the Reggio Emilia schools as communities

> in which each child's intellectual, emotional, social, and moral potentials are carefully cultivated and guided. The principal education vehicle involves youngsters in long-term engrossing projects, which are carried out in a beautiful, healthy, love-filled setting.... Nowhere else in the world is there such a seamless and symbiotic relationship between a school's progressive philosophy and its practices. (1998, p. xvi)

Fieldnotes and audio-taped data were analyzed utilizing interactional ethnographic methods (Castanheira, Crawford, Dixon, & Green, 2001) in collaboration with the teachers. By co-constructing with the teachers' and students' interpretations of salient events, theoretically defined as telling cases (Mitchell, 1984), I sought a holistic view of the sociocultural climate of these classrooms by uncovering the emic and often hidden moral meanings that can be found in everyday classroom life. My purpose is to add to descriptive theories about how classroom sociocultural and moral climates are established, by showing both *what* moral understandings are constructed over time and *how* they are constructed by members of the classrooms through language.

The descriptive analysis of telling cases made evident dilemmas that can be conceptualized as a tension in the potential or performed actions of teachers. Each possible action along the continuum of this tension presents benefits and drawbacks, and the teachers are called upon to manage the dilemma by constantly evaluating the consequences of their actions with respect to the goals and aims they have for the students in their care. In addition to evaluating their actions, they look for evidence that students are taking up what they aim to teach and then make adjustments to their teaching methods accordingly. Sometimes they purposefully plan for a teaching opportunity, but often teachable moments occur serendipitously.

Fenstermacher (2001) identified six methods that teachers use to convey virtues, enhance moral relationships, and develop intellectual dispositions in their classrooms. These methods for making manner visible (viz., construction of the classroom community, didactic instruction, design and execution of academic task-structures, private conversations, calling out for a particular conduct, and showcasing specific students) are relevant to this study and have served to guide analysis, as multiple examples of these approaches are found when teachers are managing dilemmas. Understanding manner, in part, entails examining the dynamic processes of social interactions in the classroom that reveal what moral and intellectual virtues are valued and what they mean to individuals as they become contributing members of the classroom community.

THE ANNA FRANK SCHOOL

It is difficult to put into words the intense anticipation and excitement I felt when I visited the Anna Frank School for the first time on a chilly, gray January afternoon. As I entered the classroom of Valeria Berselli[3] and Arda Giglioli, fold-up bunkbed cots with blankets, pillows, and stuffed animals were being dismantled all over the room as children slowly woke up from an afternoon nap. Just as I went over to Valeria to greet her, a girl named Elisabetta came up to me with a friendly, *"Ciao!"* and suddenly we were engaged in a conversation about the new Harry Potter movie, which she had just seen. The students were gathered around the few large tables in the room for a fruit snack, and Valeria reviewed their names, asking them to keep track by giving her a point, which they counted aloud together, for every name she remembered correctly and subtracting a point for any name she forgot. It was her first day back at school after an extended medical leave, and although normally she would have been the teacher of this group of children since they first arrived at the school at the age of 3, for various reasons she was their teacher for the first time. This was also the first time that Valeria and Arda had team taught in the same classroom, although they had been colleagues at the school for 7 and 9 years, respectively, and each had two decades of teaching experience. Each classroom's team of two teachers worked on a weekly alternating and overlapping schedule, so that one teacher was at school from 8:00 am until about 2:00 pm, while the other arrived at 8:30 am and stayed until 4:00 pm.

Valeria introduced me to the group once students moved to sit on three large steps against a wall of the classroom where they usually gathered for whole-class meetings, sharing, and storytelling. When they were settled and quietly attentive, two boys, Flavio and Samuele, excitedly shared their experiences at an amusement park as Valeria interjected with comments or questions, or to help other students share and participate in the storytelling. A rhythm developed with the boys talking as others listened and Valeria's voice punctuating the narrative, with a crescendo of side conversations leading to lots of talking all at once, until finally someone called out, *"Basta!"* ("Enough!"), and the cycle began again. When Flavio exclaimed, "Then we went in the belly of the whale!" several students chorused together, "I did too!" Finally, when it was understood that the story had arrived at its end, there was applause, but Flavio lamented that he had more to say, so Valeria promised that they would hear part two the following day.

Instantly the students jumped up to go and play in various corners of the room, while Valeria talked with Adele. She was wearing her father's tie that day so she would look like Harry Potter and wanted to talk about Harry's Nimbus 2000 broomstick. Giovanna approached me and said, "We heard you have a voice that melts ice. Will you sing for us?" I was so charmed by this invitation that I sang the first thing that came to mind, which was the alphabet song, and Amalia came along to say that her sister knew how to sing it. Soon we were deep in conversation, this group of girls and I, gathered around a world map posted above the steps where we sat to talk about the United States, Michigan, and where I lived with respect to Italy. In a somber tone, Amalia pointed to Afghanistan and said they had been talking about the war there. Fathers and mothers drifted in, collecting children and chatting with Valeria, asking, "Did you have fun today?" and, as they slowly left, children called out, "Ciao!" and exchanged hugs and kisses goodbye. I found myself participating in these exchanges, and promised Piero, who asked me to sing as I was meeting his mother, that we would sing together soon.

Why do I begin with this narrative account of my first experiences at the Anna Frank School? Perhaps it is because I am aware of the fact that despite all that has been written about the remarkable municipal preschools of Reggio Emilia, as Mardell pointed out, "a full understanding may still be elusive" (2001, p. 278). Like the group of researchers from Harvard University's Project Zero, I too feel an "urgency" to convey my ideas about what I discovered and learned as a participant observer in Valeria and Arda's classroom. Yet it is difficult to reconstruct the whirlwind of thoughts and feelings from that first afternoon. I want desperately to convey the irresistible invitations of those vivacious children to engage me not just in conversation, but in song, and the lovely remembered metaphor of a voice melting ice; the excited and detailed descriptions of their amusement park experiences inside a giant whale; the seriousness with which the girls spoke of war in a faraway place; the warmth of the embraces and goodbyes at the end of the day. I want to give life and meaning to the concepts so often cited as central to early childhood education in these Reggio schools, such as community and parent/school relationships, the "hundred languages"[4] of children in evidence everywhere I looked, and the image of the young child as capable and endlessly fascinating.

But the task I have set for myself in this chapter is to zero in on particular teaching events: to seek out telling cases where the teacher, in managing the dilemmas of teaching, uses a teaching opportunity in order to realize her goals of developing students' intellectual and moral virtues. A second goal is to show how the absence of gender stereotyping creates a classroom climate conducive to learning for all students.

THE REGGIO EMILIA CONTEXT

It is important to point out a few historical aspects of how these schools developed and the philosophies that have informed and inspired their experiences of early childhood education. It is hard to do justice to the complexity of three decades of a rich history and to explain the key features that have made the schools so famous throughout the world. Most explanations of the so-called "Reggio approach" touch on the image of the child, the role of expressive arts, projects, the environment, documentation, and teacher inquiry and collaboration (see Edwards, Gandini, & Forman, 1998; Katz & Cesarone, 1994; Valentine, 1999), but in addition to some brief history, my focus will be on the central role of community relations and parental involvement in the life of the schools. Finally, I will return to the values of subjectivity and difference before proceeding with my findings.

In the introductory pages to their seminal text, *The Hundred Languages of Children,* Carolyn Edwards, Lella Gandini, and George Forman explain the three principal influences that gave rise to these municipal schools:

> The Reggio Emilia approach to early childhood education is founded on a distinctive, coherent, evolving set of assumptions and perspectives drawn from three important intellectual traditions: European and American strands of *progressive education,* Piagetian and Vygotskian *constructivist psychologies,* and Italian postwar *left-reform politics.* All of these are blended together

with elements of past and present history and culture, such as the strong regional traditions of participatory democracy; that is, citizen alliances for solidarity and cooperation. (1998, p. 8)

This last point cannot be overstated, and it explains in part why the transfer of Reggio-inspired practices to other contexts is not always fully successful. In an effort to capture something of the spirit of the people in that part of Italy, and the history preceding the establishment of the municipally funded schools, Loris Malaguzzi recounts how in the spring of 1945, in the aftermath of World War II, a school was built just outside the town of Reggio Emilia at Villa Cella with salvaged bricks and some funding from the sale of a war tank.

> Within 8 months the school and our friendship had set down roots. What happened at Villa Cella was but the first spark. Other schools were opened on the outskirts and in the poorest sections of town, all created and run by parents. Finding support for the school, in a devastated town, rich only in mourning and poverty, would be a long and difficult ordeal, and would require sacrifices and solidarity now unthinkable. When seven more were added in the poor areas surrounding the city to the "school of the tank" at Villa Cella, started by women with the help of the National Liberation Committee (CLN), we understood that the phenomenon was irreversible. Some of the schools would not survive. Most of them, however, would display enough rage and strength to survive for almost 20 years. (Malaguzzi & Gandini, 1998, p. 50)

Certainly Malaguzzi's visionary leadership from those early years also paved the way for what was to become, starting in 1963, a network[5] of exemplary municipally funded schools for Reggio Emilia's youngest citizens. That the school of Villa Cella still exists (today it is known as "XXV Aprile") and is flourishing was not surprising to Malaguzzi, who remarked, "Its valuable history confirms that a new educational experience can emerge from the least expected circumstances" (p. 57).

Today the city of Reggio Emilia, with a population under half a million, continues its noble tradition of civic participation and social services for the needy and is experiencing an influx of immigration from the south of Italy, Asia, and Africa. The city's website, for example, http://www.municipio.re.it, offers a variety of helpful links, and there are indications that the city of Reggio is especially accommodating to its newcomers: for example, there is a link to an online Italian dictionary, and the city's printed guide to preschools includes translations into Arabic and English. During the enrollment period in January, the municipal schools are open to the public after-hours and teachers are available to confer with parents. The culture of participation in improving the lives of young children is evident everywhere.

I provide this contextual background to emphasize the strong social norm of making community and conversation a top priority of civic life, which is constantly reinforced in the daily life of the municipal schools. The physical environments invite parents in, welcoming them with comfortable corners to sit and chat, look at student work, or read a recent publication. Life revolves around the central space of the schools: the classrooms, atelier, kitchen, and office are all connected to this plaza-like area, where children are often running around and playing together while parents talk together with teachers. Teachers and staff all eat lunch together, sitting down at a large table to enjoy good food prepared by the school's cook and animated conversation. Children too enjoy a leisurely two-course meal and take turns as waiters, setting the tables with tablecloths, plates, silverware, and glasses, and cleaning up at the end of lunch. Politically, every 3 years each school elects parents, teachers, staff, and community members to its Childhood-City Council, which oversees the promotion of family participation, so vital to the success of the school's mission. Building relationships and communication networks is central to maintaining this thriving and dynamic community, overcoming obstacles, and making improvements. As Malaguzzi and Gandini (1998) explained,

> The strength of our system lies in the ways we make explicit and then intensify the necessary conditions for relations and interaction. We seek to support those social exchanges that better ensure the flow of expectations, conflicts, cooperations, choices, and the explicit unfolding of problems tied to the cognitive, affective, and expressive realms. (p. 68)

The emphasis on belonging and recognition, so central to the work with children, permeates all other levels of the schools, and it is this central belief that everyone matters and can help to make a difference in the life of the community that seems to fuel and energize the participation.

Equally important are the values of subjectivity and difference. Believing that individuals self-construct their identities but are also socially constructed within specific contexts and cultures, Reggio Emilia educators seek to understand how learning occurs through and with others. As Loris Malaguzzi put it, "It is not so much that we need to think of a child who develops himself by himself but rather of a child who develops himself interacting and developing with others" (Rankin, 2004, p. 82). Tied to the notion of what makes an individual unique is what makes us different with regard to gender, race, culture, and religion, for example. Grappling with differences raises many difficult questions for both pedagogy and politics. As Carla Rinaldi said,

Dealing with differences is difficult and requires commitment and hard work. In confronting differences, we are faced with otherness, but also with "outsideness" (extraneousness). Differences are sometimes painful, and always challenging. We tend to be more attracted by the idea of sameness, by that which makes us the same. But this is a great risk, and the questions consequently raised are of vital importance. (2001, p. 40)

In the examples that follow, we shall see how two teachers at the Anna Frank School deal with the dilemmas inherent in managing student differences, navigating the risky territory of standardization and the temptation to revert to sameness as a proxy for equity, particularly with regard to gender, by keeping their focus on the unique qualities and needs of the children in their care.

A CASE OF TWO CHILDREN: GIORGIO AND ELENA

By design, teachers in the Reggio Emilia municipal schools are paired within the classroom and given opportunities to plan and talk about their students and teaching together on a regular basis. Known in Italian as *aggiornamenti*, which might translate in English as "updates," these discussions often occur while students are napping after lunch, but sometimes happen when students are engaged in various group activities and don't necessarily require sustained adult guidance or intervention. In my first days in the classroom, I was struck by the richness of these conversations between Arda and Valeria that they seemed to snatch up whenever an opportunity presented itself, so on Friday of the first week, I asked if I might tape their discussion while children worked busily in various centers and corners of the room. Because Arda was trying to catch Valeria up on the needs and interests of each of the students, their conversation revealed the challenge of intellectually engaging all the students, particularly those with less developed verbal skills who tended to be quiet during group discussions and needed extra encouragement to draw out their ideas and thinking. In this discussion, they focused primarily on two children: Giorgio, a boy whose family was from the South of Italy and had recently moved to Reggio; and Elena, who spoke only minimally and only when absolutely necessary. I joined their conversation just as Valeria had begun to ask Arda about Giorgio.

> Valeria: And she was telling me that Giorgio has had a great desire to answer. But he was lacking actually the tools and she explained that in his family, it's a family of people who have always spoken with him in the southern dialect, and when he arrived

Arda: Like words, vocabulary, he didn't understand them, so it was a very difficult job also with him. And now he has changed a lot, but clearly with respect to the majority of other 5-year-old children he still has to try a bit harder to get there. Yet he's a very intelligent child. He's a child who listens to everything, always. He is, except for the beginning of last year that, since he didn't have many rules at home, was able—there he is, Giorgio.

Valeria: With the black cape in his hand.

Arda: He sometimes went to bed even at 1:00 in the morning because his parents didn't care that much, he said no, he cried, so sometimes he fell asleep. Because he was tired, he was tired. After this first, let's say, phase that he got over and I had talked with his parents, I said that no, that is, at a certain time one goes to bed because otherwise, here, instead of listening, to be a participant in what is going on, he was falling asleep. So a little bit him, a little bit the other thing, he listened always to everything. So he had a desire to learn, to know, to understand, to also, anyway to feel closer to others. And I have to say that, yes, now, to someone who arrives now, it might not seem so, but he has made great strides ahead.

Valeria: I remember even if he wasn't among my students.

Arda: He was really, well, a little disadvantaged, not because he didn't have

Valeria: A question of language.

Arda: Really the tools, because even his parents are very simple people.

Valeria: Because they maybe then they didn't talk that much with him, they didn't enrich him with vocabulary, with knowledge. This morning we had just talked about the rooster when I said to him the wife of the rooster makes the eggs, and so he, he didn't, he looked around, so everyone was saying to him, "But come on! But it's easy!" and the more they said that, the more he was lost.

Arda: Of course.

Valeria: A little later I called him, I got him close to me, and I told him to say it very, very quietly and I told him, "Good for you. You got it." I encouraged and supported him and I was saying then to her [Arda] that in this case it was really just about having an opportunity in the morning in which there are no special projects, and she and I are available to be with the big group, to create occa-

sions in which even a one-on-one relationship, me and
him, she and him, or she and another with him, so a
relationship with an adult or two children, you can open
this dialogue in a fairly calm situation in which information, competences are incorporated into the discussion,
reading a book, speaking, telling, etc. Because really he
just needs enrichment.

Arda: That's so true, so true.

The rooster incident that Valeria mentioned occurred that morning as
the children were having their morning snack of fresh fruit. Valeria began
a game of animal riddles in which she gave a few clues plus the first and last
letter of the animal's name, and asked specific children for their guess so
as to finish distributing the leftover fruit. When students started to call out
the answers, she suggested that they might instead provide their classmate
with an extra clue or two. Her solution to the problem of Giorgio's public
embarrassment at not immediately knowing the answer was "hen" was to
use the proximity and support of a private conversation to elicit his guess,
which was correct.

The conversation continued with comments that were punctuated by
interruptions of children who momentarily needed the attention of either
Arda or Valeria, or both, before Arda moved on to discussing Elena.

Arda: And Elena lately has so many, she has many more understandings of herself, including, among other things, the
understanding that she has difficulty with language. And
so for a few months now, she uses the strategy of not talking. She talks the indispensable minimum. Because
before she came to this realization, she talked continu-
ously, she even said nonsense, but because she wasn't
aware, she spoke freely. Since she is aware of this thing,
she is ashamed and so she tries to speak as little as possible. Yesterday, for example, at lunch, they were each
explaining what pet they have. Some had animals like
dogs and cats, canaries, crickets at home, no? And she
had a bunny, Elena (*Arda paused for an interruption*). At
some point Elena had a bunny rabbit. But then she was
allergic, she developed conjunctivitis.

Valeria: Ah, yes, yes.

Arda: And her mother gave it away. So when they said to her,
"Elena, what pet do you have?" she said nothing. I mean
really silent.

Valeria: Yes, yes.

> Arda: And so she, um, Silvana said to her, "But you had a bunny rabbit!" and she said, "I don't anymore." And so they were curious—what? You had it, he's gone, he is dead, isn't dead—until finally I said, "Tell them what happened." At that point she took some deep breaths.
>
> Valeria: Yes.
>
> Arda: Because really, suffering, anyway, to get into something with respect to a thing you aren't fully aware of.
>
> Valeria: But do you know that the other afternoon she cried about this?
>
> Arda: You told me.
>
> Valeria: Giovanna came and made fun of her because she didn't know how to say…
>
> Arda: Dreamcatcher?
>
> Valeria: Yes, exactly. She cried with sobs, I mean, despairing. Without making a sound, she cried really heavy tears, you know when you are really in silence and you cry like that.

What is striking about this conversation is that the teachers used two recent events, when Giorgio couldn't name the hen and when Elena couldn't explain about her rabbit, to illustrate how painfully aware these children were of their own language limitations. They were, in a sense, making the children's problems their own problems. They were figuring out how to take action. While the underlying issue the teachers were grappling with is one of student differences, and more specifically, of developmental differences with respect to more verbal children, we can see the dilemma of the ongoing tension between private versus public actions in Valeria's account of soliciting Giorgio's knowledge of the hen and in Arda's encouraging Elena to share the story of her rabbit with her friends. There is also a second dilemma, a tension between maintaining a safe space free of public humiliation and encouraging risk taking and meeting high expectations. Valeria tried to lessen Giorgio's embarrassment at not knowing the answer was hen by asking for a whispered guess, while Arda encouraged Elena to tell her story even though it was challenging for her. We shall see the other strategies that Arda and Valeria employed to manage these dilemmas in the examples that follow. Before doing so, it is important to note here that the teachers made no gender-based assumptions, and rather than dwelling on the deficits of Giorgio and Elena, they spoke of their needs for enrichment and more conversation in pairs or small groups.

To better understand some of the methods employed by Arda and Valeria to both enhance the intellectual development of Giorgio, Elena, and other students, and to help avoid any public humiliation while still encouraging them to participate in discussions, it is useful to examine two events that occurred during the morning meeting when the whole class was gathered on the steps. In addition to understanding how Arda and Valeria managed the two dilemmas described above, I hope to illustrate how in the whole-class context they used two of Fenstermacher's methods, showcasing and academic task structure, to further the intellectual growth of students.

One morning Valeria brought to school a special "talking stick" made by Native Americans. As students waited in anticipation, she ceremoniously held up a white sack and explained that for American Indians, "everything that comes out of the mouth is sacred and it's important to be very silent and listen." She explained how the elders sit in a circle while young people sit behind them to listen and learn. "Now I will present to you the talking stick," she said as she pulled the stick out of the sack to the oohs and aahs of the students. Valeria explained how the talking stick was chosen in the woods, and the tree that gives up a branch gets a sacred gift. Whoever held the stick could speak while everyone else would listen attentively. One at a time, students held the stick carefully aloft as they shared their ideas about how the wise elders could speak to the trees and know which would give up a branch to make the talking stick, before passing it on to the person next to them. Sometimes a student had a question for the previous student, and the stick would momentarily return to that person before being passed along again. Theories began to emerge: "Maybe that tree is a little magic to be able to talk to the wise elder. It was very kind," and "All the trees could speak." When the stick reached Elena, she held it and was silent and pensive. Students waited patiently, but finally Gabriele muttered, "I've been waiting an hour," which prompted Elena to give up and to pass the stick on to Silvana. Then Gabriele finally got the stick and wondered, "Maybe because the tree moved its smallest branches to speak to the Indian." Adele asked about the feathers, and Giorgio said they were bird feathers. Teo picked up on an earlier question from Dario as to why they were called tribes, and proposed it's because the drums go "boom boom." Dario responded, and then Elena took the stick to add, "As the heart goes boom boom." At this moment, Valeria took the stick to tell the group that Elena had said something important and closed by telling them that they could discover many things about these interesting people. She put the stick near the mailboxes as students took a short break.

What was fascinating was that once the conversation began and the stick was passed around, Valeria did not contribute to the conversation except when a question was directed at her about a bead necklace she had promised to bring to school. She had introduced the use of the talking stick to cultivate in students a way of talking slowly and listening carefully, and then observed and recorded how their questions and speculations built on previous questions. They were learning to develop and articulate their theories, and they were explaining how those ideas connected to their previous knowledge, such as Elena's, that the heart, like a drum, goes "boom boom." Valeria had designed an academic task structure that would develop an intellectual disposition toward discussion where listening carefully to each other and building on each other's ideas was important to developing theories. She did not do this didactically by telling the students that this was a good or virtuous way to have a discussion, but imaginatively used the aura of the magical stick as a tool to help them experience the power of a discussion where students spoke one at a time, and everyone listened carefully to each other's contributions and theories.

The documentation of conversations such as these is an essential part of what teachers do in Reggio's municipal preschools, for they use it not only as a point of departure for further inquiry and to assess their students, it is also shared with the community, especially with parents. For example, each day either Arda or Valeria would write up the main events and post them together with digital pictures in a newsletter (for parents, children, and other visitors), known as the *leggenda quotidiana*, outside the classroom's entrance. That day's newsletter began with the talking stick and with a picture of three children, one of whom held the stick. "The talking stick is an object used by some tribes from North America," explained the newsletter.

To teach the children how to speak one at a time, respecting and listening to the friend who is talking in silence. The friends learn to wait their turn calmly.

We explained that the stick was made by the head elder of the tribe.

> Amalia: The elder is a person who knows many things. And then my mother also told me that if people stay too close to things, they can speak with their thoughts and feel what they are thinking.
>
> Vincenzo: Amalia, but do you know how the elders can talk with the trees?
>
> Amalia: With the trees? Maybe that tree [of the stick] was a special tree and it spoke and he could hear it.

In this brief summary of the talking stick discussion, the teachers have let the parents know both what the children have been talking about and the rationale for what they have been doing in the classroom that day.

Valeria's intentional strategy to introduce the magical talking stick, imbued with sacred meaning and tales of exotic people living far away, to enable students to learn to speak one at a time, to listen very carefully, and to build on each other's ideas was purposeful and successful. It also reveals her aim to develop in students a certain intellectual disposition to discussion, one that, she hopes, cultivates values of respect and patience. I interpret this aim to lie at the intersection of academic, social, and civic goals, and to be both moral and intellectual. Valeria explained to me that once students begin to experience discussion in this way, they eventually become less reliant on the presence of the talking stick because they have learned the value of being patient and respectful during discussions. Although Elena did not speak the first time the stick came to her, she followed the subsequent train of thoughts that linked the word *tribù* (tribe) with the sound of drums, and she added her own analogy of the heart, which also goes "boom boom." Valeria used the strategy of showcasing her contribution (and the risk taking involved) when she pointed out that Elena had said something important. Giorgio also made a contribution to the discussion by answering Adele's question about the feathers on the talking stick. What the stick did most dramatically was to slow down the pace of conversation, and even the stick itself was passed from student to student slowly and with great ceremony. This not only helped the students to focus on what was being said, it gave time for students like Giorgio and Elena to think and permission to share when they were ready to say something. More dominant students might otherwise have overshadowed their fragile participation.

The daily newsletter was another showcasing strategy, meant to keep parents and others informed about significant events and conversations in the classroom. It is possible to imagine parents reading these newsletters as their children prepared to leave at the end of the day, and beginning a conversation in the car ride home about the talking stick. In other words, showcasing and designing academic task structures can not only help students to learn to value each other's ideas and contributions, and to see each other as resources for their learning, in this case the showcasing also involved parents in extending and becoming a part of the conversations that were developing in the classroom.

However, showcasing occurs in even more substantial ways than just a teacher's comment about a student's contribution, or in the daily newsletters. On my fourth day in the classroom Arda explained that Grazia had a special performance to share with the class and that Amalia would accompany her on her trumpet. As Grazia went to retrieve a red sack filled with props for her storytelling performance and Amalia got her trumpet, Arda asked the students, "Should we make the room dark, just like in a real theater?" and students enthusiastically said yes, and squeezed themselves on the steps audience-style in anticipation, while Arda reminded them how to act in the theater. Grazia sat on the floor in front of them, and pulled out a little chick from her sack as she began her story and Amalia quietly played in the background. The story explained how the little chick, Giacomino, walking in the forest saw a cave. A snake came out (at this point, she pulled a snake from her sack) and followed him, but then went back to the cave. One fine day Giacomino became a rooster (and now she pulled out a large stuffed rooster) and found the cave he remembered from when he had been little. Still curious, he went inside. There was a big fight (at this she stuck her hand inside the sack and made it move around) in the cave with the serpent, and then Giacomino came out like this! Grazia held up a rubber chicken as the room exploded in shrieks of laughter. Suddenly everyone was hugging and kissing and laughing and tumbling down from the steps into a big heap on top of Grazia and Amalia. Rather than quiet everyone down, the teachers enjoyed the sheer joy in the room until it settled down naturally. Arda said that it was such a magnificent performance that they must do an encore. The students shouted in agreement as they returned immediately to their positions on the steps, and Grazia and Amalia began the story again. The rubber chicken was an equally funny finale the second time around. Amalia had some time to explain to everyone how her trumpet worked, and she played another song. This led to more singing with a small group and then the whole class, and the teachers commented on how Amalia was really listening in her accompaniment, pausing when the singers paused. The whole event ended in more hugs, jumping, and joy that palpably exploded all over the room.

I've included this example of showcasing because it further illustrates how the teachers use the students (and their differences) as resources for each other's learning. Certainly Arda and Valeria believe that providing opportunities for students like Amalia and Grazia to share their storytelling and musical talents with the whole group will provide the kind of enrichment they seek for students like Giorgio and Elena. What is also noteworthy is the authenticity of this experience, first because it featured the students and the talents they wished to share with the class; and second because of the teachers' strategic moves to make the room dark like the real theater, to seat the students as an audience and to remind them of audience politeness, to allow the unrestrained and enthusiastic response at the end, and to call for an encore, merited by the delight everyone expressed when the performance came to its finale. These were subtle but significant teacher interventions that enhanced the learning opportunity afforded by the girls' performance and developed in students a deepening appreciation for theater as well as the storytelling talents of their classmates. It stands in contrast to a typical American "show and tell" where each student is afforded equal minutes of floor time, for Amalia and Grazia truly had ownership of the event, which was the focal point of that morning's class meeting. Students also learn that the risk of humiliation in such a public performance is mitigated by the delight expressed by their peers, and this learning can be used by the teachers in managing both of the dilemmas described earlier.

FINAL THOUGHTS

In these telling cases we have seen the complex nature of the process of managing dilemmas, which cannot be described as linear or even as a matter of means and ends. We have also seen that within the telling case of Giorgio and Elena, two dilemmas were present. Arda and Valeria were constantly engaged in observing and documenting the learning of students, all the while being very sensitive to the fragility of their take-up and adjusting their methods while keeping in mind their goals, aims, and the benefits and drawbacks of particular actions.

We have also seen how the moral and intellectual are virtually inseparable dimensions of life in Reggio Emilia's municipal preschools, and how the construction of the classroom community and maintaining its vitality requires full participation of everyone: students, their parents, teachers, and staff. Even an event as seemingly straightforward as a student's birthday is rich with moral and intellectual overtones. The cook makes a cake that is decorated by the birthday boy or girl with help from a few friends; the cake is shared at lunch and photographs are taken to document the happy festivities. These go into a class book that is often read and enjoyed by students in the classroom. If the child has a birthday party at home, an invitation for everyone in the class is posted at school, and there is extended discussion afterward of presents and games and all the other details of the celebration. For 5-year-olds, learning that birthdays are recurring cultural annual events involving family and friends is intellectually significant, and for the teachers, it provides multiple opportunities to talk about many wonderful things and to share stories of birthdays past and present. Students learn that they are loved and valued, and in turn they learn to love and value others. What goal could possibly be more important than that?

There are several implications of these findings. These cases call for a careful focus on the nature and frequency of teacher interventions. Children in this classroom are given freedom to pursue their questions and curiosities, to express freely their thinking in words, drawings, paintings, constructions, plays, songs, and dance. The teachers carefully construct an environment that invites children's engagement in this way, and they provide academic task structures that facilitate their learning. Then they spend a lot of time carefully watching and recording what happens—they too become learners. Caroline Pratt, a visionary early childhood educator, wrote over half a century ago:

> The children know what they are doing. They are as sure of themselves as the man who reproduces his model from a working drawing. They are sure of themselves *as long as adults leave them alone.*

If I labor the point, it is because I have learned its importance by experience. The over-helpful adult is no help, is actually a hindrance to the child. What perceptive adult has not seen a child's face go blank like a closed door at the very moment when he is receiving the most helpful attention? Who has not had the humiliating experience of having a child walk idly away in the middle of an answer to his question? (1948/1970, p. 49)

We saw that these Reggio educators seem to understand this fundamental notion that the children know what they are doing, and that this understanding helps them know how best to manage the tensions between being public and private actions, and between creating a space free of public humiliation while encouraging risk taking, as in the case of Giorgio and Elena.

Furthermore, they have a deep conviction of the central role of imagination in children's moral and intellectual growth, which resides in the foundational ideas of Malaguzzi and his "hundred languages of children." The imagination also generates humor and silliness, as in the imaginary defeathering of the rooster Giacomino by the snake in Grazia's storytelling performance. Because children are free to express themselves within the full range of their capacities and strengths, unbound by gender or other forms of stereotype and discrimination, and because the teachers carefully document and reflect on the meaning of the differences of all their students, and then strategically use those differences in pedagogically advantageous ways, the learning of all participants flourishes. It also allows all children to become full participants in the world as they imagine it could be, a place of peace.

NOTES

1. Since teaching is a historically feminized profession and the participants in this study are all women, teachers are referred to here with female pronouns.
2. In Italy, children enter the first year of elementary school at age 6.
3. Permission was granted to use the real names of teachers, but student names are pseudonyms.
4. Malaguzzi captured this idea in a famous poem entitled "No way. The hundred is there" (Invece il cento c'é).
5. Today there are 21 preschools and 13 infant/toddler centers.

REFERENCES

Castanheira, M. L., Crawford, T., Dixon, C., & Green, J. (2001). Interactional ethnography: An approach to studying the social construction of literate practices. *Linguistics and Education, 11*(4), 353–400.

Corsaro, W. A., & Emiliani, F. (1992). Child care, early education, and children's peer culture in Italy. In M. E. Lamb, K. J. Sternberg, C. P. Hwang & A. G. Broberg (Eds.), *Child care in context.* (pp. 81–155). Hillsdale, NJ: Erlbaum.

Edwards, C. P., Gandini, L., & Forman, G. E. (1998). *The hundred languages of children: The Reggio Emilia approach—advanced reflections* (2nd ed.). Greenwich, CT: Ablex.

Fenstermacher, G. (1992). The concepts of method and manner in teaching. In F. K. Oser, A. Dick & J.L. Patry (Eds.), *Effective and responsible teaching : the new synthesis* (pp. 95–108). San Francisco: Jossey-Bass.

Fenstermacher, G. D. (2001). On the concept of manner and its visibility in teaching practice. *Journal of Curriculum Studies, 33*(6), 639–653.

Gardner, H. (1998). Complementary perspectives on Reggio Emilia. In C. P. Edwards, L. Gandini, & G. E. Forman (Eds.), *The hundred languages of children: The Reggio Emilia approach—advanced reflections* (pp. xv–xviii). Greenwich, CT: Ablex Publishing.

Katz, L., & Cesarone, B. (Eds.). (1994). *Reflections on the Reggio Emilia approach* (Vol. 6). Urbana, IL: ERIC Clearinghouse on Elementary and Early Childhood Education.

Krechevsky, M., & Stork, J. (2000). Challenging educational assumptions: Lessons from an Italian–American collaboration. *Cambridge Journal of Education, 30*(1), 57–74.

Malaguzzi, L., & Gandini, L. (1998). History, ideas and basic philosophy: An interview with Lella Gandini. In C. P. Edwards, L. Gandini, & G. E. Forman (Eds.), *The hundred languages of children: The Reggio Emilia approach—advanced reflections* (2nd ed., pp. 49–97). Greenwich, CT: Ablex.

Mardell, B. (2001). Moving across the Atlantic. In C. Giudici, C. Rinaldi, & M. Krechevsky (Eds.), *Making learning visible: Children as individual and group learners* (pp. 278–283). Reggio Emilia, Italy: Reggio Children.

Mitchell, C. J. (1984). Typicality and the case study. In R. F. Ellens (Ed.), *Ethnographic research: A guide to general conduct* (pp. 238–241). New York: Academic Press.

New, R. (1993). Italy. In M. Cochran (Ed.), *International Handbook of Child Care Policies and Practices* (pp. 291–311). Westport, CT: Greenwood Press.

Pratt, C. (1948/1970). *I learn from children.* New York: Cornerstone Library.

Rankin, B. (2004). The importance of intentional socialization among children in small groups: A conversation with Loris Malaguzzi. *Early Childhood Education Journal, 32*(2), 81–85.

Rinaldi, C. (2001). Infant-toddler centers and preschools as places of culture. In C. R. C. Giudici & M. Krechevsky (Eds.), *Making learning visible: Children as individual and group learners* (pp. 38–46). Reggio Emilia, Italy: Reggio Children.

Valentine, M. (1999). *The Reggio Emilia approach to early years education.* Glasgow, Scotland: Scottish Consultative Council on the Curriculum.

CHAPTER 6

EARLY MATHEMATICS

Learning in the Block Center

Barbara Polnick
Carole Funk

As early as nursery school, boys and girls sitting in the same classroom with the same teacher, using the same materials, have different learning experiences. These differences persist through their pre-college education and beyond. (Sanders, Koch, and Urso, 1997, p. 3)

Are early learning experiences different for boys and girls in mathematics? If so, how are they different? How do early learning experiences relate to later success in mathematics and mathematics-related fields? What might teachers, day-care centers, parents, and other caregivers of young children do to encourage success in mathematics for both genders? These questions represent the central discussion presented in this chapter regarding gender differences in early learning of mathematics. Because human beings grow and develop more rapidly from birth to 8 years old than at any other period in their lives (National Association for the Education of Young Children, 2003) and because this early development is complex when viewed from a "whole child" perspective, including cognitive, verbal, physical, emotional, and social development, the authors recognize that this chapter alone cannot address all aspects of early childhood influences on the learn-

Gender and Schooling in the Early Years, pages 99–112
Copyright © 2005 by Information Age Publishing

ing of mathematics. In this chapter, we chose to focus on the experiential factors that can influence the way young children learn to feel and think about mathematics, specifically as they relate to gender.

To this end, the chapter is organized into four parts. First, we discuss current research in cognitive development of young children as it relates to mathematics learning and gender. The second and third sections of the chapter focus on play in centers as it relates to mathematics learning. These sections include a review of experiences found in the block center contrasted with those in the home center. Through this reflective process, the reader is asked to revisit his or her own early childhood experiences in centers, as we discuss the kind of mathematical thinking associated with pretend play. While no research has confirmed a cause-and-effect relationship between pretend play and cognitive development, it is more likely that pretend play engages many areas of the brain because it involves emotion, cognition, language, and sensorimotor actions, and thus it may promote the development of dense synaptic connections (Bergen & Coscia, 2001). The fourth part of the chapter includes a summary of recommendations for supporting high-quality mathematics learning for young children of both genders and concludes with summary statements regarding recommendations for gender equity in early mathematics learning.

INTRODUCTION

Because of the gendered brain that is sexed by different hormones before and after birth, female students and male students generally exhibit different learning needs and styles based on the differing uses of the left and right brain hemispheres that affect the way they learn (deSimone & Durden-Smith, 1983). It is through our early learning experiences that some of our first concepts about mathematics form and because of this, these experiences have the potential to affect our later success or failure in this subject (Sanders & Rocco, 1994). Learning how experiences differ for boys and girls in early education settings is critical to understanding how educators, parents, and other stakeholders can support the development of a child's ability to understand and apply mathematics concepts in school and throughout their lives. For example, studies support that both spatial relations and problem solving are areas of mathematics in which gender differences are often demonstrated. The level of success in higher-level mathematics courses in high school and college is dependent on how well students are able to solve problems. Myra and David Sadker, in their book *Failing at Fairness: How America's Schools Cheat Girls* (1994), synthesized a number of behaviors from studies on gender performance in mathematics and science. We analyzed the NCTM Principles and Standards to compare characteristics associated with good problem-solvers to those behaviors generated from gender studies, like those developed by the Sadkers. Table 6.1 offers a graphic comparison of those characteristics as they parallel those behaviors exhibited less often by girls when compared to boys.

Table 6.1.

According to the National Council of Teachers of Mathematics (2002), Good Problem Solvers exhibit...	In Mathematics, Girls When Compared to Boys ...
risk taking	are less comfortable taking risks in the secondary mathematics and science classrooms
persistence	are less persistent when seeking solutions to problems
confidence in their own abilities	have less confidence in their own innate abilities to solve problems
high expectations for success	believe that others hold lower expectations for them to succeed and/or advance in mathematics studies
resourcefulness	are less likely to find alternative strategies for solving mathematics problems when their first attempts to solve a problem fail

For purposes of clarity, the authors use the term "gender equity" in a collective sense, gleaning our definition from several authors reknown in the field of gender and gender equity. Grossman and Grossman (1994) viewed gender equity in terms of "treatment of students, gender differences in roles for which schools prepare students and gender disparities in educational outcomes" (p. 119). In a similar vein, Koch and Irby (2002) described gender equity as being "fair and just toward both men and women, to show preference to neither, and concern for both" (p. 4). Walker and Foote (2001) also defined gender equity within a culture described by the following: "all individuals having freedom from limits imposed by self or society that would prohibit both males and females from pursuing the fields of knowledge and skills suited for them" (p. 101). In light of these viewpoints, we support the belief that gender equity in the educational environment occurs when not only opportunities are provided to individuals but, also, real efforts are made to equalize, reform, and improve learning for all (Dougherty, 1997).

Although there are more similarities than differences between the sexes, many of the differences in male and female brains are related to differential brain structure and function (deSimone & Durden-Smith, 1983; Halpern, 2000). While we recognize that both socialization and developmental differences between the sexes exist, the consistent debates as to who is getting shortchanged the most continues (American Association of University Women, 2001; Hoffman, 2001; Independent Women's Forum, 2001). Girls have historically scored lower on mathematics, science, and technology achievement tests than boys (Sanders et al., 1997, p. 3). Courses such as calculus and statistics often serve as "gatekeepers" for those fields and professions that are traditionally dominated by white males: mathematics, chemistry, engineering, business, advanced medicine, and technology. Data indicate that girls participate less in higher-level mathematics courses than do boys in high school (American Association of University Women Educational Foundation, 1998). Unless girls "prepare for paid work by selecting and obtaining the neecessary education and training for an occupation that interests them, they [girls] are more likely than males to be limited to low-paying, uninteresting jobs that provide little opportunitiy for economic self-sufficiency or advancement" (Bitters & Fox-well, 1993, p. 8). Because of these missed opportunities and experiences, a limited number of girls (when compared to boys) have access to high-paying and often more personally satisfying jobs (Brody et al., 2000). Issues around why girls do not take advantage of the opportunities that are provided are wrapped up in self-esteem and curriculum preparedness. When girls do not perceive themselves as being "good at" (successful) in mathematics, they tend to shy away from taking advanced mathematics coursework (Grossman & Grossman, 1994). Girls who do not take advanced mathematics courses are often less prepared to score well on mathematics portions of college entrance exams and less likely to get into major, prestigious universities (Goodlad & Keating, 1990). "Mathematics, specifically, then becomes 'the great divide' that must be crossed in order to achieve and succeed in financially-enhanced and challenging jobs" (Polnick, 2002). Educating both genders to be successful in mathematics is critical. We can no longer use the excuse that *girls are better at language-related subjects and boys are better at mathematics and science* and that's why Janie can't engineer (McNees, 2004).

Even if one accepts that biological differences exist in male and female brains and are associated with genetic mapping and hormonal levels, and that these in turn influence cognitive processing (Hoffman, 2001; Sanders & Rocco, 1994), should we accept the belief that this "prewiring" (or lack of) toward a given talent or interest in mathematics should direct children's exposure to experiences related to learning mathematics? Overall, studies about issues related to gender equity have been subjects of debate and have not provided enough empirical evidence to provide definitive answers to the gender equity equation. Until more is known about this area of study, disagreements between existing research continue to hinder systematic implementation of interventions designed to balance this equation. What we do know is that while schools debate the issues of nurture versus nature, girls and boys alike may be missing opportunities to grow and benefit from experiences that support high-quality mathematics learning, such as in the case of the block and home centers. Issues around the role of parents, teachers, and day-care providers in facilitating these centers arise when we begin to examine how gender-related decisions about what experiences boys should have and what experiences girls should have as they relate to future success in mathematics.

Play is an important vehicle for children's social, emotional, and cognitive development, as well as a reflection of their development (NAEYC, 2003). Vigotsky (1978) believed that play leads development, with written language growing out of oral language through the vehicle of symbolic play that promotes the development of symbolic representation. Mallory and New (1994) supported the belief that play provides the context for children to practice newly acquired skills and attempt novel or challenging tasks, as well as solve complex problems.

In the second part of this chapter, we invite the readers to reflect on their earliest school experiences involving play—described in this chapter as it might occur in centers. *Centers,* sometimes called "play centers" or "learning centers," are defined in this chapter to be a certain type of classroom arrangement, constructed or organized in special ways to enhance learning, usually through child-initiated play (Frost, Wortham, & Reifel, 2005). Early childhood experts agree that learning occurs primarily through projects, learning centers, and playful activities that reflect current interests and needs of children (Beaty, 2002; Morrison, 2004; Patton & Mercer, 1996). Learning centers enable young children to engage in active learning and support learning in all the developmental domains. Planned well, centers enable teachers to meet state and national standards for what children should know and be able to do (Morrison, 2004). We recognize that learning centers, especially child-initiated learning centers, are considered the domain of preschool and kindergarten; however, we recognize that since the National Association for the Education of Young Children (NAEYC) defines early childhood as birth through age 8, there are opportunities for center work in first-, second-, and sometimes third-grade classrooms as well (Patton & Mercer, 1996). These centers may become more skill-specific, such as "the literacy center," but the concept of students working in small groups with hands-on materials around a certain theme is still utilized during part of the day. Closely associated with "centers" are "center choices" that generate a number of issues around gender and gender equity, because children at very early ages begin to separate themselves into same-gender groups (Beaty, 2002) when going to centers.

MATHEMATICS WE LEARNED
FROM THE BLOCK CORNER/CENTER

For many of us, our earliest memories of learning mathematics are those where we were counting—maybe our birthday candles, our buttons, jumping rope, skipping rocks, or bouncing a ball. But mathematics learning actually began earlier than that; it began in the block corner/center. The kind of mathematics we learned in the block center (if you were lucky enough to get over there!) would build skills that later helped us solve problems about objects in space, topics that in later years would puzzle the girls and fascinate the boys (Bush & Kincer, 1993; Kennedy, Tipps, & Johnson, 2004; Noble & Bradford, 2000). This part of mathematics learning, called spatial relations, would propel us through intelligence quotients (IQ) tests, the Armed Services Vocational Aptitude Battery (ASVAB; Wiesen, Siegel, & Wilfong, 1979) and various screening tests for engineering and architecture schools. It would be the kind of learning that would make us feel smart because over half of us would find spatial exercises extremely challenging (Halpern, 2000), so much so that we would avoid these kinds of activities and tests at all costs, including not applying for certain programs that required them for admissions. Eventually, these skills would become muddled in our mind and in the minds of others as "things we just aren't very good at" or on the positive side, "things we ought to do when we grow up." For those of us who spent a lot of time in the block corner/center and developed these spatial skills, our options were pretty open when it came to the big-salaried careers, such as engineering, architecture, medicine, computer science/programming, and chemistry.

Playing in the block center would teach us how to make larger shapes out of smaller shapes and how to rotate, flip, and slide pieces of objects into place with our eyes before we even moved them with our hands. It enabled us to look over our friend's shoulder a few feet away and say "It won't fit!" before he or she even picked up the Lego block. And, it would later facilitate our ability to draw pictures of robots, monsters, and planes that leaped off the page with their intricate detail and 3-D effect.

Those of us that spent a lot of time in the block center also learned that there are some things that just won't reach no matter how hard you stretch them. We learned that a 3-foot piece of string would wrap around the trash can (which was in easy reach) three times and that all those smaller cubes would almost fill that pitcher that was taken from the sand table. We would have learned a lot more about how smaller things fit into larger spaces, except the teacher kept making us put things we had gotten from the other centers back. Thank goodness we had pockets, so that we could use stuff we brought from home. Learning in the block center provided a foundation for understanding concepts later introduced in geometry, including graphical representations, topology, and solving word problems involving figures ("If a 50 foot tree casts a shadow on a 4-foot-tall boy standing 15 feet from the tree, how long would his shadow be?").

We also learned about how we learned, mainly that the more you played there, the better your buildings began to look and the more other people admired you for your work—not necessarily for how you behaved. Creating solid and tall structures went hand-in-hand with the highly cultivated skill of making sounds. The more you played in this center, the more sounds you learned to make with your mouth as you propelled rockets to the moon, rolled dump trucks to landfills, and, of course, made spewing earth-quakes that toppled 3-foot-high structures to the ground. This sense of what sounds objects make as they move through space would later help us learn how machines run and allow us to create much more intricate items in science and after-school activities, such as robots and rocketry for sci-ence fairs and competitions like Odyssey of the Mind (Micklus, 1978). Cre-ating these sound effects, however, was a skill that was admired by the boys but admonished by the teacher (Beaty, 2002).

MATHEMATICS WE LEARNED FROM THE HOME CORNER/CENTER

Those of us who liked the way the teacher smiled at us when we played qui-etly enjoyed the home center. We learned a lot of skills in the home center from things that were not available in the block center. The telephone was a popular item, especially since it had a notepad and pencil on a string tacked on the wall. (The pencil on the string was sometimes missing, but was later found in the block corner.) We learned to take orders for pizza over the phone ("That will be ten dollars and twenty-six cents, with tax, please!") and we also learned that, like the block center users, we could make noises too, but the noises were more subtle and melodic. (Rrringg! Rrringg! "Would someone please get that, I'm busy!"). Unlike in the block center, sounds in the home center were much more efficient. One sound could double for another, such as the telephone ring doubling as a door-bell to announce that the repairman arrived or as an alarm clock alerting lazy dolls to get up in time for school and come down to breakfast. Money was a nice feature of the home center. We learned that some coins were worth more than others and from the newspaper fliers and catalogs that the teacher placed in the center we learned that there were printed words and symbols that went along with buying things and that the value of money (not the number of coins) had a lot to do with what you could buy. For example, you needed a lot of dollars (paper money) if you wanted to buy a car (which was over in the block center). Some of us learned about banking in the home center, when the teacher put some "checks" in there, and those of us in the home center who liked to "write" would make lists of needed groceries and take our checks to the grocery store. At one time there were a lot of cool things in the grocery store center, but they soon got borrowed for use in the other centers. For example, the cans made great wheels, a basket made a fantastic spaceship, and the cash register was taken apart so that the "chink chink" sound could be put in a truck. The aprons in the store were needed in the home center, and the little plastic food was confiscated by the sand and water table, where the people at that center learned a wealth of measurement skills, such as volume displacement, conservation of space, and how to pour from a larger container into a smaller one. Having these skills would later identify you as "group leader" when we went to the science lab. Another attribute for identifying these future scientists was their ability to get dirty or to get their clothes messed up without their parents getting upset with the teacher; thus, the overalls, old dark T-shirts, and jeans were uniform at the water/sand table. Yes, the water/sand table held a lot of appeal, but for many the pressure for neatness was just too much. So many opted for the home center as a viable alternative.

The home center had its limitations in that there were a lot of things that did not do much. Nothing really ever came apart that would easily go back together. We could not fit things into other things without breaking something, and everything was kind of flat—the pictures on the walls, the covers on the doll bed, paper dolls (very popular in the 1950s and 1960s), and even the napkins at the table. Even the dress-up clothes were all kind of flat and you couldn't shape them into other things or do something totally different with them like you did with things from the block corner/center. Everything in the home center had a specific purpose and a specific place where it was to be used. Even the dishes were flat, except for the large pitcher in which you could create exotic juice drinks, except that the pitcher was usually being used at the sand table—which only the people in overalls or jeans and dark T-shirts were allowed to play at.

At the home center, like the sand/water table, we learned to measure things, like how tall someone was or how long something had to be to fit across the floor or on the wall. These skills would be later valuable when working with linear measurement, a skill at which many of the girls would excel (Noble & Bradford, 2000). We in the home center also learned to count really well (accurately and fast) because in the home center you had to count out four or five sets of everything—one for each person in the center; or if there were only two of you, you had to count out multiple sets for all the children (dolls). Those of us who spent a lot of time in the home center developed a familiarity with what would later become known as our "math facts." Learning our math facts was fun and a skill for which we received a lot of praise and recognition, like stars on a class chart.

We also learned to read the clock pretty well if you were in the home center, because when the "big hand" was straight up and the "little hand" was pointing to the door, you knew it was time to clean up. It took a long time to get everything picked up in the home center. There was a specific place for everything and everything fit "exactly perfect," if we did it right. Fitting things into their exact place was a skill that we did not have to know in the block center, and we could play longer in there because it did not take as long to clean up. Also in the block center, it was not as important that all the like things went together and stored in separate bins, because the materials would get all mixed up the next day when you tried to build something different. But, for those of us in the home center, learning where and how things fit into categories would serve as a very useful skill later in school, such as staying organized and finding your place in the book and keeping track of your finished and unfinished papers, as well as having the right supplies for the right activity. This particular skill was a real teacher pleaser, and if we did not develop it (as many of the block corner/center folks didn't), we were always in trouble with the teacher and we usually got bad grades on our report cards.

Being organized and knowing how to categorize things by their verbal descriptions helped many of us who spent time in the home center in future mathematics lessons, too. When we had to learn the names and descriptions of shapes and symbols and even later when we were first introduced to word problems and eventually algebra, we did well (Halpern, 2000). The step-by-step, organized way of solving problems really worked well for us from the home center, and as long as the process stayed linear and matched the examples given, we understood how to solve the problems. Being organized helped us when applying deductive reasoning to solve geometry proofs and logic problems.

There were other skills that we learned in the home center that could have launched future careers as mathematicians had we known that we were doing mathematics when we were using them. These included finding and completing patterns (with numbers, shapes, objects), making organized lists, sketching a picture to solve a problem, working backward to think through a problem, and working collaboratively to find solutions to problems.

WHAT WE COULD HAVE LEARNED
FROM A VARIETY OF EXPERIENCES

In reflection, all of us could have acquired the skills to be successful mathematicians—had we been given the opportunities to develop the habits, ways of learning, character traits, and flexible viewpoints of the world needed to solve problems. Had we learned in our early learning experiences how to express ourselves explicitly in our written and oral language, we would have been better at communicating our ideas about mathematics. And if we had learned to have high expectations for our own personal success, along with a sense of self-efficacy, we would have learned the value of being able to control and manipulate our environment to solve problems and to believe that we have the potential to be great mathematicians. The folks in the block center could have learned the importance of cooperating with each other by working toward a common vision and they could have learned the importance of taking care of supplies, materials, and other tools so that they would be successful in school early on, especially when dealing with the teacher. And maybe those in the home center could have learned what those in the block center/corner learned—that you need to take risks (especially to try new things), ask a lot of questions, be assertive by getting the materials we need to solve a problem, and be creative and flexible about the way we view the world (it is alright to use the green cloth napkins in the home center for mountains in the block corner/center). Likewise, the folks in the block center could have learned how to organize their work to solve problems, how there are patterns in the world that develop out of predictability, and that it's important to both follow and give directions and use explicit language when describing objects and events as we collectively seek solutions to problems. The mouth sounds were still an important communication tool that let everyone in the room know when something special was happening and how important it is to be spontaneous if we are to seek creative solutions to problems.

HIGH-QUALITY, EQUITABLE CLASSROOMS

In their recommendations for 3- to 6-year-old children, the National Council of Mathematics (NCTM) and the National Association for the Education of Young Children (NAEYC) published a joint position entitled *Early Childhood Mathematics: Promoting Good Beginnings.* This figure describes specific curriculum and instructional strategies regarding what teachers and other key professionals can do to provide/support high-quality mathematics education (NAEYC, 2003). One of these recommendations included making high-quality, challenging mathematics accessible for all 3- to 6-year old children (NAEYC, 2003). Ten recommendations were included in this chapter, outlined in Figure 6.1.

In conclusion, we know that there is still room for individuality in early learning environments and that the search to be one's own self will surface and submerge many times as we develop throughout their lives in school, home, and work environments (Puckett & Black, 2005). Like the children

To achieve high-quality mathematics education for 3- to 6-year-old children, teachers and other key professionals should:

1. Enhance children's natural interest in mathematics and their disposition to use it to make sense of their physical and social worlds.
2. Build on children's experience and knowledge, including their family, linguistic, cultural, and community backgrounds; their individual approaches to learning; and their informal knowledge.
3. Base mathematics curriculum and teaching practices on knowledge of young children's cognitive, linguistic, physical, and social-emotional development.
4. Use curriculum and teaching practices that strengthen children's problem-solving and reasoning processes as well as representing, communicating, and connecting mathematical ideas.
5. Ensure that the curriculum is coherent and compatible with known relationships and sequences of important mathematical ideas.
6. Provide for children's deep and sustained interaction with key mathematical ideas.
7. Integrate mathematics with other activities and other activities with mathematics.
8. Provide ample time, materials, and teacher support for children to engage in play, a context in which they explore and manipulate mathematical ideas with keen interest.
9. Actively introduce mathematical concepts, methods, and language through a range of appropriate experiences and teaching strategies.
10. Support children's learning by thoughtfully and continually assessing all children's mathematical knowledge, skills, and strategies.

Figure 6.1. Achieving high-quality mathematics education.

at the sand/water table, some of us may see ourselves as being future scientists or architects, doctors, theologians, politicians, teachers, and artists, each with our own quirky way of identifying with the world around us, but we all have the need and right to opportunities when we are young that help us develop the skills to be anything we want to be when we grow up.

SUMMARY

While there is no evidence that encouraging pretend play in many different arenas will increase higher levels of cognition in mathematics, facilitating center experiences so that girls and boys have equal opportunities to take things apart, move objects through space, organize and classify parts and pieces, manipulate sets of objects such as when ordering patterning, and counting and encouraging the use of mathematical language in pretend writing, reading, and dialogue, can enhance all children's mathematical understanding as well as the way they relate to the world of mathematics. Experiences in solving problems through play help children develop curiosity and patience, along with thinking skills such as flexibility and understanding of cause and effect.

In this chapter, we are proposing that children have equal access to a variety of experiences through center play. But equal access is more than equal choice because choice may be predetermined by a history of "who usually goes where," thereby discouraging some girls and boys to venture outside their social boundaries. We are not encouraging that boys put on aprons and that girls wrestle each other to the ground as some critics of gender equity authors would propose we are suggesting, but rather that educators and other caregivers be aware of those early experiences that can either enhance or limit mathematical understanding. Providing a variety of materials for interaction in a small group setting can enhance children's desire and ability to learn mathematical concepts. Through a variety of play experiences, children also learn to work toward achieving a goal and gain confidence in their ability to find solutions to problems. Offering a variety of experiences to enhance mathematical thinking may be as simple as providing a variety of manipulatives, toys, blocks, and tools for the centers where the children are, as they need them, as opposed to changing where children go in the room. We leave it then to the reader to determine the specific classroom structure for implementing learning centers and to decide to what degree, if any, a child should be guided in their play.

REFERENCES

American Association of University Women. (2001). *Beyond the "gender wars."* Symposium organized by AAUW National Press Club, Washington, DC.

American Association of University Women Educational Foundation. (1998). *Gender gaps: Where schools still fail our children.* Washington, DC: Author.

Beaty, J. (2002). *Observing development of the young child* (5th ed.). Columbus, OH: Merrill Prentice Hall.

Bitters, B. A., & Foxwell, S. (1993). *Wisconsin Model for sex equity in career and vocational education.* Milwaukee: Wisconsin Department of Public Instruction.

Bergen, D., & Coscia, J. (2001). *Brain research and childhood education: Implications for educators.* Olney, MD: Association for Childhood Education International.

Brody, C., Fuller, K., Gosetti, P. P., Moscato, S. R., Nagel, N. C., Pace, G., et al. (2000). *Gender consciousness and privilege.* London: Falmer Press.

Bush, W., & Kincer, L. (1993). The teacher's influence on the classroom learning environment. In R. Jensen (Ed.), *Research ideas for the classroom: Early childhood mathematics.* (p. 311–328). Reston, VA: National Council of Teachers of Mathematics.

deSimone, D., & Durden-Smith, J. (1983). *Sex and the brain.* New York: Warner Books.

Dougherty, B. (1997). *Changing roles of men and women: Educating for equity in the workplace.* Madison, WI: Vocational Studies Center School of Education.

Frost, J., Wortham, S., & Reifel, S. (2005). *Play and child development.* Upper Saddle River, NJ: Pearson Education.

Goodlad, J., & Keating, P. (Eds.). (1990). *Access to knowledge: An agenda for our nation's schools.* New York: College Entrance Examination Board.

Grossman, H., & Grossman, S. H. (1994). *Gender issues in Education.* Boston: Allyn & Bacon.

Halpern, D. F. (2000). *Sex differences in cognitive abilities* (3rd ed.). Mahwah, NJ: Erlbaum.

Hoffman, C. (2001). *The war against boys: How misguided feminism is harming our young men.* New York: Simon & Schuster.

Independent Women's Forum, (2001, September). *The XY files: The truth is out there . . . about the differences between boys and girls.* Paper presented at the IWF Symposium, Washington, DC.

Kennedy, L., Tipps, S., & Johnson, A. (2004). *Guiding children's learning of mathematics,* (10th ed.). Belmont, CA: Wadsworth/Thomas Learning.

Koch, J., & Irby, B. (2002). *Defining and redefining gender equity in education.* Greenwich, CT: Information Age.

Mallory, B., & New, R. (1994). Social constructivist theory and principles of inclusions: Challenges for early childhood special education. *Journal of Special Education 28*(3), 332–337.

McNees, P. (Jan 6, 2004). Why Janie can't engineer: Raising girls to succeed. *Washington Post,* p. C9.

Micklus, C. S. (1978). Odyssey of the mind. Gloucester City, NJ: Creative Competitions. Retrieved February 12, 2005, from http://www.odysseyofthemind.org/

Morrison, G. (2004). *Early childhood education today* (9th ed.). Englewood Cliffs, NJ: Prentice Hall.

National Association for the Education of Young Children. (2003). *Executive summary of early childhood mathematics: Promoting good beginnings.* Retrieved October 20, 2004, from http://www.naeyc.org/about/positions/pdf/Mathematics_Exec .pdf on October 20, 2004.

National Council of Teachers of Mathematics. (2002). *Principles and standards for school mathematics, E-Standards.* Reston, VA: Author.

Noble, C., & Bradford, W. (2000). *Getting it right for boys...and girls.* New York: Routledge.

Patton, M. M., & Mercer, J. (1996). Hey! Where's the toys?: Play and literacy in 1st grade. *Childhood Education, 73*(1), 10. Retrieved February 23, 2005, from http://www.questia.com

Polnick, B. (2002, Fall). Crossing the great divide: Changing the culture of women through gender equity in mathematics teaching and learning. *Advancing Women in Leadership Online Journal* [Special Issue].

Puckett, M., & Black, J. (2005). The young child: Development from pre-birth through age eight (4th ed.). Columbus, OH: Pearson-Merrill Prentice Hall.

Sadker, M., & Sadker, D. (1994). *Failing at fairness: How our schools cheat girls.* New York: Simon & Schuster.

Sanders, J., Koch, J., & Urso, J. (1997). *Gender equity right from the start.* New York: Erlbaum.

Sanders, J., & Rocco, S. (1994). *Bibliography on gender equity in mathematics, science and technology: Resources for classroom teachers.* New York: Center for Advanced Study in Education, CUNY Graduate Center.

Viereck, G. (1929, October 26). What life means to Einstein: an interview. *Saturday Evening Post.* Retrieved from www.some-guy.com/quotes/einstein.html

Vigotsky, L. S. (1978). *Mind in society: The development of higher psychological processes.* Cambridge, MA: Harvard University Press.

Walker, C., & Foote, M. (2001, March). *Equity in excellence for all learners: An unobtrusive look at racism, classism, and the differently abled in residence's for portfolio growth summaries.* Paper presented at the 53rd annual meeting of the American Association of Colleges for Teacher Education, Dallas, TX.

Wiesen, J., Siegel, A., & Wilfong, H. (1979). Armed Services vocational aptitude battery (ASVAB). Washington, DC: U.S. Department of Defense.

CHAPTER 7

SCIENCE EDUCATION AND GENDER

The Early Years

Linda Plevyak

SCIENCE IN AN ELEMENTARY CLASSROOM

Joseph, Brandon, Megan, and Sarah, second graders at Howard Elementary School, are talking about their plant experiment and trying to pick which question they want to answer from the list they had generated with their teacher. Some of the questions include:

- Do plants need light to grow?
- Will plants grow in different materials such as soil, sand, water, rocks, or clay?
- Will plants grow if wetted by something other than water such as soda, vegetable oil, or coffee?

Their conversation went on:

> Joseph: "I think we should plant our seeds in all the different stuff, it will be fun to mess around with the sand and clay!"

Gender and Schooling in the Early Years, pages 113–125
Copyright © 2005 by Information Age Publishing
All rights of reproduction in any form reserved.

> Megan: "Let's do the light thing, I think we could put seeds in different places where there is little light."
> Brandon: "Aw, man, I like Joseph's idea, it will be cool to fool around with all that junk!
> Joseph: "Yeah!" "Hey, Mrs. Adams, we want to plant our seeds in all of the different stuff!"

Mrs. Adams comes over to the group and asks if everyone is in agreement with the decision. Sarah says nothing and Megan, under her breath, mumbles she would rather not, but Mrs. Adams doesn't notice.

> Mrs. Adams: "All right, gather the materials you need and plant your seeds in the five different pots." Joseph and Brandon rush off to get the materials, and Megan and Sarah quietly talk about the light experiment and wonder what would have happened if they had put seeds in the closet to grow.

Positive aspects of the above scenario include:

1. Students are in a cooperative-learning group that is divided equally by gender. With less-assertive girls, however, where increasing self-confidence and promoting positive attitudes toward science are major goals, single-gender groups may work better.
2. Mrs. Adams is using the inquiry approach that allows for independent problem solving and development of process skills such as communicating, hypothesizing, and experimenting.
3. Students were given the opportunity to select a question to study.
4. The content being studied—plants and how they grow—can be emphasized in relation to the students' lives such as the foods they eat, how food is grown, and plants in the natural world.

Negative aspects of the above scenario include:

1. No clear rules of conduct were emphasized when the students were interacting. Mrs. Adams exacerbated the problem when communicating only with Joseph. Having an assertive boy in the group will generally silence the girls if there isn't an assertive girl present. Allowing everyone an equal voice and having a specific plan for disagreements will help girls who often prefer discussion and exploration.
2. Mrs. Adams responded to Joseph's outburst that relates to boys' tendencies to demand teacher attention by using body language and being verbally loud. Having a specific protocol for responding to students would help Mrs. Adams identify students' needs and concerns.

OVERVIEW OF SCIENCE IN THE EARLY GRADES

It is clear from the research on science and gender that there are numerous variables affecting who succeeds and who becomes discouraged in pursuing scientific understandings as a lifelong endeavor. Parental attitudes, media, stereotyping, textbooks, clothing, peers, toys, teacher bias, societal influences, discrimination, curriculum, and classroom dynamics are some of the variables that influence attitudes toward science. In the last decade there have been many reports and studies published on the gap between male and female students' performance in science (American Association of University Women Educational Foundation, 1998; Kahle & Meece, 1994; National Science Foundation, 1990). The influences on both boys and girls' knowledge, behavior, and attitudes toward science are so enormous that it is easy for teachers and researchers to become overwhelmed. However, there are many educators around the country who are actively working on solutions to solving the problem of inequitable representation of students pursuing science.

Researchers are experimenting with different types of science programs, including some that focus on gaining active participation of parents and highlighting role models in science (Hammerich, Richardson, & Livingston, 2000). Teachers are receiving in-service training to reevaluate how they relate to both boys and girls when teaching science. Teachers are beginning to hold high expectations for all students, restructure groups so that girls can play active roles, and showcase women who have chosen careers in science. Unfortunately, the quality programs and teacher training efforts reach only a small audience and are needed on a larger scale than what is currently being produced. Teacher training in creating gender-equitable classrooms also needs to begin with preservice teachers before their teaching behaviors become ingrained (Levine & Orenstein, 1994).

Not only are teacher training and quality programs required in science education, but focusing on the knowledge, behavior, and attitude levels of both genders between preschool and third grade is crucial because intervention is more difficult after third grade (Entwisle, Alexander, Cadigan, & Pallas, 1986). More importance has to be placed on the specific variables that influence both genders early in their lives in how they relate to and understand science. The socialization that occurs in the early grades from topics studied and types of pedagogy remains with students over time and influences subsequent behavior. This means that as early as kindergarten, gender differences in course-taking patterns, which will become apparant in later years, are starting to develop (Baker, 1990).

Another variable that impacts students' relationship to science is the portrayal of science as a masculine activity (Harding, 1986). The major reasons that science is viewed as masculine are that more men are actual scientists; science curriculum and materials are packaged to portray a masculine image; and the way in which science is taught (student–student and teacher–student interactions) focuses on more masculine traits (Kelly, 1985). Thus, girls are socialized early on to believe that science is not a subject area for them; they begin to focus on other topics. This socialization can be reinforced at home as parents tend to arrange boys' and girls' social and physical environments differently. Boys are typically bought toys by their parents that emphasize gross motor skills such as building towers or moving cars, and girls are bought toys that emphasize playing house with dolls. Parents also engage in more science with boys such as buying them a science kit or taking them on science field trips.

Finally, this chapter places emphasis on the practice of science in schools. Teachers may be aware that equity is required when focusing on science, but that awareness has not changed their behavior (Levine & Orenstein, 1994). The "hidden curriculum," which includes the daily routine and procedures of the classroom and the interactions between teacher and students, greatly impacts the achievement and attitudes of both boys and girls (Marshall & Reinhartz, 1997). Teachers have to consider how they relate to boys and girls during the science lesson. For example, some teachers call on boys more, engage boys in more problem-solving activities, give boys more feedback, praise boys more often than girls, or ask girls to perform inferior or subordinate tasks while boys set up equipment, problem solve, or define how the group will work together.

Grouping of students also impacts achievement levels since typically girls succeed in more cooperative, noncompetitive activities and high-achieving boys tend to do well in whole-group activities (Tobin & Garnett, 1987). How teachers relate to students while teaching science, especially in early childhood education (ECE), is an important consideration for which students can understand, appreciate, and actively pursue science beyond third grade. This chapter focuses on the variables that impact gender equity and how teachers and students can succeed in science within ECE.

TEACHERS AND TEACHING

Currently, over 90% of preschool through third-grade teachers are women (Gurian & Ballew, 2003). Since research shows that men and women teach differently, the teaching and learning in the early grades will be impacted by having women as the majority of ECE teachers (Grossman & Grossman, 1994). Women tend to be more student-centered, interact with students more often, and create a climate for discussion and indirect teaching. Men tend to be more direct and controlling of instruction, with an emphasis on subject teaching. Women tend to give less feedback on student responses while men give more explanation and direction when students are incorrect. Women also teach in a way that relates better to how girls learn, while men's teaching style emphasizes how boys learn. Even though students tend to do better when their learning style matches the teaching style, research has not shown that girls have the advantage in ECE classrooms (Grossman & Grossman, 1994).

So what is considered the most effective way to teach science in the early grades? Regardless of the gender of the teacher, the most effective science instructors care deeply and build a rapport and trust with their students (Van Sickle & Spector, 1996). Having all students learn how to operate computers, use equipment, discuss ideas, and be leaders supports the idea that science is for everyone. As girls tend to give up fairly easily when trying a difficult task, it is up to the teacher to create an atmosphere where risks are supported. This environment might promote student–student interactions that emphasize peer help. Support dialogue and make multiple attempts until students find success.

The following vignette relates to what might happen in this type of setting:

In a first-grade classroom Mrs. Jacobs had recently introduced primary colors to the class. The students were working in pairs and given eyedroppers; individual cups with the primary colors: red, yellow, and blue; and a large plastic tray with small holes. The students were only told that they had to use their colors to try and make new colors; no directions were given on how to create the new colors. Tracy and Elizabeth were having a hard time figuring out how much of each color was needed to create a new color. They were randomly mixing the colors and not considering the amount of each color that was being used. They also wanted to make orange, purple, and green and were having a hard time creating the exact colors they wanted. Ready to give up in frustration, the girls asked Mrs. Jacobs for help.

Mrs. Jacobs: "Why are you upset?"

Tracy: "We don't understand what to do! We mix the colors but the purple is too dark and the orange is too red."

Elizabeth: "I don't want to work on this anymore, it's stupid."

Mrs. Jacobs: "I understand your frustration, but I know you both can be successful! Let's see what you have so far. How much red and yellow are you using to make your orange?"

Elizabeth: "Well, we hadn't really thought about the amount of each color. We didn't know that really mattered."

Mrs. Jacobs: "Based on what you have, how do you think you can mix red and yellow to get the orange you want?"

Tracy: "Maybe we could start by putting in a couple of drops of each color and adding a drop or two until we like the orange color." Tracy used the dropper to put in two drops of red and two drops of yellow. She tried several combinations of the colors while counting out the drops. "This last one looks really orange!"

Elizabeth: "Let's try that idea to make a good purple!"

Tracy: "Yeah! Let's see how many cool colors we can make by counting out the drops!"

In the above scenario the girls were close to failure and having insecurities about completing the task. Mrs. Jacobs was able to get them back on track with a supportive comment and a few questions. The girls may need further guidance in trying to mix the colors, but they are able to move on with renewed self-confidence. Talking about the students' feelings, giving encouragement, providing a slightly different way of looking at the exercise, and asking questions that leads the students to think of their own solutions are effective teaching strategies, especially with girls.

Girls tend to require "sideline" encouragement and support, whereas a boy might be able to focus his energies on solving the problem no matter what. Familiarity with the subject and the context in which the problems are set, both social and cultural factors, are the major reasons for these gender differences. Encouragement from peers can go a long way in helping a girl complete a task instead of abandoning it. Risk taking is not a strength for girls so they need to be supported more when trying something new. Teachers can model taking risks and have students practice doing unfamiliar tasks. They can help students practice peer tutoring in order to support each other, making student–student interactions commonplace and of higher quality.

SOCIALIZATION AND PORTRAYAL
OF SCIENCE AS MASCULINE

Prior to beginning formal schooling, boys and girls have been socialized by parents, relatives, society, media, and religion to act and think in gender-specific ways. If teachers perpetuate the idea that girls should act one way and boys another, the students' views on gender will deepen and grow over time. As science has been promoted as a masculine subject that requires spatial, technical, mechanical, and mathematical skills and fosters behaviors such as objectivity and emotional reserve, many girls have avoided focusing on science as a topic of interest. If the "image" of science as masculine can be altered to include more accurate representations of scientists who are women then more people, including girls, will feel included in science. Those representations of scientists could include oceanographers and how they go about discovering a new type of fish in the ocean or archaeologists and how they decide where to dig to find fossils.

In ECE, teachers have the opportunity to begin a positive foundation for girls in science before the stereotypical view of science begins to develop by 6–7 years old (Jarvis, 1996). One of the first things that early childhood teachers must do is consider their own bias about gender and science. Videotaping and having colleagues observe science lessons and then analyzing them for gender inequities can help teachers to change their own behaviors. It is important for teachers to discuss their beliefs about learning, teaching, control, self, and constraints in relation to gender equity in science. Empowering students so that they feel open to discuss and monitor their own opportunities to learn science will also help in providing an atmosphere where all students can participate and learn.

GROUPING

Grouping has become most essential at the early childhood level, as cognitive and social development are intertwined when students are in primary grades (Gurian & Ballew, 2003). Group learning supports cognitive development by utilizing processing and reflection. Allowing the students to work in pairs or small groups emphasizes varied learning experiences that are important for both boys and girls.

Research has shown that working cooperatively in a group also promotes social skills, discussion, inference, and the ability to give knowledgeable conclusions (Dunne & Bennett, 1990). Collaborating with peers in a group setting on a shared task that involves communication and negotiation has also been shown to help students confront their misconceptions and make adjustments (Howe, 1990). Cooperative learning enables students to express their ideas about science experiences and broaden these ideas in conversations with their peers. It is a social experience from which girls and boys both benefit.

As essential as grouping is to students in the early grades, group dynamics has a powerful influence on attitudes of girls. Grouping of students can either diminish positive attitudes of girls toward science (as seen in the opening vignette) or reinforce girls' excitement and interest in science. To create an atmosphere of success, teachers should carefully consider how they group students in science. Specific roles should be assigned to each student so that more aggressive students do not dominate the group activity. Teachers can keep a record of these roles and rotate the students so they experience all positions. Students can be exposed to how these group positions (journal writer) relate to actual science jobs (science researcher).

Before beginning group work, students need to be taught how to conduct themselves while working with others. Students can practice giving feedback to each other, following rules, mediating disagreements, and so on. Keeping groups together for a few weeks while rotating jobs can help students form bonds with each other. Both mixed-gender and same-gender groups can be used successfully in primary grades as long as they are closely monitored. The focus should be on having students take responsibility for their own work while cooperating with others to complete an inquiry project.

SCIENCE IN PRESCHOOL/KINDERGARTEN

When children are between the ages of 3 and 5, the teacher greatly influences both boys' and girls' perceptions of what they can and cannot do in relation to play choices and whom they interact with on a daily basis (Gurian & Ballew, 2003). Students' confidence levels are also impacted by how the teacher interacts with children throughout the year. Since teachers play such an important role in the lives of preschoolers and kindergarteners, it is crucial that teachers consider how they will facilitate learning. As boys and girls will enter formal education with already established ideas about play, they will likely gravitate to separate parts of the classroom when choosing activities. It is important that two separate curriculums not develop, one for boys and one for girls, which results in different activities and materials being emphasized by each gender. Teachers should evaluate each center for gender bias. The dramatic play area should include props that would interest both genders such as different types of hats and kitchen, office, and gardening supplies. The block area can include stuffed toys, dolls, and signs for props.

Boys enjoy movement-based games such as manipulating or building towers that develop gross motor skills. Girls tend to enjoy playing with things that develop fine motor skills such as cutting, painting, or writing. As teachers want to make sure both genders receive development in both fine and gross motor skills, they can include a more personal aspect to science that focuses on stories or scenarios about people. For example, constructing a building out of large blocks and then using it as a grocery store where items are sold to classmates provides a context for the project. The development of the building requires movement, communication skills, and knowledge about weight, balance, and perception of the final product. It would also require working in a cooperative group that girls tend to enjoy. Fine motor skill development in boys can be promoted through problem-solving scenarios. For example, boys could use paints to see how many different colors they can make or create different types of game pieces by cutting construction paper.

It is important that teachers use the interests of both boys and girls when teaching about science. For instance, exploration of how insects eat might come from a student's question during a class outing. There might be a group of students who want to learn about butterflies so they find a few caterpillars, create an appropriate habitat, and watch them go through metamorphosis. The butterflies can then be released back into nature. The more control and self-direction that students have, the better the mind will develop, particularly in a supportive, well-directed environment (Gurian & Ballew, 2003).

Games can be successfully used with both boys and girls as boys like the spatial learning and competition, while girls enjoy the social interaction and will cooperate with others in open-ended or strategy-type games. In science, games can be created at the sand and water tables where students can employ "guessing" as a game when using a measuring cup to see how many scoops it takes to fill up a container. In the woodworking center the students can use a plastic hammer and investigate how long it takes to hit in nails of various sizes. Using the sense of smell, students can blindfold each other and see who can identify different smells such as peppermint, banana, or lemon.

Observation of how boys and girls interact during a game will help a teacher to see whether gender attributes hinder learning and the forward progress of the game. For example, if someone comes up with a rule change or a new rule, all participants should be allowed to decide if the rule is appropriate. Girls, who tend to be able to reason or explain their actions, can model for boys who can learn from this type of communication. It can help when students are learning through experience to have boys talk through what they are doing or draw conclusions from their activities. This will help them with vocabulary, verbalizing ideas, and communicating with others. Girls will likewise develop more spatial awareness when participating in active learning experiences, and they can still talk about the process.

SCIENCE IN PRIMARY GRADES

Just as with younger children, students in primary grades need to verbalize their ideas. Thinking out loud for both boys and girls helps them to consider the best solutions to a problem. Having students share their ideas by communicating with each other supports the research that suggests that using varied teaching strategies to encourage participation helps all students (American Association of University Women, 1999; Napper-Owen,

1994). For example, hands-on activities, emphasizing tasks that are mean-ingful and relate to the students' lives, collaborative learning, and group-work that have practical applications can draw on all students' strengths (Kahle & Damnjanovic, 1994).

Having an equitable curriculum means relating science to individual interests and abilities. Gardener (1999) identified eight different types of intelligences (linguistic, logical-mathematical, musical, spatial, bodily-kines-thetic, interpersonal, intrapersonal, and naturalistic) that students use to help themselves better understand content and skill development. The dif-ferent intelligences allow students to approach the same curriculum in diverse ways. For example, a primary class that is developing an outdoor gar-den could have a student who has a tendency toward spatial intelligence map or create a picture of the garden. A student with a propensity toward natural-istic intelligence could plant the bushes and flowers. This differentiated cur-riculum focuses on the strengths of individual students and allows them to be guided by their own ideas in relation to science.

As in the example of the outdoor garden, applying learning to the real world can foster success in science. Females are more apt to apply their sci-ence learning to practical, everyday situations and will feel success when what they are learning relates to their lives (Baker & Leary, 1995). Inquiry-oriented projects can be designed to integrate science skills into everyday experiences of both males and females. In the primary grades these projects could include why butterflies like some flowers but not others, why butter has to stay in the refrigerator, why we get goosebumps when we get out of a bath, and so on. The curiosity and wonder that is natural to all human beings can be extended and deepened when both boys and girls see the relevance to their own lives.

So what role does a primary teacher play in not only enabling students to have freedom to investigate the world but make sure they are construct-ing appropriate understandings in science while eliminating misconcep-tions? Primary teachers have to be part researcher, facilitator, investigator, as well as partners in learning (Landry & Forman, 1999). A teacher must learn what a student is thinking and what brought about this understand-ing. A teacher can then help the student reduce/replace misconceptions by introducing alternative ideas that are credible and support the student with reevaluating his or her theories (Driver, 1995). It is also crucial that a teacher be skilled in asking questions and dialoguing with students so that both teacher and student can engage in productive analysis of what is being learned (Chinn & Schaveren, 1996).

In relation to gender equity in this student-centered science classroom, the more the teacher relates science to social, emotional, and cultural experiences, the more students, especially girls, will be able to connect with the content (Shapiro, 1994). Including organized cooperative learning where discussions are monitored and students have been taught to work together will also facilitate achievement by girls. When holding whole-group discussions, using long pauses (wait-time) after questions are asked and having a system that requires all students to reply (checklist with student names) will increase the likelihood that all students will develop some type of response. Scantlebury and Kahle (1993) found that the above strategies not only work in providing success for girls, but promote achievement for boys as well.

CONCLUSIONS

The desire for many science researchers is to have a gender-inclusive curriculum where being equitable often requires differential treatment yielding equality of outcomes and positive attitudes toward science are nurtured and developed. The hope is that all students will see science as a rich part of their lives. From the research and readings in science education, it is clear that teachers, parents, and the science curriculum are the main factors in determining whether children will view science positively during their formal education years and beyond. This chapter attempted to share the important variables that affect students and their attitudes toward science and how teachers might positively impact both boys and girls in relation to science education.

As both educators and researchers we need to view equity in science from the perspective of the student. What do students see as important in their lives? An issues-driven curriculum that starts with students' questions and builds on their previous knowledge and experience requires a major shift from the way science is currently taught. Even though this type of teaching has been discussed for a couple of decades, it has not reached the majority of teachers and students. School administrators and school boards often determine curriculum and unconsciously may be gender biased in how they structure what the teachers can and cannot do in the classroom.

A grassroots initiative for equity in the science classroom that comes from the students and teachers may be one of the ways to achieve more freedom. Equity education will remain political until schools are restructured to support an inclusive curriculum. Teacher educators have to encourage, model, discuss, and involve their preK–12 preservice teachers in inclusive science education as well.

The question is ultimately, how will we know when we have achieved success in making science learning equitable for both genders? Maybe success relates to equal representation of females in all science professions or having both males and females view science as always being a part of their lives. Or maybe we will know success when we aren't focused on gender equity at all, when we are looking beyond the gender issue to the freedom of science and where it will take us next.

REFERENCES

American Association of University Women Educational Foundation. (1998). *Gender gaps executive summary*. Washington, DC: Author

American Association of University Women Educational Foundation. (1999). *Gender gaps: Where schools still fail our children*. New York: Marlowe & Company.

Baker, D. (1990). *Gender differences in science: Where they start and where they go*. Paper presented at the meeting of the National Association for Research in Science Teaching, Atlanta, GA.

Baker, D., & Leary, R. (1995). Letting girls speak out about science. *Journal of Research in Science Teaching, 32*(1), 3–27.

Chinn, C. A., & Schaveren, L. (1996). Children's conversations and learning science and technology. *International Journal of Science Education, 18*(1), 105–116.

Driver, R. (1995). Constructivist approaches to science teaching. In L. P. Steffe & J. Gale (Eds.), *Constructivism in education* (pp. 234–286). Hillsdale, NJ: Erlbaum.

Dunne, E., & Bennett, N. (1990). *Talking and learning in groups*. London: Macmillan.

Entwisle, D. R., Alexander, K. L., Cadigan, D., & Pallas, A. (1986). The schooling process in first grade: Two samples a decade apart. *American Educational Research Journal, 23*(4), 587–613.

Gardener, H. (1999). *Intelligence reframed: Multiple intelligences for the 21st century*. New York: Basic Books.

Grossman, H., & Grossman, S. H. (1994). *Gender issues in education*. Boston: Allyn & Bacon.

Gurian, M., & Ballew, A. (2003). *The boys and girls learn differently: Action guide for teachers*. San Francisco: Jossey-Bass.

Hammerich, P., Richardson, G., & Livingston, B. (2000). *Sisters in science confronting equity in science and mathematics education*. Paper presented at the annual American Educational Research Association Conference, Seattle, WA.

Harding, J. (1986). *Perspectives on gender and science*. Philadelphia: Falmer.

Howe, C. (1990). Grouping children for effective learning in science. *Primary Science Review, 13*, 26–27.

Jarvis, T. (1996). Examining and extending young children's views of science and scientists. In L. H. Parker, L. J. Rennie, & B. J. Fraser (Eds.), *Gender, science and mathematics* (pp. 29–40). Norwell, MA: Kluwer Academic.

Kahle, J. B., & Damnjanovic, A. (1994). The effect of inquiry activities on elementary students' enjoyment, ease, and confidence in doing science: an analysis by sex and race. *Journal of Women and Minorities in Science and Engineering, 1*, 17–28.

Kahle, J. B., & Meece, J. (1994). Research on gender issues in the classroom. In D. Gabel (Ed.), *Handbook of research on science teaching and learning* (pp. 542–557). New York: Macmillan.

Kelly, A. (1985). The construction of masculine science. *British Journal of Sociology of Education, 6*(2), 133–153.

Landry, C. E., & Forman, G. E. (1999). Research on early science education. In C. Seefeldt (Ed.), *The early childhood curriculum: Current findings in theory and practice* (pp. 133–158). New York: Teachers College Press.

Levine, E. Z., & Orenstein, F. M. (1994). *Sugar and spice and puppy dog tails: Gender equity among middle school children* (Report No. PS023836). (ERIC Document Reproduction Service No. ED389457)

Marshall, C. S., & Reinhartz, J. (1997). Gender issues in the classroom. *The Clearinghouse 70*(6), 333–337.

Napper-Owen, G. E. (1994). And justice for all: Equity in the elementary classroom. *Strategies 8*(3), 23–26.

National Science Foundation. (1990). Women and minorities in science and engineering. Washington, DC: Author.

Scantlebury, K., & Kahle, J. (1993). The implementation of equitable teaching strategies by highschool biology teachers. *Journal of Research in Science Teaching, 30,* 537–545.

Shapiro, B. L. (1994). *What children bring to light: A constructivist perspective on children's learning in science.* New York: Teachers College Press.

Tobin, K., & Garnett, P. (1987). Gender related differences in science activities. *Science Education, 71,* 91–103.

Van Sickle, M., & Spector, B. (1996). Caring relationships in science classrooms: A symbolic interaction study. *Journal of Research in Science Teaching, 33*(4), 433–454.

CHAPTER 8

THE ROLE OF EDUCATORS IN COMMUNICATING GENDER EQUITY TO PARENTS

Laverne Warner
John Barerra

Parents play the largest and most important role in shaping their children's sense of themselves and supporting them through the barrage of cultural and peer pressures that do so much to distract them from what is truly important: the kinds of people they are and the contributions they can make to family, friends and the world. (Brody, 1997, p. 7)

Nationwide, educators are attempting to achieve a consistent bond of cooperation between home and school. The primary focus of any kind of parent involvement program is on children and their well-being. Educators learn information through everyday classroom occurrences that will influence parent involvement and promote an understanding of gender equity during a very important stage in students' development. Clearly, the challenges of education are ones neither schools nor families can meet alone; educators and families must support one another. Parent involvement can be addressed through many lenses, but gender equity is vital.

In 1994, the U.S. Congress added parental involvement to the National Educational Goals. Goal 8 stated that by the year 2000, every school would

Gender and Schooling in the Early Years, pages 127–148
Copyright © 2005 by Information Age Publishing
All rights of reproduction in any form reserved.

develop partnerships that will increase parental involvement and participation in promoting a better understanding of how parents are impacted by gender equity. The factors that impact gender equity could come from many sources, including cultural emphasis or regional differences. Though this deadline is long past, some students, teachers, and staff have not had any diversity, multicultural, gender, or equity training.

Recognizing that parents are a child's first teacher, numerous education laws require meaningful parent involvement, including Title 1 of the Elementary and Secondary Education Act of 1965 (ESEA), Title IX, the National Education Goals, Head Start, the Americans with Disabilities Act, and the Individuals with Disabilities Education Act (IDEA). Along with the historical factors of the role of parent involvements, educators must also understand the crucial elements of gender equity, as gender equity begins with a multifaceted classroom where there are no gender barriers. Children in today's schools can provide communication to parents by saying: "Mom, my teacher said that I can be anything I want."

Prior to the 1990s, educators dealt with Title IX, landmark legislation prohibiting exclusion from educational programs on the basis of sex. Title IX, part of the Educational Amendments of 1972, eliminated federal funding in three areas if local school districts fail to provide athletic financial assistance, accommodation of athletic interests and abilities, and other program components. In 1997, statistical figures showing advancement for women as a result of Title IX were positive:

- 41% of medical degrees awarded (as compared with 9% in 1977);
- 44% of law degrees awarded (as compared with 7% in 1972);
- 41% of doctoral degrees to U.S. citizens (as compared with 25% in 1977).(www.now.org/issues/title_ix)

For parents to understand gender equity in a meaningful way, educators must illuminate ideas and foster strong beliefs in children's dreams about their futures. The role of educators is to create a comfortable setting for children to create career avenues without violating any gender equity issue. As an example, parents may not have any idea that they could run a restaurant until they try it or are taught by someone how to do it, and this attitude, without intervention by schools, would be passed on to their children. Teachers without gender equity training and sensitivity to gender equity issues are often at fault in continuing gender inequities without even knowing that they are doing an injustice to the students.

Gender equity should, in fact, be equitable to all, causing concern that male students in the United States face problems that females and others around the world do not face.

Patten (2000) reported the following facts about boys growing up in America:

- 90% of violent acts committed in America are perpetrated by males;
- the majority of children who are murdered, neglected, homeless, in foster care, and otherwise institutionalized are male;
- 90% of the children who are prescribed Ritalin are boys;
- 90% of incarcerated citizens are male;
- boys and young men comprise the majority of child-abuse victims and are less likely to tell authorities that they need help. (http://npin.org/pnews/2000/pnew300/int300a.html)

Robertson (1996) summarized a study completed by the American Association of University Women (AAUW) on gender bias in schools. AAUW's report suggested that education for both boys and girls needs to be improved. Proposed remedies included teacher professional development on gender sensitivity, more personal attention for children from teachers and school staff, and giving students confrontational mediation skills, as well as encouragement to participate in student government and other school activities. Both genders require leadership skills, and parents and professionals must work together to understand children's issues and provide children with the knowledge and experience to acquire and hone those necessary skills.

Fostering young students' aspirations can begin with a simple "Look What I Can Do" thematic unit (or it could be written into a classroom mission statement or common language the district adopts). Later, the title may change to "Look What I Will Do," signifying progress. Collaboration with a university professor can be another avenue in addressing gender equity issues. This can occur when she sends her students to observe in and participate in classroom experiences. Children come to schools with ideas about gender roles because of their cultural traits. To instill gender equity does not mean saying that only Suzie can make dresses. The instillation of gender equity can be accomplished when tteachers say, "Whoever wants to make dresses for their dolls can work in the Art Center."

EFFECTS OF UNDERSTANDING GENDER EQUITY ON PARENT INVOLVEMENT

Parents must be able to support their children's aspirations, and understanding gender equity can assist parents in supporting their children's dreams. Baiamonte (1995) noted that by giving teachers and administrators an opportunity to listen to what their students have to say, they can promote better school-to-home, home-to-school communications as well as to foster parental involvement. Children come to our classrooms with notions given to them by their environments. Consequently, having a simple recipe that can address all gender issues is impossible. What gender equity implies is that all children wear on their personalities elements of *who* and *where* they came from, and these thoughts need to be confronted, affirmed, and/or changed.

An administrator's understanding of current issues with gender equity will pave a road to the recognition of certain needs in children. Sensitivity to cultural characteristics is an important characteristic for administrators because of the diverse feelings of various cultures toward gender roles. Laosa (1982) defined population sensitivity as "an orientation that seeks to make services, institutions, or policies harmonious with the basic values, needs, and characteristics of diverse populations" (p. 34). Loasa also believed that the family environment has a significant effect on the child's educational development. In order to reduce differences in achievement, programs must address not only the child's inherent abilities but also her or his family environment.

Comer (1984) discussed the emotional support that children need in order to learn, indicating that such an environment of support is optimally created when families and school personnel cooperate. Bennett (1986) cited the benefits to parents themselves as they gain greater confidence and expertise in helping their children succeed academically. Parent involvement with gender equity can be woven together with support for parents and children in the following ways:

1. Include examples of male and female accomplishments throughout teachers' lesson plans and explain to parents why they are included (explanations can be done by having a gender equity museum at the school or even in the classroom).

2. Model acceptance of gender equity by administrators and teachers (accomplish this strategy by having simple daily announcements about famous people who stepped out of their gender to achieve; e.g., "Did you know that Amelia Earhart was the first woman to fly around the world?").

3. Plan training sessions to help parents understand elements of gender equity (sessions must give opportunities for parents to discuss their perspectives before any training takes place—hearing their peers is a powerful strategy).

4. Involve both male and female parents in discussing sensitive issues through focus groups and seminars and including gender equity issues in teacher/staff development sessions (gender equity observations will come from teachers, and they must have time to share their story treasures).

Nationwide, the U.S. is beginning to witness a variety of promising changes and current trends in the attitudes and the perceptions of school personnel and culturally and linguistically diverse parents toward one another. Basterra (1998) presented a list of recommended policies and practices to support parent/school relationships:

1. States need to develop policies that encourage and enable school districts and schools to promote successful school–home partnerships that are responsive to the diverse populations they serve;

2. Train teachers at the undergraduate and graduate levels to recognize the importance of gender equity and to gain cross-cultural skills needed to make this partnership work;

3. Provide training to parents on how to best use their talents to help their children succeed in school; and

4. Focus on establishing true partnerships in which both school personnel and parents learn from each other and find ways in which they can mutually support efforts in educating children. (p. 1)

The four elements described above can initiate a common language or foundation in understanding gender equity. Levine and Lezotte (1995) reported that high levels of parental involvement are characteristic of effective schools and "...that effectiveness is positively associated with involvement" (p. 530). Comer and Haynes (1991) emphasized that parent involvement with a child's education is an essential component to have effective school programs. Within a multicultural perspective, Hidalgo, Siu, Gight, Swap, and Epstein (1995) noted that parental support and encouragement of educational efforts result in children's increased academic achievement. Hidalgo and colleagues indicated that when educators encourage minority parents to become partners in their child's education, parents develop a sense of efficacy that influences the child and results in positive academic outcomes. Involving parents supports the school community, although it is usually just "mom" providing time for academic challenges. Encouraging fathers to participate is vital, as both parents create an atmosphere that is sensitive and well equipped for gender challenges.

Both parents may not be present, but a child needs to know they care and be recognized by having his or her parents come to the school. Some conflicts may not be solved and changing cultural characteristics may be more difficult. For example, what strategies would a school community utilize to support a girl who wants to play football when the parents totally oppose her involvement? This is an important question to be considered because a school community does not want to be remembered by parents saying, "Look at the ideas the school put in my child's head!" However, with positive communication, there can be a stronger understanding between parents, students, and the school community.

A contemporary school initiative would lack substance if it did not include a parent-involvement component. The main purpose of parent-involvement programs is to have parents actively engaged in the education of their children. Studies have shown a positive relationship between parental involvement and increased student achievement (Clark, 1983; Comer, 1980; Dornbusch, 1986).

Parents have a strong desire to improve their schools and to help their children receive a better education than they did. Parent involvement should be a special focus of any successful school. National education goals have stressed the importance of parents and families in children's learning. The following statistics were disseminated by the United States Department of Education in 1994:

1. Forty percent of parents across the country believe that they are not devoting enough time to their children (Finney, 1993),
2. Teachers ranked the parents' role in their children's learning as the issue that should receive the highest priority in public policy over the next few years (Louis Harris & Associates, 1991),
3. Among students ages 10 to 13, 72% said they would like to talk to their parents more about schoolwork and 48% of older adolescents agreed (National Commission on Children, 1991).

When federal initiatives required parent involvement as an integral part of new grant applications, schools placed a renewed emphasis on parental involvement (Sosa, 1997).

Ascher (1987) defined parental involvement as a range of activities from promoting the value of education in the home to the actual role of team decision-maker in policy, curriculum, and instruction issues. Parents can participate at various levels, including taking advocacy roles, sitting on councils and committees, and participating in the decision making and operation of schools. Parents can serve as classroom aides and accompany a class on a field trip or assist teachers in a variety of other ways.

More recently, Sosa (1997) stated that parent involvement includes the initiation of learning activities at home to improve their children's performance in school (e.g., reading to them, helping them with homework, playing educational games, or discussing current events). Clearly, parent involvement is now seen as a greater aspect of student achievement than having parents just participate in a "bake sale" (Sosa, 1997). The role of the parent is a complex one because so many different types of households exist in today's society.

Attempting to impart the ideology of gender equity is a delicate task for the teacher. To understand gender equity in every child's household would be a monumental task. Each household encompasses different cultural aspects that may address gender equity in different ways, a circumstance that clearly defines the role of the teacher.

In some cases, parent–teacher organizations meet during working hours and material sent home is English, only causing conflicts for many parents. In 1994, United States Secretary of Education Richard Riley stated, "Teachers must also learn new ways to involve parents in the learning process. Thirty years of research tells us that the starting point of putting children on the road to excellence is parental involvement in their children's education" (Shartrand, Weiss, Kreider, & Lopez, 1997). The partnership that addresses gender equity builds a bridge with the parents to showcase accomplishments and should attempt to include everyone.

CO-PRODUCTION OF CHILDREN'S EDUCATION

A number of parent involvement program models are built on the idea that the education of children should be viewed as a partnership between the school and the home; that students and parents are co-producers of education, not simply passive recipients of educational services. Co-production refers to those activities, individual and collective, in the school or at home, that contribute to school efforts to instruct pupils more effectively and raise pupil achievement. Efforts to ensure gender equity need to occur co-productively as well. Such efforts include:

1. Extracurricular activities designed for children with special interests and talents (such as music, sports, clubs, or citizenship experiences).
2. Frequent and specific reporting of children's strengths and skills by the teacher to families with suggestions as to how classroom efforts can be reinforced at home.
3. Parent education programs designed to make parents more knowledgeable about what schools are trying to do and how specific school endeavors are able to broaden children's opportunities.
4. Home visitor programs to provide special help and advisement to low-income and immigrant families.
5. Parent volunteers assisting teachers in the classroom by preparing instructional materials and observing teachers encouraging children to maximize their potential.

Most of these activities involve initiative by teachers and principals and coordination by the school (Davies, 1987). Advocates have viewed co-production or partnerships as a way to organize resources both inside and outside public school systems to achieve higher levels of learning and accomplish gender equity in the process. The co-production concept places responsibility for learning on students, parents, and the broader community, allowing schools to become the agent of change.

SCHOOLS THAT PROMOTE CHANGE

Research has conclusively shown that parent involvement in education benefits students, parents, teachers, and schools. This collaboration creates the bridge between home and school. Whether the program is at the preschool, elementary, or high school level, the most basic statement that can be made about parent and family involvement in education is that when it happens, everyone benefits (Epstein, 1987).

For parents to benefit, the collaboration must be, without a doubt, in a comfortable setting. A discussion of gender equity strategies should be conducted to emphasize children's differences. Hosting a family town hall meeting with a presentation would be a possibility to initiate the discussion. A gender equity co-production should be centered on current accomplishments in school settings, and all district officials can be on the invitation list.

Proactive parent involvement policies and practices at the district, state, and national levels are prerequisite. From school boards and district offices to state and national departments of education and national professional associations, principals and educators need to know their leaders are willing to support and encourage them as they seek to implement change. Although a few studies have addressed what kind of educational support parents provide for their children, additional research is needed to identify efficient supportive parental behaviors (Ebener, 1995).

Several keys are available for a principal of a public program to successfully involve parents in education that address the gender-equitable school climate and communication:

1. Create a gender equity survey that children do together with parents.
2. Investigate to learn if there are communities/businesses with women leaders or managers.
3. Train a parent liaison about gender equity strategies.
4. Invite a local personality or public official to discuss personal challenges as a female role model.
5. Implement a cultural fair to showcase the roles of males and females in a country of origin.

6. Design a gender equity issues book (or newsletter) created by the students to share with the parents.

7. Exhibit a bulletin board where children can share their understanding of gender equity issues.

8. Highlight family members' accomplishments by having them share stories on their job.

9. Plan staff development with gender equity issues as a topic and use role play and discussion as techniques to enhance their awareness.

The principal is to measure the effectiveness of caring family involvement programs and activities on a regular basis in order to evaluate school climate and communication. Creating a mission for caring family involvement at any school level can do this. The mission of a parent involvement program is to provide resources to parents and schools to form partnerships that will help improve the involvement of families to increase student achievement. The administration must provide resources for gender equity to be included within those partnerships.

Gender equity can be included through the creation of a gender issue committee or a Shared Decision-Making Committee member can be in charge. Despite significant growth, increased ethnic diversity, escalating poverty, and pronounced learning differences that have impacted the state's standardized examinations, parents must become involved to increase overall student performance. The school can:

Empower parents. Parenting is a tough job, and parent education programs can provide much-needed support. Staff members should not assume that they are experts who know what's best for caring parents. Instead, they should work along with parents to help carry out goals and activities jointly determined by parents and staff.

There needs to be an interdependence for any gender equity issues to be discussed in order to show the difference between the ideas that men have for themselves and those they have for their mothers, wives, sisters, and daughters. A discussion where parents can share how they perceive they have been deprived of their rights in the school setting can be helpful.

Focus on the needs of both parents and child. Research confirms that parents who face dire problems of their own (e.g., unemployment, lack of housing, or lack of support from other adults) are not likely to be able to meet their children's needs. We must recognize that parents' needs may be so great that they overshadow any attention to children.

Adjust to the specific needs of parents in the program. There is no "one-size-fits-all" parent education program, and the principal must adjust to meet the needs of each parent. What works well in one school may not work in another. Effective parent programs respond to the cultural traits and values of ethnic populations, which, in turn, supports the literature of cultural sensitivity (Laosa, 1982). All staff members should be sensitive to the realities faced by low-income parents. As an example, low-income parents are unlikely to respond to a learning activity that begins, "As you are planning your summer vacation."

Allow plenty of time for parent discussion. The best parent education programs allow plenty of time for open-ended, parent-dominated discussions to foster positive school climate and communication. Administrators must solicit caring parents in their community about new ideas.

Many activities are available to parents that are interested in becoming involved with their children's education. All school districts value both the at-home contributions and those that take place at school and in the community. Reading to children at home and talking with them at a family meal are as important as volunteering at school and serving on advisory committees. Many types of parent involvement are needed in school/home and community partnerships that will help the principal of a public school to succeed.

School communities can establish such programs to encourage strong parental involvement through communication at a schoolwide level about gender equity. The following examples illustrate different types of parent activities and programs that promote strong communication about gender-related issues:

1. A school newsletter created by students, teachers, and parents.
2. School community projects with staff facilitating the endeavor.
3. Parent awareness workshops.
4. School policy decisions made with parents' input.
5. Resources for parents/volunteers to feel welcomed.
6. Adult basic education.
7. Technology training.

Effective parent involvement programs match the needs of school and community. Principals in programs should work to build comprehensive family communication about gender issues. The following are recommendations based on the high response means for the construct of communication for a school with a gender-equitable program.

Families and schools as communicators. Parents and schools should communicate with each other about school activities and programs, discipline codes, learning objectives, and children's state of knowledge. This sharing of information can be accomplished through newsletters, school handbooks, parent–teacher conferences, open houses, informal messages, and telephone calls. Schools can work through community-based organizations to develop relationships with caring parents from diverse backgrounds and others who previously have not been involved actively in school–parent activities.

Caring families and schools as supporters. Parents support schools and children's learning in many ways: as volunteer tutors; as field trip supervisors; as classroom assistants and curriculum resources; as lunchroom, health room, and administrative office assistants; as organizers of school events and assemblies; and by attending student performances, sports events, and other school-related activities. Schools have an opportunity to support caring students and their families by forming collaborative relationships with the assistance of public and private agencies that provide family support services.

These relationships may include partnerships with public health and human services agencies; local businesses; higher education systems; youth-serving organizations; and religious, civic, and other community-based organizations. When having a town meeting or PTO gathering, it is best to have both male and female speakers.

Caring parents and schools as learners. Parents can participate in programs to foster the development of their knowledge and skills. These learning activities may include literacy instruction, basic adult education, job training, continuing education, child development instruction, and parenting education. To support the findings for communication, schools can also offer the use of facilities and other resources. Schools can also encourage teachers and other personnel to learn about the cultural and community values and practices that are common to their students and their families.

Parents need to know that gender equity issues begin in the home. Mutual obligations of the sexes are critical in the organization and conduct of the home, as both genders need to be acknowledged. Have a "memorial" appealing to equal rights, not only on behalf of women, but men also.

Families and schools as teachers. Parents have the opportunity to model and support caring children's education through home-learning activities. This includes ensuring that children's health and environmental conditions are conducive to learning. Caring parents can supervise children's homework and model support for education through their own continuing education activities.

Educators can play an important role in teaching caring parents about the school's expectations for student learning, including curriculum options, graduation requirements, and the school and community-based services that support student growth and learning. We have to create an "ability to achieve" forum for gender equity issues to be removed.

Shared governance with caring parents. As members of advisory councils, PTAs, or other groups, parents can advocate for change, help develop school improvement plans, and participate in school governance. These groups can lead the community in assessing school needs and developing goals.

Caring families and schools in collaboration with community organizations. Schools can reach out to link caring families to needed services and community organizations, which in turn can strengthen home environments and increase student achievement. Communication between the school, businesses, cultural organizations, and community groups creates a shared responsibility for the well-being of children, families, and schools by all members of the community. Conduct role-playing scenarios of people being taken advantage of by men and women employees and/or have representatives from the EEOC office present to talk to parents.

The recommendations that would support school climate are school communication and parents as collaborators, problem solvers, advisors, and decision makers. Principals should always welcome parents. In order for parents to feel appreciated and welcomed, volunteer work must be meaningful and valuable to them and the school. Capitalizing on the expertise and skills of caring parents provides much-needed support to educators and administrators already taxed in their attempts to meet academic goals and student needs. Although there are many caring parents for whom volunteering during school hours is not possible, creative solutions like before- or after-school "drop-in" programs or "in-home" support activities provide opportunities for those parents to offer their assistance as well. See a recommended list of strategies that principals should consider for helping parents feel appreciated in Figure 8.1.

---

1. Ensure that office staff greetings, signage near the entrances, and any other interaction with parents create a climate in which parents feel valued and welcome.

2. Survey parents regarding their interests, talents, and availability, then coordinate the parent resources with those that exist within the school and among the faculty.

3. Ensure that parents who are unable to volunteer in the school building are given the options for helping in other ways (at home or at their place of employment).

4. Organize an easy, accessible program for utilizing parent volunteers, providing ample training on volunteer procedures and school protocol.

5. Develop a system for contacting all parents to assist as the year progresses.

6. Design opportunities for those with limited time and resources to participate by addressing child care, transportation, work schedule needs, and so forth.

7. Show appreciation for parents' participation and value their diverse contributions.

8. Educate and assist staff members in creating an inviting climate and effectively utilizing volunteer resources.

9. Ensure that volunteer activities are meaningful and built on volunteer interests and abilities.

Figure 8.1.   Strategies for helping parents feel appreciated.

With so many students, how can principals in schools build effective gender-related strategies with each of the parents? One teacher can set aside 10 minutes a day to telephone, e-mail, or send postcards to parents. Once a month the teacher can make at least two contacts with each family represented in the class. Most conversations should focus on student successes and upcoming activities for parents and families. Because of the consistent contact and accessibility, parents will be more eager to respond and support the student/class goals that are supportive to families they serve and efforts will be determined effective and worthwhile. Parent and family involvement related to gender equity is a wise investment for communities.

Communication between home and school is to be regular, two-way, and meaningful: Communication is the foundation of a solid partnership. When parents and principals communicate effectively, positive relationships develop, problems are more easily solved, and students make greater progress. Effective home–school communication is the two-way sharing of information vital to student success. Even potentially beneficial parent–teacher conferences can be one-way if the goal is merely to report student progress.

Partnering requires give-and-take conversation, goal setting for the future, and regular follow-up interactions. Communication in public schools should:

1. Use a variety of communication tools on a regular basis, seeking to facilitate two-way interaction through each type of medium.

2. Establish opportunities for parents and principals to share partnering information such as student strengths and learning preferences.

3. Provide clear information regarding course expectations and offerings, student placement, school activities, student services, and optional programs.

4. Disseminate information on school reforms, policies, discipline procedures, assessment tools, school goals, and include caring parents in any related decision-making process.

5. Conduct conferences with parents at least twice a year, with follow-up as needed.

6. Accommodate the varied schedules of parents, language barriers, and the need for child care when scheduling conferences.

7. Encourage immediate contact between caring parents and teachers when concerns arise.

8. Distribute student work for parental comment and review on a regular basis.

9. Translate communications to assist parents.

10. Communicate with parents regarding positive student behavior and achievement, not just regarding misbehavior or failure.

11. Provide opportunities for parents to communicate with principals and other administrative staff.

12. Promote informal activities at which parents, staff, and community members in the near community can interact.

13. Provide staff development regarding effective communication techniques and the importance of regular two-way communication between the school and parents.

At the beginning of the school or program year, the school should offer outreach sessions with a parent involvement coordinator that include the following: (a) course or program expectations and goals of a caring program; (b) information on how and/or when to contact program staff or administration in a school setting; (c) the process for handling program questions and/or concerns; (d) strategies to support learning at home; and (e) testing and assessment information and procedures for parents. Always include a time for questions and answers to address specific parent or family concerns. If possible, provide a video recording of the event to share with those unable to attend.

School outreach sessions can stimulate action in bridging efforts with community resources. Consider several of the following gender-specific recommendations:

1. Distribute information regarding cultural, recreational, academic, health, social, and other resources that serve parents within the community.

2. Develop partnerships with service groups and local businesses run by females and males to advance student learning and assist parents.

3. Encourage employers to adopt policies and practices that promote and support parent participation in children's education.

4. Foster caring student participation in community service by both females and males.

5. Involve community members in school volunteer programs.

6. Disseminate information to the school community, including those without school-age children, regarding caring school programs and performance.

7. Collaborate with community agencies to provide family support services and adult female and male learning opportunities, enabling parents to more fully participate in activities that support education.

8. Inform staff members of the resources available in the community and strategies for utilizing gender resources for parents.

As the momentum for ongoing, organized parent involvement at the school and district level increases, so does the demand for family involvement program information for parents. After a complete review of the demographic characteristics, the following recommendations, in question form, are supported by the findings for schools where gender equity is valued. See Figure 8.2 for questions assessing the degree of parental involvement in school programming.

To ensure ongoing effective parent participation in the decision-making process, principals of programs can work to create an environment where female and male parents can: (a) attend open meetings on school/program issues for the student; (b) receive clear program goals and objectives for caring programs; (c) have information available about the process for dealing with concerns; (d) have access to the steps to problem solving; and (e) feel that the principal is genuinely interested in responding to their concerns in a constructive and fair manner.

Effective parent involvement programs will be comprehensive and coordinated in a gender-specific nature. They will include, but not be limited to, the following components of successful, caring parent involvement programs:

1. Meaningful communication between home and school is regular and two-way.
2. Responsible parenting is promoted and supported.
3. Parents play an integral role in assisting student learning.
4. Parents are welcome in the school, and their support and assistance are sought.
5. Parents are full partners in the decisions that affect children and families.

---

1. To what extent do parents participate in parent–teacher conferences?
2. How are parents and the community assisted in understanding the parent involvement program?
3. What types of materials are made available to parents?
4. How is parent involvement evaluated on an annual basis?
5. How will the data be used in the implementation of the parental involvement program?
6. How are parents kept informed when their children are performing well (i.e., school rating)?
7. How are parents kept informed when their children are not performing well?

Figure 8.2.   Parental involvement assessment questions.

Principals want to establish partnerships with female and male parents and with the community. It is expected that parents be seen as valued partners in the educational process, serving as the child's teacher in the home. All school and district activities will give proper considerations to the involvement of parents. Everyone gains if school and home work together to promote high achievement by our children. Parents play an extremely important role as children's first teachers.

It can be useful to develop a survey to gather parent volunteer information including special skills or talents from both moms and dads. The program should provide opportunities for those who are able to volunteer during the day, those who are able to commit to regular service, and those who can participate occasionally at home or at work. The principal should follow up with volunteers on a timely basis and have female and male focus groups; provide a consistent place and process for parent volunteers to sign in and list the hours served; and invite parents to join their child for lunch whenever convenient, and, if possible, provide a free lunch during the year.

Volunteers should be trained regarding school or program protocols, routines and procedures, volunteer expectations, and equipment usage. In addition, provide a central location for volunteers to work with secure places for personal belongings. Give clear instructions for completing volunteer tasks as well as the appropriate staff or teacher contact name if more information is needed. The principal must look for creative ways to show appreciation for female and male volunteer support on an ongoing basis.

As part of the volunteer participation in public schools, procedures and resources containing the following will create a stronger gender-important climate:

1. School or program handbook for volunteers
2. Sign-in and out policies for all volunteers
3. Suggestion forms for parents
4. Volunteer welcome letter and list of benefits for parents
5. Volunteer work locations of parents

The principal of a public school, where gender issues are discussed, should provide:

1. Support for the efforts of parents, including training parents, to the maximum extent practicable, to work with their children in the home to attain the instructional objectives of the program and to understand the program requirements.
2. Training for parents, teachers, and administrators to build a partnership between home and school.

3. Training for teachers, principals, and other staff members involved in working effectively with parents of participating children.

4. Consultation with parents, on an ongoing basis, concerning the manner in which the school and parents can work together better to achieve the program's objectives.

5. A comprehensive range of opportunities for caring parents to become informed, in a timely way, about how the program will be designed, operated, and evaluated, allowing an opportunity for parental participation, so that parents and educators can work together to achieve the program's objectives.

The process of developing female and male parent policies should include community-based organizations, teachers, administrators, business, families, students, and other key stakeholders to have a successful outreach program.

1. Opportunities need to be available for all parents to become involved in decision making about how the family involvement programs will be designed, implemented, assessed, and strengthened.

2. Encouragement of participation of parents who might have low-level literacy skills and/or for whom English is not their primary language is vital.

3. Regular information for parents about the objectives of educational programs and regarding their child's participation and progress in those programs should be provided.

4. Professional development for teachers and staff should be required in order to enhance their effectiveness with parents.

Schools need to recognize the myriad diverse family structures, circumstances, and responsibilities, including differences that might impede parent participation. The person(s) responsible for a child may not be the child's biological parent(s), and policies and programs should include participation by all persons interested in the child's educational progress.

The principal of a public school should sponsor program or community events that allow educators and parents to interact on a social basis in addition to standard parent–teacher conferences or school/program meetings. The principal plays a pivotal role in making parent and family involvement a reality. Educators and other staff need to sense the level of priority administrators give to involving parents in their children's education. The climate in a school is created, to a large extent, by the tone set in the office of the principal. If principals collaborate with both female and male parents, educators will be more likely to follow suit. Sometimes there is a misperception that partnering with parents, particularly in the decision-making process, will diminish the principal's authority. Yet the top management models in America are open and collaborative, encouraging subordinates to share their concerns and engage managers and workers in cooperative problem solving, rather than making decisions through strict hierarchical systems. Such an approach need not diminish the manager's authority, but can lead to better decisions in businesses or in schools with female and male parents.

Without administrative leadership, long-term progress in parent–school partnerships is difficult to achieve since genuine change requires systemic solutions and coordinated efforts of consistent leadership support without gender bias. Working together to implement the program standards, principals and teachers can accomplish a great deal. When female and male parents become involved, they develop a mutual goal and substantial progress results.

Not only are programs called upon to serve culturally gender-diverse populations, but also to serve the structures and supports for caring parents that are continually changing as well. The predominant scenario in most households includes both caring parents working outside the home. In addition, single-parent families are on the rise, as well as the number of grandparents who serve as primary caregivers for their grandchildren. These patterns of change in family structure indicate that the current needs of families are indeed diverse, requiring heightened sensitivity to the increasing demands of home life. As our society increases in the numbers and groups of diverse populations represented, only those programs willing to be flexible, sensitive, and supportive to the parents, children, and families they serve will be determined effective and worthwhile.

Parent programs offer many opportunities for the community. Female and male parent and family involvement is a wise investment for communities. If female and male parent involvement traditions and habits are to be transformed, there must be adequate support from the principal as the school leader. Figure 8.3 illustrates some examples of parent programs that support gender equity.

There is not unanimous agreement about the definition of "parent involvement in education." Different groups and organizations hold different perspectives. Historically, two traditions, each operating with a totally different set of assumptions and values, have influenced the development of parent involvement (Rodriguez, 1999). The parent education tradition reflects a child-centered, professional orientation. This tradition is based on the assumption that both female and male parents need access to knowledge in order to perform adequately as parents. The other tradition, the citizen participation approach, is based on the assumptions that adults have the right and competence to share in making decisions that affect their own lives and the lives of their children. Below are some of the barri-

1. Provide understandable, accessible, and well-publicized processes for influencing decisions, raising gender issues, or concerns.

2. Encourage the formation of PTAs or other caring parent groups to identify and respond to gender issues of interest to parents.

3. Include parents on all decision-making and advisory committees, and ensure adequate training for such areas as policy, curriculum, budget, school reform initiatives, safety, personnel, and gender-related issues.

4. Provide parents with current information regarding school policies, practices, and both female and male student school performance data.

5. Encourage and facilitate active parent participation in the decisions that affect students, such as student placement, course selection, and individual personalized education plans.

6. Treat parental concerns with respect, and demonstrate genuine interest in developing solutions.

7. Promote female and male parent participation on school district, state, and national committees and issues.

8. Provide training for staff and caring parents on collaborative partnering and shared decision making.

Figure 8.3.   Characteristics of programs that support gender equity.

ers to parent involvement and some possibilities the principal may use to overcome these.

1. *Time.* Be flexible when scheduling meetings. Try different times of the day or week to allow both female and male parents to take part.

2. *Location.* Meetings at community centers, apartment buildings, and places of worship are convenient.

3. *Value.* Personally welcome female and male parents, especially those who appear to be withdrawn or uncomfortable.

4. *Learn their interests and abilities.* Actively seek opportunities for mothers and fathers to use their experiences and talents to benefit the school.

5. *Don't know how to contribute?* Conduct a talent survey, then think of ways to use both moms' and dads' many talents.

6. *Encourage parents to share information on careers, hobbies, and pets.* Arrange for workshops and seminars for parent and community members on leadership and organizational skills.

7. *Don't understanding the system?* Write a parent's handbook covering the rules, procedures, and sources of information to answer their questions.

8. *Child care.* Find an available room in the school for child care. Hire students to babysit if your districts allows.

9. *Language barrier.* Arrange for an interpreter at meetings and conferences as needed.

10. *Cultural differences.* Be sensitive to other cultures' values, attitudes, manners, and views of the school.

11. *Transportation.* Visit parents in their home. Hold small group meetings in a community center, at a caring parent's home, or another convenient place. Arrange carpools and walk pools.

12. *Planning.* Mothers and fathers should be involved in the planning stages of a program, rather than after the majority of the decisions have been made.

13. *Arrange for training in caring parent involvement for all school staff.* Make sure that caring parents are welcome to drop in at school during the day. Have a parents' room at school.

14. *Parents have overwhelming problems.* Provide information and advocacy to help mothers and fathers secure the services they need, such as food stamps, job training skills, medical treatment, child care, etc.

15. *Low literacy.* Contact your library to find literacy groups or tutors of English as a second language to do programs. Plan a family literacy program as part of your parent involvement program for moms and dads.

Include a mini-poll (one question) of caring parent opinions covering a wide range of gender topics over time. Utilize caring parent feedback in making school/program decisions.

Principals of public schools should include family involvement policy-making membership. The following examples will prevent any gender bias issues that may occur in a school setting:

1. Recognition of diverse family structures, circumstances, and responsibilities, including differences that might impede parent participation. The person(s) responsible for a child may not be the child's biological parent(s) and policies and programs should include participation by all persons interested in the child's educational progress.

2. A child's education is a responsibility shared by the school and family during the entire period the child spends in school. To support the goal of the school district to educate all students effectively, the schools and parents must work as knowledgeable partners. To address the issue of a caring staff is an implication for future studies.

Although parents are diverse in culture, language, and needs, they share the school's commitment to the educational success of their children. This school district and the schools within its boundaries, in collaboration with parents, shall establish programs and practices that enhance parent involvement and reflect the specific needs of students and their families. Principals should support the development, implementation, and regular evaluation of a parent involvement program in each school, which will involve both females and males at all grade levels and in a variety of roles.

REFERENCES

Ascher, C. (1987). *Improving the school-home connection for poor and minority urban students*. New York: ERIC Clearinghouse for Urban and Minority Education, Teachers College, Columbia University. (EDU 300 484)

Baiamonte, B. (1995). Spanish speaking parents' perceptions of their role in school activities: An experimental stud. *Dissertation Abstracts International, 56*(08A), 3028. (UMI No. 2036784).

Basterra, M. (1998). *Involvement of parents of diverse cultural and linguistic background.* Paper presented at the American Education Research Association Symposium, San Diego, CA. Retrieved November 10, 2001, from http://www.maec.org/parntlep.htm

Bennett, W. (1986). *First lessons: A report on elementary education in America.* Washington, D.C: Department of Education. (ED279205)

Brody, J. (1997, November 11). Personal health: Parents can bolster girls' fragile self-esteem. *New York Times,* p. F7.

Clark, R. (1983). *Family life and school achievement: Why poor black children succeed or fail.* Chicago: University of Chicago Press.

Comer, J. (1980). *School power: Implications of an intervention project.* New York: Free Press.

Comer, J. (1984). Home-school relationships as they affect the academic success of children. *Education and Urban Society, 16*(3), 323–337.

Comer, J., & Haynes, N. (1991). Parent involvement in schools: An ecological approach. *The Elementary School Journal, 91*(3), 271–277.

Davies, D. (1987). Parent involvement in the public schools: Opportunities for administrators. *Education and Urban Society, 19*(2), 147–150.

Dornbusch, S. (1986). *Helping your kids make the grade.* Reston, VA: National Association of Secondary School Principals.

Ebener, R. (1995). Supportive behaviors of low-income parents of academically successful children. *Dissertation Abstracts International, 56*(6A), 2079. (UMI No. 9534332)

Epstein J. (1987). What principals should know about parent involvement. *Principal, 66,* 6–9.

Finney, P. (1993, May 17). The PTA/ Newsweek national education survey. *Newsweek.*

Hidalgo, N., Siu, S., Gright, J. A., Swap, M., & Epstein, J. (1995). Research on families, schools, and communities: *Handbook of research on multicultural education* (pp. 498–524). New York: Simon & Schuster, Macmillan.

Laosa, L. (1982). School, occupation, culture, and family: The impact of parental schooling on the parent-child relationship. *Journal of Educational Psychology, 74,* 791–827.

Levine , D., & Lezotte. L. (1995). Effective schools research. *Handbook of research on multicultural education* (pp. 535–547). New York: Simon & Schuster, Macmillan.

Louis Harris and Associates. (1991). *The metropolitan life survey of American teachers: Strengthening links between home and schools.* New York: Author.

National Commission on Children. (1991). *Speaking of kids: A national survey of children and parents.* Washington, DC: Author.

National Educational Goals Panel. (1994). *The national education goals report: Building a nations of learners.* Washington, DC: Government Printing Office.

Patten, P. (2000). Girls, aggressive? *Parent News* [Online], *6*(4). Retrieved August 23, 2005, from http://npin.org/pnews/2000/pnew

Robertson, A. (1996, November). *Fostering school success in adolescents: Girls' issues / boys issues.* Retrieved August 23, 2005, from http://npin.org/pnes/1996/pewnw96/pnewn96h.html

Rodriquez, A. (1999). The parent involvement practices of a selected group of Hispanic parents in Hillsboro County, Florida. *Dissertation Abstracts International, 60*(8A), 2775. (UMI No. 9940937)

Sosa, A. (1997). Involving Hispanic parents in educational activities through collaborative relationships. *Bilingual Research Journal, 21,* 1–8.

Shartrand, A. M., Weiss, H. B., Kreider, H. M., & Lopez, M.E. (1997). *New skills for new schools: Preparing teachers in family involvement.* Retrieved March 221, 2005, from www.gse.harvard.edu/hfrp/pubs/onlinepubs/skills/chptr1.html

U.S. Department of Education. (1994). *Riley calls for family involvement to increase learning: Announces nation-wide partnerships.* Washington, DC: Author.

CHAPTER 9

GENDER EQUITY IN EARLY CHILDHOOD ASSESSMENT

Genevieve Brown
Beverly J. Irby
LingLing Yang

In recent years, Congress and national organizations have focused attention on assessment practices for young children. In 1994, the U.S. Congress charged the National Goals Panel to "create clear guidelines regarding the nature, functions, and uses of early childhood assessments, including assessment formats that are appropriate for use in culturally and linguistically diverse communities, based on model elements of school readiness" (Shepard, Kagan, & Wurtz, 1998). The National Association for the Education of Young Children (NAEYC) and the National Association of Early Childhood Specialists (NAECS) recommended that assessments, as a central part of early childhood education programs, be (a) ethical, appropriate, valid, and reliable; (b) developmentally appropriate; (c) culturally and linguistically responsive; (d) related to the child's real world; (e) understood by teachers through their own professional development; (f) inclusive of families; and (g) connected to best practice and research in teaching and learning, interventions, and program improvement (NAEYC & NAECS/SDE, 2003). The National Association of School Psychologists (2004) agreed that early childhood assessment practices should be nondiscriminatory in terms of ethnicity, native language, family composition, and/or socioeconomic status. However, this group added the critical component of gender to the expectations of appropriate assessment

Gender and Schooling in the Early Years, pages 149–163

for young children. The addition of gender is significant, as there has been limited focus on this equity issue in early childhood assessment.

Gender equity should be an integral part of developmentally appropriate practices in early childhood assessment. Ignoring gender in assessment is equivalent to designing solutions "to meet everyone's needs," which "risk meeting no one's" (Wellesley College Center for Research on Women, 1992, p. 9). Addressing gender, along with other equity factors that impact school performance, is important to ensure that all students will succeed to the best of their ability.

Assessments are frequently used in making decisions related to curriculum and instructional strategies for young children. When assessments become the basis for placing students in various programs, such as gifted, bilingual, or special education, or for determining promotion status of students, they are then considered high stakes. On such high-stakes assessments, gender has not been given adequate consideration (Core Leaders Group, 2004). Our chapter reviews gender-related assessment practices in early childhood education and recommends the most appropriate early childhood assessment practices for combating gender bias.

ASSESSMENT PRACTICES
IN EARLY CHILDHOOD EDUCATION

Two forms of assessment are prevalent in early childhood education. The first is traditional assessment, generally taking the form of standardized tests. The second is assessment based on the observable performance of children.

Traditional assessment practices—Standardized assessment. For decades, norm-referenced, standardized tests (i.e., achievement tests) have been used to assess the development of young children (NASP, 2004). This type of evaluation is usually viewed as objective, unbiased, and as providing equal opportunity, because standardized tests do compare the test taker to a normative group of children of the same age, gender, geographic location, income level, disability, and/or cultural background (Angela & Angela, 2004). Despite the fact that standardized tests have comparative norms, inequity still exists in standardized tests. For example, the development of standardized tests is subjective (i.e., who develops the test, what content is covered and from whose perspective, what questions are included, what terms are used, the level of difficulty, and how the scores are interpreted).

The disparity of scores between males and females and between white and minority test takers on standardized tests reveals that in many cases the test is flawed, gender-biased, and discriminatory (NASP, 2004). Furthermore, there are disparities between classroom performance and test scores related to gender. Although girls do better than boys in their classroom performance at all levels of schooling, they score lower than boys on key standardized tests (Mid-Atlantic Equity Center, 1993). Multiple explanations related to why males out-perform girls on standardized tests are given. They include: (a) males and females approach learning differently and, therefore, analyze and solve problems differently; (b) tests may be designed in a manner more conducive to the way males solve problems; (c) both girls and boys do better on questions with content familiar to them (if more items favor boys, they have an advantage); (d) references to males in standardized test items consistently outnumber those to females; (e) girls complete fewer items and are more likely than boys to check an "I don't know" option and, thus, fail to complete the test (Becker, 1990; Linn, DeBenedictis, Delucchi, Harris, & Stage, 1987).

Traditional assessment practices with young children. Despite concerns of inequity in standardized testing, schools continue to use standardized test scores of female students, children from minority and low-income families, or children whose first language is not English to label and track them into "slow," "learning disabled," or "remedial" classes where they fail to make good progress. The younger the children are when assessed by norm-based standardized tests, the more likely it is that they will be incorrectly labeled. Research also demonstrates that once labeled, children tend to bring their behavior into line with that label. This suggests that repeated standardized assessments could be damaging to children (i.e., in the level of anxiety they might experience, in possible negative self-perceptions based on poor test performance; Bowman, Donovan, & Burns, 2001), and in inappropriate placements in special programs.

Standardized assessment should be used with great caution in educational decision making about young children for several reasons. First, such tools are even less accurate and less predictive when used with young children (NASP, 2004). Second, it is difficult to assess children in the early years of life (i.e., from birth to age 8) because during this period, young children's physical, motor, and linguistic development outpaces all other stages. Third, young children are not good test takers. In principle, the younger the children are, the poorer their test-taking skills will be. Therefore, the younger the child being evaluated, assessed, or tested, the more errors are made (Ratcliff, 1995; Shepard, 1994). Fourth, standardized tests are not capable of demonstrating how or what students are learning, the kinds of help they need, the classes to which they are assigned, and the quality of teaching they receive. Fifth, because standardized tests are equated with high standards, they are falsely considered to be the true representation of children's learning levels (Peterson & Neill, 1999). Sixth, administered over only a minimal time period, standardized tests fail to measure much more than test-taking ability. Seventh, and as mentioned earlier, these assessments tend to be gender, culturally, linguistically, and socio-economically biased (NASP, 2004).

Performance assessment practice defined. Performance assessment is the direct, systematic observation of an actual student's performance and the rating of that performance according to previously established performance criteria (Bredekamp, Knuth, Kunesh, & Shulman, 1992). In this type of assessment, students are asked to perform a real task or to create a product and are assessed on both the process and the end result of their work. Performance assessment is authentic, in that it conveys the idea that assessments should engage students in applying knowledge and skills in the same way they are used in the real world (Wiggins, 1991). It strongly recommends the use of more open-ended problems, hands-on activities, and portfolios of student work (Linn, Baker, & Dunbar, 1991). Authentic assessment requires teachers to think differently about how they can determine what a child knows.

Different from standardized assessments, performance assessments provide an alternative approach to assessing young children, focusing on what children know and can do rather than on how they compare to other children. Although some degree of subjectivity may be present in performance assessments, we contend that they are more equitable than standardized assessments because performance assessments address young children as individuals, giving them an equal opportunity to demonstrate and apply their knowledge. Therefore, the benchmark of achievement is based on the individual child's growth from one assessment point to another. As each child is assessed, the teacher can also have a deeper understanding of how each child learns and even how the learning progress of each child compares to other children in the classroom. In this sense, the assumption is that authentic assessment is more valid than standardized testing in that comparisons are made by the teacher and are based on the observed performances within the same environment by the same teacher, who impacts the learning of each child and recognizes individual diversity.

Performance assessment is appropriate for use in early childhood education; it is a viable basis for a variety of educational decisions that affect the child, including planning for groups and individual children and communicating with parents. Furthermore, performance assessment may be used to adjust instruction, yielding real benefit to the children and the program as well (Katz, 2001).

Performance assessment practices promoting equity. Performance assessment promotes equity because it is: (a) meaningful, (b) linguistically appropriate, (c) developmentally appropriate, (d) instructionally sensitive, and (e) fair. Meaningfulness is addressed through contextualized assessments as students deal with meaningful problems. Furthermore, the purpose and content of the assessment are understandable to both boys and girls at the same academic level. Linguistic appropriateness occurs as the language used in tasks is free of gender bias, and the students use their own language competency to demonstrate their knowledge (Baker, 1994); the level of language maturity and readiness are also considered. Performance assessment addresses developmental appropriateness through consideration of the maturation level of the child and gender influences related to recent brain research. Instructional sensitivity is attained as performance assessment emphasizes the relationship between assessment and instruction and responds to the learning efforts of the child rather than to innate qualities. When the content, skills, and strategies are taught in nongender-biased ways, no instructional bias will be revealed on the assessment (Baker, 1994). Fairness is achieved through performance assessment as the progress of each individual child is assessed as demonstrated through work samples and attached records collected by the teacher over time.

APPROPRIATE EARLY CHILDHOOD ASSESSMENT PRACTICES FOR COMBATING GENDER BIAS

Early childhood assessment practices must allow for accurate and non-biased identification of the developmental needs of infants, preschoolers, and young children and facilitate interventions that involve school administrators, teachers, parents, and other caregivers (NASP, 2004).

Girls and boys do not mature equally in verbal and spatial capacities and are different in their learning styles (Darling-Hammond, 1994). The explanations of gender differences are based on cognitive, social, and cultural factors and congruity between the teaching style and students' learning styles (Terregrossa & Englander, 2000). For instance, girls, regardless of the subject matter, tend to have a comparative advantage in verbal skills and boys in mathematical skills. Furthermore, traditional "chalk-and-talk" modes of teaching favor girls, who are more ready to sit down and start with a task, while boys' alienation from education may be explained by the fact that at primary-school level they are taught almost exclusively by women and few strong and active male role models can be found as a lead character in the reading materials.

In addition, learning in young children is the result of interaction between a child's thoughts and experiences with materials, ideas, and people. These materials and ideas should be not only age-matched, but also should be gender, linguistically, culturally, and socioeconomically appropriate (Meisels, 1985; Standards for Educational and Psychological Testing, 1985; Uphoff & Gilmore, 1985).

Portfolios

The type of performance assessment that we find is the most comprehensive and equitable is the portfolio. The portfolio is a collection of thoughtfully selected work samples, artifacts, and accompanying reflections indicative of a child's learning experiences, effort, and progress toward and/or attainment of established curriculum goals (Irby & Brown, 2004).

Children's portfolios are an important tool for accomplishing authentic assessment and gender equity in the early childhood classroom because every child is given an equal opportunity to perform at his or her best level and is judged in a fair, consistent, nonarbitrary, and nonprejudicial way (Johnson & Rose, 1997). Portfolio assessment is individualized and reflects evidence of children's growth, development, and learning (Albrecht & Miller, 2004; Irby & Brown, 2004).

The approaches to portfolios vary considerably, but they all rest on records and collections of the student's work that is done over a long period of time, rather than on a few hours' test. Brown and Irby (2004) take the approach one step further. They contend that a portfolio is not a portfolio unless it has reflection (self-assessment) from the student included. This piece of the portfolio addresses gender bias in that it allows for free expression of the child related to his or her own work. A male child is not being compared to a female child; rather, each child is reflecting on his or her own work.

Portfolio assessment enables teachers to share information with students about their own performance as well as with parents, peers, or other interested people over time without interpretation of scores and allows teachers and parents to follow the children's progress in order to identify areas of growth and necessary improvement (Hill, 1995). Portfolio assessment also involves children in their own learning and assessment when they choose work samples for their portfolios. They begin to have a notion of evaluating their own work, thus initiating the development of reflective self-assessment skills (Irby & Brown, 2004).

Portfolios Assist Teacher Reflections

Bias is combated in the portfolio in that the portfolio process not only requires that the young child begin to use a reflective process over time, it also requires that teachers reflect consistently on the quality of student work (Peterson & Neill, 1999), their own classroom pedagogy, and selection of curriculum materials that promote gender equity (Irby & Brown, 2004).

Additionally, teachers should be trained to be aware of gender issues in curriculum planning, classroom teaching, and assessment. First, they should create developmentally appropriate curriculum and teaching practices, in which they use their knowledge of growth patterns of young children, along with an understanding of individual children, their interests, and their cultural backgrounds to set up the appropriate environment and deliver learning experiences. Second, they should be able to respond effectively to individual differences and gender differences. For example, they should make toys and materials free of gender bias, avoid the sex-biased language in communicating with young children, and avoid providing the context unfamiliar to students of one sex and with fewer references to persons of one gender. Third, they must be aware of the importance of equity issues in assessment.

Reflection on classroom pedagogy. As the instructional decision maker in his or her classroom, the teacher has various options in deciding physical organization of his or her classroom, teaching methods, instructional styles, grading, and assessment. Reflection encourages the teacher to (a) pay special attention to the stereotypes and problems that affect boys as well as girls; (b) develop nonsexist teaching and learning plans, which include the experiences and achievements of both women and men from various racial and ethnic groups; (c) create a nonsexist classroom, including the physical arrangement and organization of the classroom, verbal and nonverbal language, interaction, and activities; and (d) incorporate nonsexist teaching into their daily instruction (Sadker & Sadker, 1982).

Reflection on curriculum materials. Teacher reflection impacts the selection and use of curriculum materials. First, reflection enhances teachers' awareness of the importance of nonsexist materials and enables them to recognize and identify the sex or racial biases that exist in instructional materials. Second, reflection assists the teacher in rejecting or avoiding gender-biased materials, such as those in which (a) women are invisible or stereotyped as dependent, passive, incompetent, and docile; (b) women's roles and contributions are minimized or omitted; (c) the information pertaining to women is fragmented and isolated from the mainstream of historical and cultural development; and (d) language is sex-biased, with, for example, masculine terms and pronouns such as *policeman, mailman,* and *he* being used (Sadker & Sadker, 1982).

Components in Portfolios

The early childhood portfolio includes self-assessment and documentation of a child's experiences within the classroom and from the parents.

Self-assessment or reflection. Self-assessment is an important component of the portfolio. In fact, at the heart of the assessment portfolio is the critical piece called *reflection.* Without reflective work with the child, the portfolio is nothing more than a scrapbook. Self-assessment in young children enables them to identify their best work and their interests. It also aids in developing oral language and decision-making skills (Irby & Brown, 2004). Children can begin to use self-assessment when they are quite young and with guidance may become more effective at evaluating their performance.

According to Irby and Brown (2004), a young child can be assisted in the development of self-assessment through use of the Reflection Question Model. This model is designed to help the teacher elicit each child's "new learning" and to clarify and reinforce their "new understandings." The three steps for initiating self-assessment and reflection are select, dscribe, and interpret.

As teachers guide the children through the three steps of reflection during a portfolio conference, they may ask all or some of the questions listed at each step. Children's responses or reflections may be audio recorded or may be recorded by the teacher onto a printed form listing the three steps and the accompanying questions. The questions are designed to encourage the child to articulate what he or she has learned to enhance motivation for learning, and to build confidence related to his/her progress. Guiding prekindergarten children to engage in self-reflection takes time. Teachers report, however, that when children become accustomed to this reflective process, they are usually realistic and able to make appropriate comments and suggestions. Because time to sit down with children to lead them through the model and record their responses is limited, some teachers have trained parent volunteers or teacher assistants to record responses.

STEP 1. Select. The teacher should guide the child to select the artifacts that represent his or her best work. In this step, the teacher will ask the following or similar questions:

- Which work sample are you most proud of?
- Which example would you most like to show your parents or friends?
- Which example would you most like to talk about with me or with our class?

STEP 2. Describe. In this step the teacher will guide the student to recall the situations or activities related to the learning experience.

- What can you tell me about this project?
- What do you like about this work sample (or specific product—drawing, recording, book)?
- Where were you when you worked on this project?
- Who helped you with this project?
- How did you make this project/sample/drawing ...?
- How did you know how to do the project ...?

STEP 3. Interpret. The child has now described the project. Step three represents the actual self-assessment or reflection. The following questions may be used as a guide:

- Why do you want to share this work with others?
- Why do you think you did such a good job on this work?

- What was the hardest thing about this work?
- What was the best part of dong this project?
- Is there something that you need help with?
- What else do you want to know about this?
- Is there something else you would like to tell me about this?

Teacher documentation. Documentation has long been encouraged and practiced in many early childhood programs and is a critical component of a child's portfolio. Teacher observations, checklists, and other forms of documentation of a child's experiences are important for inclusion in a child's portfolio. By observing children's behavior in their natural environment on an ongoing basis, teachers record chronologically children's development, catalog their accomplishments, and respond to their rapidly changing needs by adjusting programs and classroom activities (Shepard et al., 1998).

Understanding of developmental differences related to gender can assist the teacher as he or she observes the child and assesses learning. Generally, observations can be divided into systematic observations and anecdotal observations. Systematic observation gives teachers insight into how each child's development is unfolding, as well as an understanding of the developmental uniqueness of each child, while anecdotal observations of children not only help teachers to understand each child's individual developmental pace, temperamental traits, and stages of development, but also to uncover children's emerging interests (Albrecht & Miller, 2004).

The Classroom Observation Form (Figure 9.1), representative of systematic observation, may be used to observe a child's performance over a period of time. Other ways that a teacher may document the child's progress for inclusion in the portfolio may include:

- Observational checklists taken over time (developmental, state or district-developed, teacher-developed, criterion-referenced)
- Conference interview notes
- Goals and objectives checklists
- Paintings or drawings
- Reading log entries
- Physical performance checklists
- Benchmark tests
- Rating scales
- Video- or audiotapes
- Photographs
- Parent–teacher conference notes
- Anecdotal notes (Irby & Brown, 2004)

Classroom Observation Form

Name Performance																
Tells stories using puppets																
Constructs with blocks																
Paints using various materials																
Traces letters																
Acts out stories																
Follow directions																
Records sketches of designs																
Uses basic graphing skills																
Labels objects according to size																

Figure 9.1.   Sample classroom observation form (Albrecht & Miller, 2004).

Below are two examples of children's drawings (Figures 9.2 and 9.3). In Figure 9.2, Myoli, a 4-year-old girl, drew a picture of her mother washing shoes and reflected on that verbally. Rogelio, a 4-year-old boy, described his actions in his drawing (Figure 9.3). These two figures include the child's reflection about the drawing and the teacher's interpretation of the child ren's 3 months into the school year. It is evident in these two examples that the male is more verbal. However, girls usually provide more sophisticated and elaborate responses than boys (Van Krayenoord & Paris, 1997). Teachers must be aware of this so that they will not underestimate the boys in their classrooms, thinking they are less able to self-assess or that they are less able to effectively communicate their thoughts verbally.

Parent documentation of a child's experiences. Parent information is usually not as detailed or extensive as are the other sections of the portfolio. Teachers will need to solicit items for this section and should encourage parents to take an active role in extending the child's learning and in recording observations of the child's learning. Some teachers hold work shops at the beginning of the year on how parents might participate in the portfolio process. Included in this section of the portfolio might be:

- Parent observations regarding their child's work
- Summaries of parent–teacher conferences from the parent's perspective
- Records or logs of home readings/activities
- Records of family experiences related to learning goals (photos, brochures, library card, and event tickets) (Irby & Brown, 2004)

Figure 9.2.   Myoli's drawing.

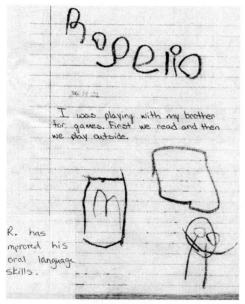

Figure 9.3.   Rogelio's drawing.

Parents' information on the child's experiences at home is an integral part of the children's portfolios. Some parents feel worried about their children's gender-nonconforming behaviors. Some parents even inadvertently implant gender-biased ideas, actions, or words in their children. The teacher plays an important role in promoting parents' gender sensitivity. Parents' gender stereotypes and attitudes may be changed by the teachers' belief in gender equity. By reviewing the children's portfolios and by meeting with their teachers, parents can learn about home environment, in which boys are allowed to have dolls and read stories about fantasy, while girls are permitted to enjoy rough games, adventure tales, war stories, and historical nonfiction.

ASSESSMENT AND DECISION MAKING

As assessment is often the basis for decisions that affect students' educational futures, assessment should provide equal opportunities for all students to demonstrate their abilities and knowledge. Being aware of the potential inequity in assessment will prepare policymakers, teachers, and parents to intelligently question the design of the assessments and the uses of the assessment results, as these strongly influence policymaking, curriculum design, classroom instruction, teacher–student interaction, and young children's learning and self-esteem levels.

Policymakers

Even an unbiased test may be used in ways that give an advantage to members of one gender. For example, a testing policy may treat test results differently for males and females (Axman, 1990). As this is the case, it is imperative that policymakers and educators look critically at current research and practices in assessment related to gender equity and student learning. This research challenges schools to create equitable environments that promote the social and academic success of all children (Brown & Irby, 2004).

It is recommended that policymakers (a) enact a policy on gender-fair testing, (b) establish procedures for reviewing all tests for equity concerns, and (c) incorporate professional development experiences that aid teachers in making instructional decisions.

Teachers

Assessment results often influence curricula and teaching strategies. Such decisions should be responsive to gender differences. For example, in making instructional decisions, teachers should (a) respond appropriately to the developmental needs of both boys and girls; (b) have the same expectations of academic achievement for both boys and girls; (c) provide gendered role models, gender-fair activities, and learning and developmental opportunities in and out of the classroom; (d) examine instructional materials for ethnic, racial, and gender bias; and (e) reflect on teaching styles to ensure sensitivity to the needs and concerns of both genders.

SUMMARY

Equity should be an integral part of any assessment. However, it is a mistake to assume that simply shifting from one type of assessment to another will eliminate all concerns about biases or that such a shift will necessarily lead to equality in assessment (Linn et al., 1991).

In this chapter, we reviewed gender-related assessment practices in early childhood education with a focus on performance assessment, and we recommended portfolios specifically for minimizing gender bias in assessments. Portfolios allow teachers to carefully select student-centered data that assess specific learning over several designated periods of time and in a variety of contexts. Such assessments more accurately, objectively, and authentically provide a comprehensive and holistic view of child growth, development, and learning from which teachers can make equitable decisions based on the performance of individual children, regardless of their gender.

REFERENCES

Albrecht, K., & Miller, L.G. (2004). *The comprehensive preschool curriculum*. Beltsville, MD: Gryphon House.

Angela, N., & Angela, L. (2004). *What assessment means to early childhood educators?* Retrieved January 14, 2005, from http://www.childcareexchange.com

Axman, C. R. (1990). Gender bias and fairness. *ERIC Digest.* Retrieved December 14, 2004, from http://www.ericdigests.org/pre-9218/gender.htm

Baker, E. L. (1994, March). Making performance assessment work: The road ahead. *Educational Leadership, 51*(6). Retrieved June 23, 2003, from http://www.ascd.org/readingroom/edlead/9403/baker.html

Becker, B. (1990). Item characteristics and gender differences on the SAT-M for mathematically able youths. *American Educational Research Journal, 27*(1), 65–71.

Bowman, B. T., Donovan, M. S., & Burns, M. S. (2001). *Eager to learn: Educating our preschoolers*. Washington, DC: National Academy Press.

Bredekamp, S., Knuth, R. A., Kunesh, L. G., & Shulman, D. D. (1992).*What does research say about early childhood education?* Retrieved December 14, 2004, from http://www.ncrel.org/sdrs/areas/stw_esys/5erly_ch.htm

Brown, G., & Irby, B.J. (2004). Women leaders creating equitable schools. *Delta Kappa Gamma Bulletin, 70*(4), 5–8. Core Leaders Group. (2004). *Early childhood equity initiative*. Retrieved December 14, 2004, from http://teaching forchange.org/DC_Projects/ECEI/edei.html

Darling-Hammond, L. (1994). Performance-based assessment and educational equity. *Harvard Educational Review, 64*(1), 5–30.

Hill, M. (1995). Self-assessment in primary schools: A response to student teacher questions. *Waikato Journal of Education 1,* 61–70.

Irby, B. J., & Brown, G. (2004). *Promoting authentic assessment: Portfolios in early childhood education* (Teacher's ed.). Columbus, OH: McGraw-Hill.

Johnson, N. J., & Rose, L. M. (1997). *Portfolios: Clarifying, constructing, and enhancing*. Lancaster, PA: Technomic.

Katz, L. G. (2001, June/July). Early learning shows benefits. *Early Care and Education, 2*(6). Retrieved December 12, 2004, from http://www.ecs.org/clearinghouse/27/21/2721.htm

Linn, R. L., Baker, E. L., & Dunbar, S. B. (1991). Complex, performance-based assessment: Expectations and validation criteria. *Educational Researcher, 20*(8), 15–21.

Linn, M. C., De Benedictis, T., Delucchi, K., Harris, A., & Stage, E. (1987). Gender differences in national assessment of educational progress science items: What does "I don't know" really mean? *Journal of Research in Science Teaching, 24*(3), 267–78.

Meisels, S. (1985). *Developmental screening in early childhood*. Washington, DC: NAEYC. Mid-Atlantic Equity Center. (1993). *Beyond Title IX: Gender equity issues in schools*. Retrieved December 10, 2004, from http://www.maec.org/beyond.html

National Association of School Psychologists. (2004). *Position statement on early childhood assessment*. Retrieved December 14, 2004, from http://wwwnasponline.org/information/pospaper_eca.html

National Association for the Education of Young Children & the National Association of Early Childhood Specialists in State Departments of Education. (2003). *Introduction on where we stand on curriculum,assessment, and program evaluation*. Retrieved December 10, 2004, from http://naecs.crc.uiuc.edu/position.html

Peterson, B., & Neill, M. (1999, Spring). Alternations to standardized tests. *Rethinking Schools, 13*(3). Retrieved December 12, 2004, from http://www.rethinkingschools.org/archive/13_03/assess.shtml

Ratcliff, N. (1995). The need for alternative techniques for assessing young children's emerging literacy skills. *Contemporary Education, 66*(3), 169–171.

Sadker, M. P., & Sadker, D. M. (1982). *Sex equity: Handbook for schools*. New York: Longman.

Shepard, L.A. (1994). The challenges of assessing young children appropriately. *Phi Delta Kappan, 76*(3), 206–212.

Shepard, L., Kagan, S., & Wurtz, E. (Eds.). (1998). *Principles and recommendations for early childhood assessments.* Washington, DC: National Educational Goals Panel.

Standards for Educational and Psychological Testing. (1985). Washington, DC: American Psychological Association, American Educational Research Association & National Council on Measurement in Education.

Terragrossa, R. A., & Englander, V. (2000). Global teaching in an analytic environment: Is there madness in the method? In R. Dunn & S. A. Griggs (Eds.), *Practical approaches to using learning styles in higher education.* London: Bergin & Garvey.

Uphoff, J. K., & Gilmore, J. (1985, September). Pupil age at school entrance—how many are ready for success? *Educational Leadership, 43,* 86–90.

Van Krayenoord, C. E., & Paris, S. G. (1997). Australian students' self-appraisal of their work samples and academic progress. *Elementary School Journal, 97*(5), 523–537.

Wellesley College Center for Research on Women. (1992). *Gender-equitable education: A focus on literacy.* Retrieved December 14, 2004, from http://www.wcwonline.org/o-rr25-2a.html

Wiggins, G. (1991). Standards, not standardization: Evoking quality student work. *Educational Leadership, 48*(5), 18–25.

CHAPTER 10

TRAJECTORY FROM BULLYING TO SCHOOL VIOLENCE

A Gender Perspective

Rebecca A. Robles-Piña
Carrie H. Butler

An examination of the path from bullying to school violence from a gender perspective is needed to understand where the emphasis should be for future school violence prevention programs and research and to determine if these should be different for boys and girls. This chapter examines the literature on school violence as it relates specifically to bullying, since it affects both boys and girls. A review of gender-related studies to bullying behavior is examined from a historical perspective, international and national prevalence, categories of bullying, psychological correlates, and social group influences. Finally, future directions and conclusions are examined.

HISTORICAL PERSPECTIVE

Initially, the focus on bullying was addressed in response to a case where males were involved as victims in Norway. The incident involved three 14-

Gender and Schooling in the Early Years, pages 165–178
Copyright © 2005 by Information Age Publishing

year-old boys who committed suicide as a result of extreme harassment from classmates (Olweus, 1993). The term "bullying," however, had been defined 30 years earlier by Olweus (1972), who coined it as "mobbing" and defined it as an individual or a group of individuals harassing, teasing, or pestering another person.

A survey from 1985 to 2004 of four U.S. newspapers that included *USA Today, New York Times, LA Times,* and *Washington Post* (Newspaper Source Database, n.d.) indicated that the first mention of school violence in the United States appeared in 1985 when two stories were written. In the 1990s, stories of school violence escalated, with 1999 as the year in which most stories were written. Since 1999, there has been a decrease in the number of stories about school violence in those newspapers. From a gender perspective, the majority of the stories documented were about school violence related to school shootings committed by boys.

One of the most notable cases in the United States of school violence involved two young men who perceived themselves to have been bullied and retaliated by shooting several students at Columbine High School in Colorado in 1999. These young men expressed to others that they were angry because they felt ostracized from the popular group. One of the students, Klebold, expressed in his journal that he felt like an outcast and that everyone was against him (Lindsey, 2000).

The U.S. Department of Health and Human Services (2001) reported that 71% of students involved in school shootings were targets of bullying. When bullying is left unmanaged, bullies as well as victims can experience a variety of emotional, social, behavioral, and academic difficulties (Moffit, Caspi, Dickson, Silva, & Stanton, 1996). Some research states that bullying behavior not only affects the overall climate of the schools (Limber & Small, 2003), but also that it poses serious academic and social-emotional risks for victims and bullies (Nansel et al., 2001).

In summary of a historical and gender perspective to school violence, attention was initially given to this issue outside the United States where males were victimized. In the United States, by major newspaper accounts, stories about school violence first occurred in 1985, peaked in 1999, and have decreased since then. From a gender perspective, the majority of the newspaper stories have focused on violence and victimization for males. Current research distinguishes between male and female violence and victimization according to types of bullying. Finally, research has identified bullying as a contributing factor to school violence and has discussed the deleterious effects on children when left unresolved.

INTERNATIONAL AND NATIONAL PREVALENCE

The first studies on the prevalence estimates of bullying, victimization, and bullying/victimization categories were conducted in Scandinavian countries. Subsequently, rates for the United States were reported. Related to the estimates for bullying in elementary, middle, and high schools, a most recent study (Pellegrini & Long, 2002) indicated that school violence has shown a curvilinear trend, with bullying and aggression increasing most at the middle school transitional period from elementary school and declining in high school.

Bullying rates in elementary schools have varied widely on the international scope. For example, studies examining bullying behaviors conducted in Finland ranged from 4.1% (Olafsen & Viemero, 2000) in comparison to 49.7% (O'Moore & Kirkham, 2001) in studies conducted in Ireland. A U.S. study (Pellegrini, Bartini, & Brooks, 2001) determined the rates of bullying to be 14% for students in elementary grades. Another study in the United States for grades 4–6 reported that 25% of the students indicated that they bullied another student during the 3 months prior to the study (Hoover, Oliver, & Hazler, 1992).

Victimization rates in elementary schools outside the United States ranged from 11.3% in a sample of 5,813 students in Finland (Kumpulainen, Rasainen, & Henttonen, 1998) to 49.8% in a much larger sample of students in Ireland (O'Moore & Kirkham, 2001). In the United States, the rate of victimization in elementary schools is reported to be 19% (Pellegrini et al., 2001).

Prevalence estimates of the bully/victim dynamic were first recorded in Finland; Olafsen and Viemero (2000) reported a school bullying prevalence rate of 2.2%, and Kumpulainen and colleagues (2001) reported a rate of 18.6%. Reports of bullying in middle schools indicated lower rates than those found in elementary grades, with a rate of 4.7% for a sample of Finnish eighth-grade students (Salmivalli, Lappalainen, & Lagerspetz, 1998) and a rate of 27% in a sample of 6,758 middle school students in the United Kingdom (Whitney & Smith, 1993). In U.S. middle schools, Hoover and colleagues (1992) reported that 88% of the junior high and high school students observed bullying and 77% of students reported being a victim of bullying.

In foreign secondary schools (grades 9–12), victimization ranged from 4.2% to 25% for Australian students (Peterson & Rigby, 1999) to 3.4% to 10% in secondary schools in Britain (Salmon, James, & Smith, 1998). A study in Scotland that examined both bullying and victimization found a prevalence estimate of 4.2% (Karatzias, Power, & Swanson, 2002). In U.S. high schools, Nansel and colleagues (2001) surveyed 15,686 students in grades 6–10 and found that 29.9% had been involved in bullying, 13%

reported being a bully, 10.6% reported being a victim, and 6% reported being a bully-victim.

With regards to gender, there is a plethora of earlier studies on bullying reporting that boys exhibit significantly higher levels of aggression than girls (e.g., Coie & Dodge, 1998). Currently, the research indicates that boys are still reporting being more victimized than girls; boys bully more boys than girls; and girls bully more girls than boys (Hay, Payne, & Chadwick, 2004). However, in regards to the validity of the prevalence data using gender, Crick and Rose (2001) have questioned how that data had been collected. The authors reported that historically many studies on aggression had excluded girls. This was especially true when aggression was studied as overt physical or verbal aggression rather than covert physical and verbal aggression, which have most often been linked to girls. Current research reveals patterns in which males exhibit more aggressive behaviors than females, although female violence in recent years has increased (American Association of University Women Educational Foundation, 2001).

In summary, prevalence estimates for bullying and victimization were first recorded in the Scandinavian counties and then in the United States. An analysis of bullying, victimization, and bullying/victimization prevalence rates in elementary schools indicated that the United States had similar rates to those in foreign schools; however, rates in U.S. middle schools were not only higher than U.S. elementary schools, but also much higher than those found in foreign middle schools. High school prevalence rates for bullying in U.S. high schools were higher than in foreign schools. Finally, boys were disproportionately represented in bullying, victimization, and bullying/victimization categories. This has led to research examining covert and overt bullying in relation to female rates of bullying and victimization.

CATEGORIES OF BULLYING

The dyadic bully–victim paradigm has been challenged by current research that suggests that bullying behaviors fall along a continuum (Bosworth, Espelage, & Simon, 1999). The traditional bully/victimization categories have now given way to subcategories of aggressive bullies, victims, bully-victims, bystanders, and normal controls (Salmivalli, Lagerspetz, Bjorkqvist, Osterman, & Kaukiainen, 1996). This new paradigm has opened up possibilities to study aggressive behaviors in both males and females. In other words, the sole view of aggressive behavior linked to males is not the only worldview used when examining aggressive behaviors associated with bullying.

Some of the possibilities that have opened up for investigation are studies of covert aggressive behaviors, such as teasing and behavior that can occur on a less frequent basis but that is nonetheless harmful. The new categories of study in bullying behavior have given rise to the study of relational aggression and indirect aggression.

When bullying is described along a continuum of covert acts of aggression related to indirect aggression and relational aggression, the gender lines become blurred. Crick and Grotpeter (1995) defined relational aggression as "behaviors that are intended to significantly damage another child's friendships or feelings of inclusion by the peer group" (p. 711). Oesterman and colleagues (1998) defined indirect aggression as "social manipulation, attacking the target in circuitous ways" (p.1).

One of the first studies to examine relational aggression was conducted by Crick and Grotpeter in 1995. In a study of 491 students in grades 3–6 in a midwestern town, a peer nomination instrument was used to measure covert or relational aggression; overt aggression, such as physical and verbal; prosocial behavior; and isolation. Students were placed into four groups: relationally aggressive, overtly aggressive, both overtly and relationally aggressive, and nonaggressive. No gender differences were found for the relationally aggressive, overtly relationally aggressive, and nonaggressive groups. Statistically significant gender differences, however, were found for the overtly aggressive group, with boys (15.6%) being more overtly aggressive than girls (.4%). Two other studies (Espelage & Swearer, 2003; Rys & Bear, 1997), however, have replicated the Crick and Grotpeter study to examine gender differences in relational aggression and found no differences between males and females.

In summary, the constructs of school violence, aggression, and bullying have undergone various iterations in identifying gender differences. The latest attempt to examine the categories of bullying and relational aggression by gender have produced mixed results and need further investigation.

PSYCHOSOCIAL CORRELATES

The psychosocial correlates that have been studied in relationship to bullying are race/ethnicity, anger, depression, anxiety, and empathy. Of those correlates, the ones that have been examined along gender lines include depression and empathy.

Of all the correlates of bullying behavior that have been examined, depression was found to be the most common mental health symptom experienced by both male and female victims (Callagan & Joseph, 1995). By comparison to boys, girls who had been victimized had higher levels of depression (Craig, 1998). Austin and Joseph (1996) add that clinical depression is not a phenomenon of those who have been victimized, but that it can also occur in high numbers of boys and girls who bully.

Elevated levels of depression have also been observed in bully-victims, in other words, those who bully and who have also been victimized (Austin & Joseph, 1996). The studies of bully-victims have revealed that this group had the highest rates of suicidal ideation (Kaltiala-Heino, Rimpela, Marttunen, & Rimpela, Rantanen, 1999). This particular phenomenon is gaining momentum among youth. For example, a recent study indicated that 78% of the attackers in high school shootings had a history of suicidal thoughts and attempts, and 6% had experienced depressive symptoms (Vossekuil, Fein, Reddy, Borum, & Modzeleski, 2002). Clearly, the dynamic between bullying and victimization is one that deserves immediate attention and action from both parents and school professionals.

Another psychological characteristic that has been studied along gender lines is empathy, and it has been studied within the context of various school prevention programs. The inclusion of empathy in prevention programs is based on the premise that empathy makes a difference in controlling bullying behavior (Miller & Eisenberg, 1988). While earlier studies investigated the sole effect of empathy in school violence prevention programs, more recent research has suggested that school violence prevention programs not only include empathy, but also prosocial and respectful behaviors (Espelage & Swearer, 2003). A study that guided this line of thinking follows.

Endresen and Olweus (2001) conducted a study of the effects of empathy on bullying behaviors on a sample of students between the ages of 13 and 16 in Norway. They used the Empathic Responsiveness Questionnaire (Olweus & Endresen, 1998) and the Olweus Bully/Victim Questionnaire (Olweus, 1989) to study the impact of empathy on bullying. Examples of questions asked to empathic responses by gender were: (a) "When I see a girl who is hurt, I wish to help her," and (b) "Seeing a boy who is sad makes me want to comfort him."

There were some interesting results along gender lines. For example, in comparison to boys, girls reported higher levels of (a) empathic responsiveness, (b) levels of emotional distress, and (c) empathic concern. A finding that was true for both boys and girls was that those respondents who displayed high levels of empathic concern were more likely to view bullying as negative and thus less likely to bully others. Those students who had a positive attitude toward bullying, or who felt that bullying was a "rite of passage," were more likely to bully others and support others who bully (Bently & Li, 1995; Endresen & Olweus, 2001; Pellegrini & Long, 2002). These findings have implications on bullying programs in that they need to go beyond teaching empathic concern to include social attitudes.

In summary, of all of the psychosocial characteristics studied, depression and empathy have the strongest relationship to bullying behavior. Depression was known to affect both boys' and girls' behavior along the bullying continuum. Girls were capable of having more empathic responses than boys; however, the research indicated that school violence programs should include not only empathic training, but also the teaching of prosocial skills and changing attitudes.

SOCIAL GROUPS' INFLUENCE ON BULLYING

The interactions between bullies and victims and those with whom they socialize, such as peers, parents, and teachers, are necessary to better understand how these social agents encourage or discourage bullying behaviors in both boys and girls.

Family Factors

When examining bullying behavior within family factors, there has been considerable support for the interaction between aggressive behavior and family characteristics (Berdondini & Smith, 1996; Bowers, Smith, & Binney, 1994; Olweus, 1993). A study that documented bullying and parental styles (Olweus, 1993) concluded that boys raised in families where there was (a) a lack of parental supervision, (b) physical violence, and (c) a lack of warmth engaged in more bullying behaviors. Another study added that families who had a high need for power were more likely to raise bullies (Bowers et al., 1994). Conversely, children who had a demanding and controlling mother, and where the family tended to be enmeshed, were more likely to be victims (Berdondini & Smith, 1996); this was especially true for boys (Rigby, Slee, & Cunningham, 1999). Families of girls who were likely to be victims tended to have families who engaged in demanding, coercive, and rejecting behavior (Finnegan, Hodges, & Perry, 1998).

Peers

Several studies have been conducted to examine the impact of the peer dynamics on bullying behaviors of boys and girls. One particular study of children, grades 4–6 (Farmer et al., 2002), tested the hypothesis that aggressive youth are members of small, isolated groups and are often on the margins of their peer group. Two findings from this study that dispelled the myth that bullies are isolated from their peers were that (1) aggressive boys had many friends, and (2) over 67% of aggressive boys and over 50% of aggressive girls were nominated as friends by nonaggressive peers. Furthermore, the authors found that aggressive girls were more likely than aggressive boys to be labeled as deviant by their peer group.

A second study, replicating Farmer and colleagues' study (Rodkin, Pearl, Farmer, & Van Acker, in press), used peer-nominated methodology to identify the three most popular students in school. They tested the hypothesis that children who vote bullies as "cool" will engage in bullying behavior themselves. The study found that more aggressive boys than girls were nominated as "cool" by their peer group. Interestingly, nonaggressive children voted bullies as "cool," and aggressive children tended to nominate nonaggressive children as "cool." This finding indicated that the term "cool" can be associated with aggressive as well as nonaggressive children.

A third study examined popular-prosocial or "model" boys and popular-antisocial or "tough" boys by peer nomination (Rodkin, Farmer, Pearl, & Van Acker, 2000). Popular-prosocial boys were seen as athletic, authoritative, studious, and nonaggressive. Similarly, the popular-aggressive boys were also seen as cool and athletic; the only difference being that the popular-antisocial boys were seen as antisocial. This study's findings suggest that boys who are aggressive, athletic, and cool can also be very popular.

Another dynamic that has been studied along peer and gender lines is the perception of peer enemies. Rodkin and colleagues (in press) studied enemy dyads, students who were enemies, in grades 3 and 4. They found that 52% of the enemy dyads were between boys and girls. This has implications on bullying behavior since boys and girls are most likely to bully their perceived enemies. This finding also has implications on a finding by the American Association of University Women Educational Foundation (2001), who found that early aggression leads to later sexually aggressive behavior toward females. More research is needed to clarify the interplay of these bullying dynamics.

Teachers

Conventional wisdom would indicate that teachers have a distinct advantage to stop bullying behavior since they supervise students throughout the day. Espelage and Swearer (2003) have stated, "Teachers need to be more aware of same- and cross-sex aggression among their students" (p. 392). Interestingly, these authors also add that while teachers are authority figures that can make a difference toward reducing bullying behavior, they often underestimate the number of bullying problems, side with the perpetrators, and fail to stop bullying behaviors.

Interviews conducted by Siann, Callahan, Glissov, Loekhart, and Rawson (1994) found that teachers concurred that girls and boys bully in different ways. Teachers believed that girls were more likely to be involved in acts of verbal violence than boys, who were most likely to be involved in acts of physical violence. Research has also been conducted on teachers' attitudes and actions toward boy/girl and girl/boy bullying (Birkinshaw & Eslea, 1998). Specifically, teachers were asked about their perceptions of physical, verbal, and indirect bullying between boys and girls; the amount of distress experienced by the victims; and the implications for intervention. Teachers were more likely to perceive bullying as physical acts, and they also felt this was overwhelmingly distressing to the victim. Moreover, teachers perceived girl acts of physical bullying against boys as more serious than when boys demonstrated physical acts against girls. Lastly, teachers were more likely to execute some form of punishment if the bullying was physical rather than verbal or indirect.

Another study surveyed teachers' and school counselors' perceptions of bullying and effective interventions to use in bullying (Robles-Piña, Nichter, & Campbell-Bishop, 2004). In regards to gender differences in bullying incidents, teachers and school counselors responded a "3" or "unsure" on a Likert-type instrument indicating "1" as strongly disagree to "5" strongly agree. Teachers and counselors were not sure whether boys and girls displayed different types of bullying behaviors. This is consistent with the literature on teachers' lack of knowledge to identify, inability to rate prevalence, and lack of competence in dealing with bullying (Boulton, 1997; Leff, Kupersmidt, Patterson, & Power, 1999; Stockdale, Hangadumanbo, Duys, Larson, & Sarvela, 2002). The Robles-Piña and colleagues study would suggest that this line of thinking is consistent for school counselors as well. Moreover, this study found no gender differences for the different types of interventions used. The three most frequently used by teachers and counselors were (1) mediation, (2) life skills taught through classroom guidance units, and (3) various types of media, such as videos, stories, books, and websites.

In summary, parenting styles affect whether or not boys and girls will bully or be bullied. The myth that bullies are loners and isolated from their peers has been dispelled by the literature. Both male and female bullies have friends and can be considered popular by their classmates. Interestingly, however, is the fact that aggressive behavior in boys is perceived as being "cool," whereas girls' aggressive behaviors are perceived as being deviant. Not surprisingly, females are more likely to verbally, or covertly, bully, and they are more likely than boys to be victims of sexually aggressive behaviors. The majority of the studies on teachers' perceptions about bullying and, most recently, school counselors, indicate that they are not aware of bullying behavior, its frequency, and how to intervene in these situations.

FUTURE DIRECTIONS

While it is important to continue the dialogue in regards to bullying from a gender perspective, there are other critical areas that need attention. Those areas are gay, lesbian, bisexual, and transgendered (GLBT) youth (Espelage & Swearer, 2003); ethnicity; and children from low-socioeconomic-status backgrounds (Wolke, Woods, Stanford, & Sehultz, 2001). There is a paucity of research in the area of GLBT youth related to bullying. The Wolke and colleagues study conducted in England and Germany, however, did find a significant relationship between ethnicity and bullying, with minorities more likely to be the victims of bullying. However, in U.S. studies, a national study (Nansel et al., 2001) and a state study (Hanish & Guerra, 2000), indicated there were no relationships found between ethnicity and bullying. More research is clearly needed in these areas.

CONCLUSION

This chapter compared bullying behaviors nationally and internationally, and simultaneously examined bullying gender differences from a historical perspective, terms of prevalence, characteristics, and psychosocial correlates.

In order to determine the direction of school violence prevention programs and research, it is necessary to investigate why bullying was first investigated in foreign countries before it was studied in the United States. The type of reasoning that kept this phenomenon from being studied until school shootings erupted is essential for a clearer understanding of direction. Bullying nationally and internationally, for both males and females, is prevalent in today's society. Currently, U.S. rates of bullying appear to be higher than in foreign countries. This is especially true for transitional times such as the transfer from elementary to middle school. More research is needed to determine why this trend is so pervasive, and school prevention programs need to be implemented and assessed in the middle schools.

Both males and females are involved in bullying behaviors. Males are more likely than females to engage in physically aggressive acts, whereas females are more likely to be verbally aggressive and are more likely to be victims of sexual assault. Socially, boys may be conditioned, or reinforced by their peers, to perceive aggression as being "cool"; but females may be conditioned by their peers to perceive aggression as deviant. One explanation for the differing characteristics between male and female bullying behaviors relates to the reinforcements they receive from others. Bullying intervention programs can ameliorate the bullying situation by promoting healthier dynamics of empathy, respect, and social attitudes among youth.

Acts of bullying perpetuate detrimental influences in schools that can have devastating consequences on individual students and the entire school atmosphere. This is not only true for boys and girls but also for students who are different in terms of ethnicity, socioeconomic status, and sexual orientation.

Parents and school professionals serve as powerful influences in the lives of young people. Parents who provide adequate supervision, and reduce the levels of family conflict in the home, can help to curtail bullying behaviors in their children. Similarly, school professionals who are attentive and monitor the aggressive dynamics between students may prevent bullying on campus. Prevention and intervention programs that aim to incorporate parents' and school professionals' support, along with the program components of empathy and respect among youth, are theoretically designed to effectively reduce bullying among school-age youth.

REFERENCES

American Association of University Women Educational Foundation. (2001). Hostile hallways: Bullying, teasing, and sexual harassment in school. Washington, DC.

Austin, S., & Joseph S. (1996). Assessment of bully/victim problems in 8 to 11 year olds. *British Journal of Educational Psychology, 66,* 447–456.

Bentley, K. M., & Li, A. K. F. (1995). Bully and victim problems in elementary schools and students' beliefs about aggression. *Canadian Journal of School Psychology, 11,* 153–165.

Berdondini, L., & Smith, P. K. (1996). Cohesion and power in the families of children involved in bully/victim problems at school: An Italian replication. *Journal of Family Therapy, 18,* 99–102.

Birkinshaw, S., & Eslea, M. (1998). *Teachers' attitudes and actions toward boy vs girl and girl vs. boy bullying.* Paper presented at the meeting of the British Psychological Society, Lancaster University, London.

Bosworth, K., Espelage, D. L., & Simon, T. (1999). Factors associated with bullying behavior in middle school students. *Journal of Early Adolescence, 19,* 341–362.

Boulton, M. J. (1997). Teachers' views on bullying: Definitions, attitudes, and ability to cope. *British Journal of Educational Psychology, 62,* 73–87.

Bowers, L., Smith, P. K., & Binney, V. (1994). Perceived family relationships of bullies, victims, and bully/victims in middle childhood. *Journal of Social and Personal Relationships, 11,* 215–232.

Callagan, S., & Joseph, S. (1995). Self-concept and peer victimization among schoolchildren. *Personality and Individual Differences, 18,* 161–163.

Coie, J. D., & Dodge, K. A. (1998). Aggression and antisocial behavior. In N. Eisenberg (Ed.), *Handbook of child psychology* (Vol. 3, pp. 779–862). New York: Wiley.

Craig, W. M. (1998). The relationship among bullying, victimization, depression, anxiety, and aggression in elementary school children. *Personality and Individual Differences, 24,* 123–130.

Crick, N. R., & Grotpeter, J. K. (1995). Relational aggression, gender, and social-psychological adjustment. *Child Development, 66,* 710–722.

Crick, N. R., & Rose, A. J. (2001). Toward a gender-balanced approach to the study of social-emotional development: A look at relational aggression. In P. H. Miller & E. K. Scholnick (Eds.), *Toward a feminist developmental psychology* (pp. 153–168). New York: Routledge.

Endresen, I. M., & Olweus, D. (2001). Self-reported empathy in Norwegian adolescents: Sex differences, age trends, and relationship to bullying. In A. C. Bohart, C. Arthur, & D. J. Stipek (Eds.), *Constructive and destructive behavioral: Implications for family, school, and society* (pp. 147–165). Washington, DC: American Psychological Association.

Espelage, D. L., & Swearer, S. M. (2003). Research on school bullying and victimization: What have we learned and where do we go from here? *School Psychology Review, 32*(3), 365–383.

Farmer, T. W., Leung, M. C., Pearl, R., Rodkin, P.C., Cadwallader, T. W., & Van Acker, R. (2002). Deviant or diverse peer groups? The peer affiliations of aggressive elementary students. *Journal of Educational Psychology, 94,* 611–620.

Finnegan, R. A., Hodges, E. V. E., & Perry, D. G. (1998). Victimization by peers: Association with children's reports of mother–child interaction. *Journal of Personality and Social Psychology, 75,* 1076–1086.

Hanish, L. D., & Guerra, N. G. (2000). Predictors of peer victimization among urban youth. *Social Development, 9,* 521–543.

Hay, D. F., Payne, A., & Chadwick, A. (2004). Peer relations in childhood. *Journal of Child Psychology and Psychiatry, 45*(1), 84–108.

Hoover, J. H., Oliver, R., & Hazler, R. J., (1992). Bullying: Perceptions of adolescent victims in the Midwestern USA. *School Psychology International, 13,* 5–16.

Kaltiala-Heino, R., Rimpela, M., Marttunen, M., Rimpela, A., & Rantanen, P. (1999). Bullying, depression, and suicidal ideation in Finiish adolescents: School survey. *British Medical Journal, 319,* 348–351.

Karatzias, A., Power, K.G., & Swanson, V. (2002) Bullying and victimization in Scottish secondary schools: Same or separate entities? *Aggressive Behavior, 28,* 45–61.

Kumpulainen, K., Rasainen, E., & Henttonen, I. (1998). Bullying and psychiatric symptoms among elementary school-age children. *Child Abuse and Neglect, 22,* 705–717.

Kumplulainen, K., Rasainen, E., & Puura, K. (2001). Psychiatric disorders and the use of mental health services among children involved in bullying. *Aggressive Behavior, 27,* 102–110.

Leff, S. S., Kupersmidt, J. B., Patterson, C., & Power, T. J. (1999). Factors influencing teachers' predictions of peer bullying and victimization. *School Psychology Review, 28,* 505–517.

Limber, S. P., & Small, M. A. (2003). State laws and policies to address bullying in schools. *School Psychology Review, 32*(3), 445–455.

Lindsey, D. (2000, May 15). A reader's guide to the Columbine report. *Salon.* Retrieved July 12, 2002, from http://www.salon.com/news/feature/2000/05/17/guide/

Miller, P., & Eisenberg, N. (1998). The relation of empathy to aggressive and externalizing/antisocial. *Psychological Bulletin, 103,* 324–344.

Moffitt, T.E., Caspi, A., Dickson, N., Silva, P., & Stanton, W. (1996). Childhood-onset versus adolescent-onset antisocial conduct problems in males: Natural history from ages 3 to 18 years. *Developmental and Psychopathology, 8*, 399–424.

Nansel, T. R., Overpeck, M., Pilla, R. S., Ruan, W. J., Simons-Morton, B., & Scheidt, P. (2001). Bullying behaviors among US youth: Prevalence and association with psychosocial adjustment. *Journal of the American Medical Association, 285*, 2094–2100.

Newspaper Source Database. (n.d.). Retrieved November 2, 2004, from http://wwwEBSCOhost

Oesterman, K., Bjoekqvist, K., Lagerspetz, K. M. J., Kaukiainen, A., Landau, S. F., Fraczek, A., et al., (1998). Cross-cultural evidence of female indirect aggression. *Aggressive Behavior, 24*, 1–8.

Olafsen, R. N., & Viemero, V. (2000). Bully/victim problems and coping with stress among 10 to 12 year-old pupils in Aland, Finland. *Aggressive Behavior 26*, 57–65.

Olweus, D. (1972). Personality and aggression. In J. K. Cole & D. D. Jensen (Eds.), *Nebraska symposium on motivation* (pp. 261–321). Lincoln: University of Nebraska Press.

Olweus, D. (1989). *The Olweus Bully/Victim Questionnaire.* HEMIL-senteret, Univesitetet I Bergen, Norway.

Olweus, D. (1993). Bully/victim problems among school-children: Long-term consequences and an effective intervention program. In S. Hodgins (Ed.), *Mental disorder and crime* (pp. 317–349). Thousand Oaks, CA: Sage.

Olweus, D., & Endresen, I.M. (1998). The importance of sex-of-stimulus object: Age trends and sex differences in empathic responsiveness. *Social Development, 7*, 370–388.

O'Moore, M., & Kirkham, C. (2001), Self-esteem and its relationship to bullying behavior. *Aggressive Behavior, 27*, 269–283.

Pellegrini, A. D., Bartini, M., & Brooks, F. (2001). School bullies, victims, and aggressive victims: Factors relating to group affiliation and victimization in early adolescence. *Journal of Educational Psychology, 91*, 216–224.

Pellegrini, A. D., & Long, J. D. (2002). A longitudinal study of bullying, dominance, and victimization during the transition from primary school through middle school. *British Journal of Developmental Psychology, 20*, 259–280.

Peterson, L., & Rigby, K. (1999). Countering bullying at an Australian secondary school with students as helpers. *Journal of Adolescence, 22*, 481–492.

Rigby, K., Slee, P. T., & Cunningham, R. (1999). Effects of parenting on the peer relations of Australian adolescents. *Journal of Social Psychology, 139*, 287–288.

Robles-Piña, R., Nichter, M., & Campbell-Bishop, C. (2004). Assessment of counselors' and teachers' perceptions about bullying in schools. *The Journal of At-Risk Issues 10*(1), 11–21.

Rodkin, P. C., Farmer, T. W., Pearl, R., & Van Acker, R. (2000). Heterogeneity of popular boys: Antisocial and prosocial configurations. *Developmental Psychology, 36*, 14–24.

Rodkin, P. C., Pearl, R., Farmer, T. W., & Van Acker, R. (in press). Sexual harassment and the cultures of childhood: Developmental, domestic violence, and legal perspectives. *Journal of Applied School Psychology.*

Rys, G. S., & Bear, G. G. (1997). Relational aggression and peer relations: Gender and developmental issues. *Merrill-Palmer Quarterly, 43,* 87–106.

Salmon G., James, A., & Smith, P. K. (1998). Bullying in schools: Self-reported anxiety, depression, and self-esteem in secondary school children. *British Medical Journal, 317,* 924–925.

Salmivalli, C., Lagerspetz, K., Bjorkqvist, K., Osterman, K., & Kaukiainen, A. (1996). Bullying as a group process: Participant roles and their relations to social status within the group. *Aggressive Behavior, 22,* 1–15.

Salmivalli, C., Lappalainen, M., & Lagerspetz, K. M. J. (1998). Stability and change in connection with bullying in schools: A two-year follow-up. *Aggressive Behavior, 24,* 205–218.

Siann, G., Callahan, M., Glissov, P., Loekhart, R., & Rawson, L. (1994). Who gets bullied? The effect of school gender and ethnic group. *Educational Research, 36,* 123–134.

Stockdale, M.S., Hangadumanbo, S., Duys, D., Larson, K., & Sarvela, P.D. (2002). Rural elementary students', parents', and teachers' perceptions of bullying. *American Journal of Health Behavior, 26*(4), 266–277.

U.S. Department of Health and Human Services. (2001). *Youth violence: A report of the Surgeon General.* Rockville, MD: U.S. Department of Health and Human Services: Centers for Disease Control and Prevention, National Center for Injury Prevention; Substance Abuse and Mental Health Services Administration; Center for Mental Health Services; and National Institute of Mental Health.

Vossekuil, B., Fein, R.A., Reddy, M., Borum, R., & Modzeleski, W. (2002). *The final report and findings of the Safe School Initiative: Implications for the prevention of school attacks in the United States.* Washington, DC: U. S. Secret Service and U. S. Department of Education.

Whitney, I., & Smith, P. K. (1993). A survey of the nature and extent of bullying in junior/middle and secondary schools. *Educational Research, 35,* 3–25.

Wolke, D., Woods, S., Stanford, K., & Sehultz, H. (2001). Correlates of bullying and victimization of primary school children in England and Germany: Prevalence and school factors. *British Journal of Psychology, 92,* 673–696.

CHAPTER 11

EMERGENT LEADERSHIP THROUGH MENTORING IN EARLY CHILDHOOD EDUCATION

Lee Turner-Muecke

Leadership development among early childhood education professionals is almost nonexistent. According to Kagan (1994), shared leadership of the type naturally found in early childhood education settings would rely on a collaborative rather than a competitive training approach. The humanistic dynamic that forms the integral quality of the early childhood profession does not lend itself to the more conventional approach to professional development found in corporate settings.

This research describes a 6-month case study of leadership development in an early childhood setting. Three dyads were part of a group of teachers and early childhood managers who were involved in a departmental mentoring process that emerged into a doctoral research project. Six early childhood education supervisors serving in a federally funded program located in the western United States were research participants. Schon's (1983) reflective supervision was employed as a model that develops professionals through facilitation and guidance toward self-defined goals. Data analysis included three taped interviews per participant, each approximately 1 hour in length, administered by the action-researcher at the

Gender and Schooling in the Early Years, pages 179–192
Copyright © 2005 by Information Age Publishing

beginning, middle, and end stages of the research; eight taped pre- and post-observational conferences (approximately 1 hour each), conducted twice a month between dyads; and reflective journals with weekly entries by each participant. The study spanned 6 months and generated over 600 pages of transcribed data, including interviews, dyadic conferences, and written journals. One transcribed tape of a mentoring support group and an anonymous survey of mentees contributed to the total database.

All six participants were involved in a mentoring experience for 8 months prior to the commencement of this research project. The design of the study focuses on two specific constructs: reciprocity and professional growth. This research was a process-oriented study that illuminates the details of interaction between mentor/mentee and potentially illuminates aspects of leadership development in the early childhood profession. The perspective of the subjects forms the data for this study. A discussion of the findings reveals emerging patterns of reciprocity and mutual benefits.

The critical need for men in the field of early childhood, as direct service staff and early childhood managers, is duly acknowledged. A recent survey by the National Education Association, the nation's largest teachers' union, found that the number of male public school teachers in the United States hit a 40-year low in 2004. Only 21% of the nation's 3 million teachers are men, and a majority of those work at the middle or high school levels. With low salary levels in early childhood, it is inevitable that we are among the lowest in percentage of male employees. This deprives very young children of the male role models and caregivers that are critical to their developmental growth outside of the home.

BACKGROUND TO THE STUDY

In the field of early childhood education, leadership preparation is a relatively recent phenomenon. Systematic and tested methods for leadership training in early childhood are not evident. Reflective practice and mentoring have been recognized as best practices in a profession that is relationship-based and interactive (see Lally, 1998). It is recommended that time be set aside for reflection and that professionals in the field be trained in reflection and its benefits, as well as peer coaching and self-assessment (Whitebook, Hnatiuk, & Bellm, 1994). However, little research is available to understand the nature of reflective practice or mentoring in early childhood. Hence, the potential value of such professional development to the field cannot be fully understood.

Schon (1987) framed a type of mentoring that embodies mutual inquiry where reflection on practice is paramount. In a cycle of pre- and post-observation routines built around observation of the intern, the active part of the mentor's work is to facilitate the mentee's (or intern's) thinking and subsequent action without bias or manipulation. This allows the mentee to develop along an individual path rather than clone the mentor. It is a constructivist paradigm relying on facilitation and mutuality as a process. This requires the mentor to be self-aware and nonjudgmental in order to enter into a process of inquiry with their mentee in a caring and relationship-based model. The mentor is unable to perform this task without self-examination and self-inquiry, setting the stage for mutual growth. The demand, therefore, is to remain open, flexible, and able to be vulnerable in order to perform the skilled artistry of mentoring.

The dyadic partners in the study had been working together in their early childhood program for up to 10 years. Three participants were newer members, having joined the team the last year or two before the research began. Although reflective practice was a familiar concept to the action-researcher and some of the other participants, the group had not engaged in formal reflective practice or mentoring prior to the commencement of the research. All participants volunteered to form the research group, with the action-researcher serving as the sixth member and completing the third dyad. The intrinsic motivation of the volunteers was considered helpful in completing the research and successfully producing data for analysis.

All participants were trained in reflection as an integral part of the mentoring process. Mentors received further training in thinking sensitively about practice while in the act of mentoring another early childhood professional. The three mentors were guided to use observational information to facilitate their mentees toward reaching self-defined goals and seeing perhaps undiscovered elements for their own reflection and integration.

This constructivist approach is integral to exploring mentoring relationships and in examining the dyadic interaction in this study of reciprocity and mutual professional growth. A possible outcome was that a continuous methodology might emerge that would rely on staff resources and, in turn, could positively impact mentoring participants' interactions and professional relationships. In this event, the potential application to early childhood professional development could be cost-effective and provide positive reinforcement to professional interaction.

Although all the research participants in this study were females, it is understood that involving men in this paradigm could only enrich the study and raise the standard of our qualitative service to children and families.

SETTING FOR QUALITATIVE STUDY

The action-researcher was a doctoral student in education. She was also the Director of Children and Family Services for a nonprofit organization operating Head Start and Early Head Start programs in an inner city on the West Coast. Her experience in education includes 9 years of classroom teaching, 3 years of college teaching in early childhood, 21 years of supervision and administration including a year as a Faculty Associate training student teachers, and 4 years as a School Associate supervising student interns. The thesis study was situated in the early childhood program in which the action-researcher was Director. The research participants ranged in age from mid-30s to mid-60s, from 5 to 30 years of early childhood experience, and 3 to 25 years of supervision experience. All participants were women, and five of the six were in management positions in the early childhood program when the research began. One participant was promoted to a management role while the research was in progress.

The design of the mentoring project within the Children and Family Services Department where this research was conducted is nested or multi-tiered. That is, every ECE staff person in the department is mentored. Managers in more senior positions are mentoring management staff that, in turn, mentors teachers and assistant teachers. A graphic of this nested model is included in Figure 11.1.

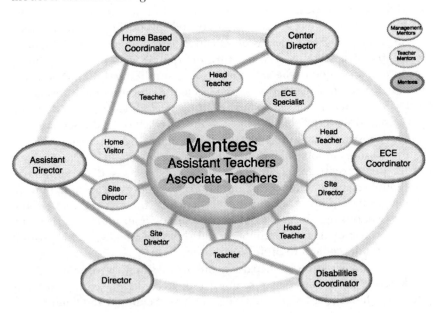

Figure 11.1.   Departmental reflective supervision model.

ISSUES FOR INQUIRY

Reciprocity and professional growth formed the focus of this study. The research design was not focused on mentor traits, which is a traditional approach; rather, it examined the process of interaction of mentor and mentee in a frame of mutual inquiry. However, in order to consider interaction and process, it is important to look at the manner in which participants relate. Traits such as openness, self-confidence, lack of competition, ability to put the mentee at ease, and a flexible and sharing orientation are all characteristics that readily come to mind in describing an effective mentor. It would be interesting to include additional traits to be considered if men were a party of a mentoring leadership study. All of these considerations need to be included when designing any training programs for mentors.

The necessity of self-reflection and analysis is an integral part of the mentoring process for both mentor and mentee (Schon, 1987).The first step for each mentoring participant is self-reflection leading to a setting of individual goals. In Figure 11.2 the goals of each mentor and mentee is depicted along with the evolution of their goal/s over the time of the study.

Rose, the Director of the Department and action-researcher, hoped to gain insight into the mentoring process from the research point of view so that contributions to early childhood education leadership could be made

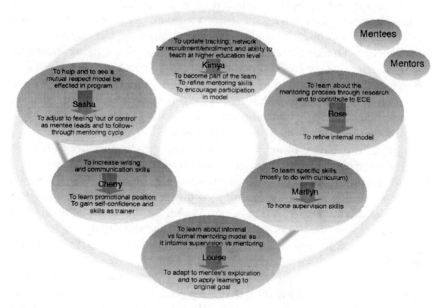

Figure 11.2.   Participants' goals and goal evolution.

through the mentoring process in a more systematic way. Louise, the Departmental Assistant Director, wanted to gain a clearer understanding of a true mentoring model in order to understand in what way a true model is different from mentoring, which is merged with direct supervision. Both Rose and Louise's later reflections did acknowledge the impact that their respective mentees had on their own processing of information and learning.

Some participants were interested in the interactive process from the outset. Sasha, Center Director for the large infant/toddler center, was focused on a link with relationship-based organizations and their impact on managerial style that then "ripple out" to families and children being served. Sasha believed that a top-down power structure does not build the same working environment and ultimate performance that a structure built on mutual respect and inclusion can. She hoped to learn more about and gain the benefits of this kind of organization in her center.

The Disabilities Coordinator (Kimya), hoped to gain a better understanding of herself and those with whom she worked. Having recently joined the department from southern California, Kimya wanted to build more trust and relationships with the people at work. She also wanted to help others, specifically her own mentees.

Cherry, who began the research as a Head Teacher at the large infant/toddler center was quickly promoted to ECE Specialist, was quite clear about what she hoped to gain. Cherry's goals became more oriented toward understanding the responsibilities related to her new position, which included making presentations and training others. Being somewhat shy in nature, Cherry had difficulties with public speaking. She wanted to be able to share the areas in her professional life that needed improvement and then receive feedback that would help her improve her practice. In this way, Cherry felt her contribution to the families and to training staff in her professional life would be more optimal.

Marilyn, the Home-Based Coordinator for the 39 preschool children receiving services at home, wanted to attain more specific skills and organize so that she could more effectively serve the program. She translated this into a desire for implementing a cutting-edge Reggio Emilia curriculum in the diverse Head Start program in which she served. After the first few weeks of meeting, it became apparent that the skills that needed development were those concerned with supervision rather than with innovative curriculum.

In each case, with a slight exception in the case of Kimya, the participants hoped to gain information that, over time, related to the formulation of their main goal/s. For example, Rose's goal remained consistent throughout the study; she wished to learn about the mentoring process through research in order to contribute to professional development in early childhood education. As the research progressed, goals evolved and changed in response to the results of and reflections on the conference cycle performed by each dyad.

As this interactive process study is rich in detail, only one mentoring dyad will be discussed in depth for the purposes of this gender equity chapter.

Sasha and Cherry had been working at the same site for a year or more. Sasha had been Site Director approximately 1 year and was a white woman of 40 some years that was married interracially with two partially grown children. She was completing the final units of her B.A., coping with a son with some developmental delay, trying to learn the Head Start system, and volunteering for a reflective mentoring research project. None of these factors dampened her enthusiasm and support of her mentee.

Her mentee, Cherry, was an African American woman from the South who was now enjoying her 60s as a Head Teacher, grandmother, and lovely and wise advisor to her friends and colleagues. Her placid personality offered a haven to colleagues in the demanding environment of child care. Cherry initially wanted to improve communication skills as her goal. Accompanying her promotion to Early Childhood Education Specialist, Cherry's goals evolved into working on her skills as a trainer, as this was a role in which she would now serve. Sasha supported Cherry's goals and wanted to create a supportive situation in which Cherry's influence and an environment of mutual enquiry and respect "would ripple out to families."

As this dyad moved through bimonthly conference cycles with observation of the mentee by the mentor, the action-researcher completed midway and final interviews and had them transcribed; once written journals were submitted, information began to emerge from the participants' reflections.

METHODOLOGY AND THE INQUIRY PROCESS

The applied methodology for the mentoring process in this research was that of reflective supervision (Schon, 1987) with pre- and post-observation conferences occurring biweekly. In conferences, mentors and mentees discussed and recorded follow-up on goals that had been set by the mentee. Mentors observed their mentees, collecting data at the mentee's specified request to aid in their self-analysis. The background, midway, and final interviews and written journals of each of the six participants were augmented by one tape of a mentoring support group that met with all departmental mentors during the course of the research. In addition, mentees in the department were surveyed anonymously for their input, and the resulting data was used in the analysis of findings. If men had been a part of this study, the data would probably have indicated some outcomes that were specific to their individual perspectives.

Participants were instructed to frame their reflective writing around reciprocal benefits and progress toward goals as well as comments on their process of sharing information and experiencing being involved in a mentoring process. Some of the interview questions specifically invited response on issues, including the engagement and interaction of the mentor; the focus on problem identification and solution, benefits, and challenges; mutuality; reciprocity; and meaningful growth. Taped conferences provided verbatim transcripts of biweekly interchange between mentors and mentees, which provided an authentic voice for the participants.

Among those were the voices of Sasha and Cherry, both of whom presented thoughtful and deliberate reflections on their mutual inquiry. Sasha observed that her mentee slowed the process down for her and that she benefited from a new way of taking time to reflect. Rather than things always happening at a fast pace as an administrator, it was beneficial to learn from someone else's style, which made you go slower and be more reflective in the process. Cherry's style was naturally thoughtful and reflective. She displayed a wisdom specific to those with the benefit of life experience. Sasha confessed that at times she felt she was "losing control." She said it took some time for her to feel comfortable with Cherry controlling her own path of self-discovery. Sasha had just taken over the position of Center Director in the last year and had never before supervised a center of such size. Cherry was older than her mentor, had a great deal of integrity, and was very committed to being professional. In the process of mentoring, Sasha learned not to give direct suggestions, but to facilitate Cherry's thinking about her choices of action through questioning. Sasha said she felt that this made her a better mentor and made her feel more confident and authentic when approaching other problems dealing with running her center. Sasha found the experience validating and stated that it helped her to overcome the insecurities she felt as a mentor.

Cherry expressed her vulnerability by stating that she wanted to share her goals and not keep them a secret anymore. She felt if they were out in the open and she could get help, and even improve, that she would feel more confident. In spite of Cherry's innate wisdom and life experience, she was shy and unsure of herself, especially in her new position as a supervisor and trainer of over 25 teachers. She even claimed that through this process she was learning to appreciate herself. Cherry had stated originally that she did not always feel confident enough to even ask questions. In speaking to her mentor about this topic, Cherry said,

> Still to know (enough) to grow...but you're okay with yourself; you're not feeling inadequate, that you don't measure up. Even comparing yourself with

anyone, I think this is really helping me a lot. I'm really pleased—pleased with it. And it does, like you say, it does spill over into other areas.

The sense of mutuality of inquiry, of reflection, and of reciprocal benefit was emerging, as evident in this dyad. Clearly, Sasha admitted to professional self-analysis as a result of guiding Cherry through her own self-analysis. Sasha readily admitted to experiencing a broadening of her vision with respect to processing and exchanging information as a result of her mentee's input. She learned that there are different ways to view reality and that there is more than one way to solve a problem. This alone would allow one to believe that mutual or reciprocal inquiry was existent.

FINDINGS OF THE STUDY

Reciprocity

Sasha and Cherry each felt that they had benefited from the mentoring process. In the final interview, Cherry commented that her mentor seemed to be pleased with her growth. Cherry stated that it seemed that she and Sasha were engaged in a relationship that, without the mentoring experience, probably wouldn't have been as close or as interactive. As the relationship developed, an increase in sharing of articles and other resources became regular and appreciated by the mentee. Sasha became more familiar with the needs and interests of her mentee and was able to reflect on and suggest meaningful resources for her on a regular basis. Sasha and Cherry discussed the reciprocal benefit of acknowledging an increased sense of self-appreciation. In a discussion about self-talk and positive affirmation as females, both acknowledged sometimes-negative concepts of themselves and that in being able to help another person, a sense of appreciation had emerged. They committed to continuing this affirmation and self-appreciation.

Sasha felt that her benefits included a consciousness of her professionalism due to her need to role model for another. She also felt that in trying out the strategies of positive mentoring, you learn something if you remain open about how things can be done in a different way. Cherry's way wasn't necessarily Sasha's way, but it was a valid way and one that caused a slowing-down of Sasha's pace, allowing for reflection. The other big benefit mentioned by Sasha was having someone to talk to about how and what professionals are doing as they go through their days. She felt this was a significant benefit because so often professionals get burned out, discouraged, ineffective, or feel as if their work is not meaningful or appreciated.

The mentoring process allows for a chance to reflect and make choices about professional direction with another colleague.

The other two dyads also expressed an experience of reciprocal benefits. Greater vision, increased confidence, organizational focus, improved relationships, an individualized developmental pace for staff growth, resources, satisfaction, a sense of helping and pride, and collegiality were among the benefits that participants felt that they experienced. Some expressed a belief that the program as a whole was beneficially impacted. In the beginning, Rose, the action-researcher, witnessed this small team working and inquiring together and producing a much more creative and accepting environment among the six participants. Trust seemed to have reached a new level and, while working, participants acquired this new level of trust interacting with one another as a result of taking the time to engage in reflective mentoring.

All participants seemed to share a commonality of some benefit from the mentor/mentee interaction, exemplifying reciprocal learning, one from the other, while mutually engaged in inquiry about their professional practice. It would have been informative to explore the expressions of male participants in this study of mutual inquiry and reflection. Their perspective would have enriched a study of early childhood leadership development.

Professional Growth

A framework of mutual inquiry and engagement while progressing toward the goals of the mentee was prevalent due to the fact that participants received training in reflective supervision at the outset of the mentoring program, prior to commencement of the research.

Sasha and Cherry each had strong hopes for gain as they entered the research project. Cherry's were much more self-oriented in terms of professional growth that would build her training and communication skills; Sasha's hopes for gain were much more organizationally focused in terms of the growth of her Center through a mutual respect versus power and control model. Yet in their mentoring and learning process, Cherry was able to help her mentor, Sasha, open up to herself and identify her own need for control. Though Sasha seemed not to mention this control issue often, she did recognize her own tendency to direct while remarking on the learning she was experiencing by letting her mentee, Cherry, lead. Her chosen goal was taking her to a place of significant learning and growth for herself as well as those she supervised.

Cherry continued to make notable progress in her communication skills as well as in training and interpersonal relationships after her promotion.

Her humble and quiet wisdom helped build the type of organization that her mentor hoped for and, in fact, reciprocally facilitated her mentor's learning and growth.

The other two dyads also reported a sense of professional growth. Rose, the action-researcher, shared on a number of occasions during her interviews and reflective supervision conferences that she felt that she was also growing and learning in ways that her multiple responsibilities as Department Head had not previously afforded her. Years before, in her role as Faculty Associate in Education at a West Coast Canadian University, Rose had learned contemporary processes for evaluating teacher interns' performances. Applying these principles as she watched her mentee present at one of the infant/toddler sites gave her reason to reflect anew. Rose was moved by the experience of observing her mentee, Kimya, using a creative and sophisticated approach to a presentation, grouping with some of her own mentees. Rose said this made her think "out of the box" when conventional strategies for presentation were abandoned by Kimya for a more innovative and progressive approach. It was a kind of epiphany to realize that simply taking the time to engage in mutual inquiry, including observation of another professional during a busy workday, could expand one's seasoned professional thinking in a new way.

Each mentor seemed to agree that their learning had involved staying open to follow the lead of their mentees and to accept alternate ways of approaching problems and puzzles. One stated that it was very important to give this credit and to "trust in the process." Louise made a rather profound confession in the final interview that she had had doubts about the reflective supervision model, as it had been introduced, really working in a way that she would find satisfying. She detailed how that doubt had been removed during the process and that she had learned the deeper meaning of the true reflective supervision approach. Although a lot of the mentor learning could be attached to the acquisition of knowledge about reflective supervision and the refinements of mentoring, the acceptance and allowance for a kind of openness and vulnerability on the part of mentors represents is in itself growth and progress toward goals as skilled facilitators. For example, two mentors shared that they learned to be open and let the mentee lead. Two of the three mentors mentioned feelings of not knowing where they were going or being "out of control," and then learning to go with that flow to see where it took them and what the real issues were. That takes courage. Participants all agreed there was no agenda except the facilitation of the mentees' growth.

The mentees, themselves, raised many areas of meaningful growth that they had experienced. Among those was the acquisition of new skills or additional resources. At the same time the individuality of the mentees and, therefore, their growth patterns, were distinct.

Out of all of the differences came a voice of positive and meaningful interaction producing significant growth and a willingness on the part of all research participants to engage further in the mentoring experience. Sasha felt that more authenticity was offered to her in her work as mentor. More depth and more meaning to her work emerged as a result of her participation. It is interesting to note that, even though the focus of the reflective supervision process is on the facilitation of mentee goals, mentors also experienced growth and progress toward their goals.

Challenges and Barriers

The research identified numerous challenges to the mentoring process. Finding sufficient time away from caregiving and administrative responsibilities is, of course, one challenge that everyone expressed. Proximity was also identified as a critical factor to support accessibility of the mentor to the mentee for scheduled routine meetings. Other challenges included mentee choice of mentor and regular meetings between mentors and mentees. The caseload of mentees became a focus for refinement over time, allowing for optimal interaction with a fewer number of mentees.

A male viewpoint on the mentoring process and interaction would enrich a model of mentoring in early childhood and study a cross-gender interaction that needs to be explored in mentoring early childhood development leaders.

Summary and Conclusions

As this research experience and the knowledge gained from all those who have participated throughout were integrated, a list of suggestions emerged for consideration in creating a mentoring program within another early childhood setting. Assuming that time for a reflective supervision and mentoring model is planned, the following are four central concepts providing the basis for a strong mentoring model:

1. Training of mentors that includes the reflective supervision model and use of journals and pre- and post-observation conferences, so that a systematic implementation is possible.
2. Allowance for choice of mentor bearing in mind accessibility issues of mentor to mentee.
3. Clarity that the evaluation process will be distinct and separate from the mentoring process is necessary.

4. Ongoing support for both mentors and mentees. A mentoring support group that meets regularly is important as a forum for ongoing facilitation of and extension of mentoring skill refinement. Mentees also need to have input and feedback venues.

Of the many outcomes listed as possible expectations in the study, some emerged as common themes among participants. Every mentor in the project, in relation to their mentee's progress, discussed self-esteem and its development. Essentially, all participants admitted to growth demonstrated by progress toward goals. Several alluded to growth beyond their original goal, actually changing their goal all together. Others experienced increased job satisfaction, as well as a deeper understanding of and learning about their own mentoring skills, and a sense of the impact on the program as a whole

A fundamental perceptual shift is necessary for reflective mentoring to be considered as a professional development intervention. The idea of taking time for significant professional exchange and reflection is foreign to the underpinnings of the service approach in a profession that nurtures and cares for the youngest members of society. A systematic approach to mentoring as a process of promotion of growth and realization of goals requires professional commitment and detailed attention to succeed.

It is important to reiterate that though men were not a part of this research study due to the scarcity of early childhood male professionals, the need for more men in the lives of young children is great. Indeed, in research such as this study and many more to follow, looking at the role of cross-gender mentoring in education and specifically early childhood education would add rich texture to the beginnings of this knowledge base. If we are to take seriously relationship-based care (see Lally, 1998), then we must take seriously relationship-based adult interaction among the professionals who provide important role models for young children. This modeling must include men as child development providers and managers.

Mentor training is essential to educate and inform best practice so that an awareness of potential pitfalls is shared. The need to catalyze movement or take a risk action was emergent in the research. In fact, due to training regarding such action, participating mentors were able to identify moments when they found themselves in a situation with no forward movement, and began to become familiar with strategies to effect a "risk-action" strategy to catalyze movement when progress was stuck.

The discussion of professional growth through mentoring has only begun. This research design may have been limited through the use of the broad question of how participants felt they had benefited or grown. Perhaps more specific detail or dissection of types of growth inherent in a mentoring experience would be useful in a further research study. Also, additional exploration of the benefits of the mentoring interaction between dyads could further describe the experience and inform mentoring intervention.

CONCLUSIONS

The research demonstrated a consensus that there were reciprocal benefits and growth toward goals for each participant. Participants saw no definite end to the growth and felt it would be ongoing as long as they were involved in the mentoring process. As final interviews ended, participants were setting new goals, reflecting on goal evolution, and looking forward to a new year and new challenges.

As stated, many other studies are needed to fully approach a more comprehensive understanding of mentoring in a reflective supervision frame. A better understanding of the layers and nuances of mentoring and potential uses of this model or others, including those that have male participants, as an intervention strategy in the development of ECE staff can only be achieved through further exploration and study.

REFERENCES

Kagan, S. (1994). Leadership: Rethinking it—Making it happen. *Young Children, the Journal of NAEYC, 49*(5), 50–54.

Lally, R. (1988). *Parent infant toddler caregiver.* Sausalito, CA: West Ed. Materials.

Schon, D. A. (1983). *The reflective practitioner.* New York: Basic Books.

Schon, D. A. (1987). *Educating the reflective practitioner, toward a new design for teaching and learning in the professions.* San Francisco: Jossey-Bass.

Whitebook, M., Hnatiuk, P., & Bellm, D. (1994). *Mentoring in early care and education, refining an emerging career path.* Washington, DC: National Center for the Early Childhood Workforce.

INDEX

A

Adolescent girls, socialization of, 51
Assessment practices, 161
   and decision making, 160
      and policymakers, 160
      and teachers, 161
   focus on, 149
   See also Gender equity in assessment
      practices

B

"Borderwork," 16
Brain research and education. *See* Neuroscience
Bullying, 174–175
   categories, 168–169
   future directions, 174
   gender perspective, 166
   historical perspective
      Columbine High School shoot-
         ings, 166
      Norwegian case example, 165–166
      surveys (U.S. newspapers), 166
   international and national preva-
      lence, 167–168
   psychosocial correlates, 169–171
   social groups' influence on, 171
      family factors, 171
      peers, 171–172
      teachers, 172–173

C

Centers, 103
Classroom power relations and gender
   expectancies, 13
Communicating gender equity to parents, 127–128, 146–147
   challenge for teachers, 133
   "co-production" concept, 133–134
   communication dynamics, 139–140
   community resources bridging
      effort, 140–141
   effects of understanding gender
      equity, 129–130
      parent involvement/support for,
         130
      recommended policies, 131
      statistics on parental involve-
         ment, 132
   issues affecting boys and girls,
      128–129
   keys (tools) for change promotion,
      134–135
      community organizations collab-
         oration, 138
      discussion time allocation, 136
      families/schools as communica-
         tors, 136137
      families/schools as learners, 137
      families/schools as supporters,
         137

Gender and Schooling in the Early Years, pages 193–197
Copyright © 2005 by Information Age Publishing
All rights of reproduction in any form reserved.